THE MANY LANDFALLS OF JOHN CABOT

On 24 June 1497 John Cabot landed somewhere on the eastern seaboard of what is now Canada, yet even today, five hundred years later, no one knows precisely where. Once an issue in diplomatic negotiations over title to a continent, Cabot's landfall has also been the subject, especially in centennial years, of competing attempts to appropriate the meaning of the event.

Beginning with the historical context of Cabot's journey, Pope traces the various landfall theories which have placed his landing in locations from the Strait of Belle Isle to Cape Breton. The very uncertainty of our knowledge, he argues, has allowed nationalists in both Newfoundland and Canada to shape the debate about Cabot's itinerary and to stake claims to the landfall that amount to the invention of differing national traditions. As well, Pope concludes, the invented tradition of 'discovery' has allowed Europeans and their descendants to overlook the fact that their possession of North America is based on appropriation from Aboriginal peoples.

Well-illustrated with period maps, engravings, and stamps, *The Many Landfalls of John Cabot* will appeal to readers interested in early European transatlantic voyages, in the nature of the anniversaries that have celebrated Cabot's landing, and in the question of how national pasts are constructed, often from ambiguous sources.

PETER E. POPE is a member of the Archaeology Unit, Department of Anthropology, Memorial University of Newfoundland.

PETER E. POPE

The Many Landfalls of John Cabot

UNIVERSITY OF TORONTO PRESS
Toronto Buffalo London

© University of Toronto Press Incorporated 1997
Toronto Buffalo London
Printed in Canada

ISBN 0-8020-0786-4 (cloth)
ISBN 0-8020-7150-3 (paper)

∞

Printed on acid-free paper

Canadian Cataloguing in Publication Data

Pope, Peter Edward, 1946–
    The many landfalls of John Cabot

    Includes index.
    ISBN 0-8020-0786-4 (bound)   ISBN 0-8020-7150-3 (pbk.)

    1. Cabot, John, d. 1498?   2. America – Discovery and
    exploration – British – Historiography.   I. Title.

    FC301.C3P66 1997   970.01′7′092   C97-930989-1
    E129.C1P66 1997

University of Toronto Press acknowledges the financial assistance to
its publishing program of the Canada Council for the Arts and the
Ontario Arts Council.

Contents

Illustrations

Preface

Several years ago, while I was still a graduate student, Brian Cuthbertson, then of the Heritage Branch of the Nova Scotia Department of Tourism, asked me to write a research paper on the early exploration of Atlantic Canada. I have him to thank for my original interest in the topic at hand, because the consequent plunge into the Cabot literature soon convinced me that the debate about Cabot's itinerary had more to do with nationalism than with navigation. I made this argument in a paper for the Atlantic Canada Studies Conference in Fredricton, in 1994. Several people made useful comments on it or its earlier incarnations; in particular, I would thank Eric Davis and Phyllis Leblanc. Gerry Hallowell of the University of Toronto Press made one of the most useful comments, when he asked me if I thought I could write a book on the theme, accessible to the educated lay reader. I have tried to do this and, as my editor, he has been a great help in refining this idea.

I have also benefited from discussions, both in and out of formal seminars, with members of the history and anthropology departments at Memorial University of Newfoundland. In particular I must thank Ralph Pastore and Robert Paine for taking the time to look at the manuscript in detail and for their helpful suggestions. I would also thank James Hiller and Shane O'Dea for sharing their close knowledge of late-nineteenth-century Newfoundland. I was assisted in my bibliographic research by Glen Brown, through the Maritime Studies Research Unit of Memorial

University, and I thank him for his hard work and the unit for financing his assistance. Research of this kind depends on the kindness of archivists, and this book owes much to the Centre for Newfoundland Studies and, in particular, the enthusiasm of Joan Ritcey. I would also thank Larry Dohey, of the Roman Catholic Archdiocesan Archives in St John's.

Many people helped me write this book, but its shortcomings are my own. To the extent that it manages to tell a coherent tale, this reflects the patience of my colleagues, friends, and family. I have to thank the Archaeology Unit and the Anthropology Department at Memorial University for providing me with a constructive institutional setting and for generously accepting this historically oriented work in progress as fit research for a historical archaeologist. I would also thank Jeannette Macey for listening patiently to endless second thoughts about the manuscript, for her sensible comments, and for her charming maps. Thanks are also due my daughters, Molly and Laura, for their help with all the things that parents who are busy writing let slide.

Peter Pope
Flatrock, Newfoundland
25 March 1997

THE MANY LANDFALLS OF JOHN CABOT

1

An Introduction

The Landfall of Cabot

There's an argument unfinished
   Twixt his Lordship and the Judge,
And the Doctor takes a hand in
   For to settle an old grudge:
It's about this Cabot landfall,
   They are making such a racket:
Some say he came as passenger
   In Billy Coady's Packet ...

Sure I turned a coat for Cabot
   Says a woman on the settle,
By the same he drank that evening
   What cold tea was in the kettle,
And he et enough of pan-cakes
   And pigs heads in the larder,
For to feed the population
   Of Quebec and Moreton's Harbour.

I remember well John Cabot
   When he didn't have a dollar,
And he used a wart was on his neck
   To button on his collar,
And a shocking hand for smoking,
   And a devil for tobaccy,

With a scattered foxy whisper
　　Like an Upper Island cracky.[1]

I was to the ice with Cabot
　　Says a man from Tilton Harbour,
He was two springs in the *Walrus*
　　And another with Joe Barbour,
And another spring with Foley
　　In a schooner called the *Blinker*,
That's the spring the crew turned manus
　　They said Cabot was a jinker.[2]

Sure I went to school with Cabot
　　Says a man named Billy Brandon,
It was called the Orphan Asylum
　　Where St. Patrick's Hall is standing;
He was duller than molasses,
　　And his tongue was like a clapper,
And his fingers were all broken
　　From the master's hardwood slapper.

Sure I knew Cabot's mother
　　Says a spinster named Kate Abbott,
And her name is Patience Morgan,
　　That's before she married Cabot;
I remember her three sisters –
　　Mary Joe and Julia Johnston,
And another married Flavin
　　That was living in Wisconsin ...

Traditional Newfoundland song (sometimes attributed to Johnny
　　Burke)[3]

The old song parodies the subject of this book: when, how, and
why Canadians and Newfoundlanders have claimed John Cabot
as their own. Johnny Burke wrote this satirical ballad (if he actually
wrote it) within the context of a particular Newfoundland debate

about Cabot's landfall, 'twixt his Lordship and the Judge,' that is, between the Roman Catholic Bishop of St John's, Michael Howley, and the jurist and eminent historian of Newfoundland, Daniel Prowse. (The Presbyterian churchman, Dr Moses Harvey, took a dissenting view.) These were among the most audible voices in the quadcentenary squabble over Cabot in 1897, but Newfoundlanders were not the only ones to voice their opinions. Neither American, British, nor Canadian scholars were silent on the matter.

The recent observance of the five-hundredth anniversary of John Cabot's voyage to North America in 1497 has confirmed the lesson of the quadcentenary: the location of his landfall is not simply a historical question. There was only one landfall that mattered, for Cabot and his crew caught their first sight of North America but once. Yet mutually exclusive claims about where he sailed and where he made his landfall are evident today, just as the quadcentenary of 1897 prompted an earlier flurry of assured speculation. A review of the maps, documents, and exhaustive analyses published to date suggests that such claims should be treated sceptically, in the absence of new evidence. The event is better documented today than it was a century ago, but we still have no secure basis to go much beyond saying that in 1497 Cabot explored part of Canada's Atlantic littoral, somewhere between Cape Breton Island and the Strait of Belle Isle and that his landfall was, therefore, somewhere on or near this coast. This book will recall what we know about John Cabot, it will investigate why and how the history of his voyage was obscured, and it will show how nationalism shaped a debate about Cabot's itinerary a century ago, at the time of the four-hundredth anniversary of his voyage. This will lead us to ponder the curious way in which late-fifteenth-century national traditions shaped the original landfall itself, which will lay the groundwork for a reconsideration of the idea of 'discovery' and some reflections on the uses of the landfall as a precedent for the European appropriation of North America.

We know only a little about John Cabot and his voyage of 1497, from a handful of documents and the debatable cartographic repercussions of his expedition. The scraps of unambiguous information that have survived the centuries bob on a confused sea of tales told by John Cabot's ambitious and influential son Sebastian. We know more about the context than about the voyage of 1497. We know something about the expansion of European trade and new developments in ship design and navigation, but we generally know little of particular Atlantic voyages, ships, or masters. Officially sanctioned explorations were more likely than fishing voyages to reach the notice of the literate and to rate a mention in contemporary documents, for the fishing trade was then, as now, unremarkable and unglamorous. Official voyages of 'discovery' were not, however, more common or even always more important than obscure fishing and trading voyages in bringing Europeans into closer acquaintance with that part of the New World which is now Canada. Poorly documented economic exploitation and informal exploration often preceded better documented official expeditions. In other words, the Native peoples of North America were not the only ones who might have questioned the originality of some famous 'discoveries.' Europe's own fishermen would sometimes have been able to do so as well.

If Bristol fishing masters were capable of reaching Iceland in the fifteenth century, why did Henry VII permit a Venetian navigator to lead an English transatlantic expedition? Despite their experience in northern voyages, English mariners were not really ready for transatlantic voyages. What distinguishes the voyages of circa 1500 from medieval Norse voyages is that some Italian, Portuguese, and Spanish pilots had learned how to use celestial navigation to take their ships far into the Atlantic and back in a single season, without stepping from island to island. Few English masters would have the necessary navigational skills and equipment until the middle of the sixteenth century. John Cabot was working at the navigational cutting edge of his time.

With due respect to the Native peoples of North America, who discovered and colonized maritime Canada, Labrador, and eventually Newfoundland at the close of the last Ice Age, it is possible to make the politically incorrect argument that Cabot's expedition was also a voyage of discovery. This is so because the relationship of Old World and New was asymmetrical. It was, after all, European mariners who visited North America, returned with news of it, and began to exploit it – not the other way around. To deny that Europeans 'discovered' North America is an effective way to criticize Euro-centred history and geography, but it is also a way to lose sight of the fact that it was (for better or for worse) western Europeans who discovered that the world has many continents and that it is possible to reach and exploit them by sea. Like the landing of Columbus, the Cabot landfall gave rise to a significant historical tradition precisely because it could be taken to symbolize the moment when Europe appropriated North America. Cabot's landfall was not that moment, of course, but the gradual process of appropriation, sometimes loosely summarized in the omnibus concept of conquest, has become a context within which we have to place the notion of 'discovery,' precisely to the extent that 'discovery' has been used, in the past, as a precedent or justification for possession. We will reconsider the Native people of the Atlantic coast, in this spirit, in a closing discussion of Cabot's place in national tradition today.

The limited and ambiguous documentation of Cabot's exploration of 1497 has, paradoxically, encouraged luxuriant growth in the secondary literature on the topic of his itinerary. This literature is often fertilized with the rich loam of nationalism. The fact that there is no conclusive evidence for any particular landfall has opened a historiographic space in which nationalists of various persuasions have pronounced on the question of what must have been. Our collective memories of John Cabot's voyage have become part of the way we construct our national past (or pasts). This sounds like an excuse to carry on in a postmodern way about texts, but the intention here is simpler: to contrast what we know about Cabot with what we think we know about Cabot, giving special attention to the invention of tradition at the time of the quadcentennial celebrations of 1897 and the ongoing debate about the location of the landfall. The topic of the twentieth-century management of the cultural resource that the Cabot tradition has become I leave to others with better access to the files of Parks Canada and provincial tourist agencies. We will consider aspects of Cabot in 1997, but only in order to clarify issues raised by the commemorations of the preceding century.

The staking of claims for Cabot's landfall, during the quad-centenary, amounted to the invention of competing traditions. Traditions about turning points in national history have as much to tell us as the events themselves, as Simon Schama reminds us in 'The Many Deaths of General Wolfe.'[4] As another cynic puts it: 'History does not repeat itself, it adjusts itself. The history of history shows, in sum, how the past sets itself up as mediator of the present.'[5] The theory of a Cape Breton landfall appears to have emerged out of anglophone/francophone cultural tensions within Canada, as much as out of competition between Canada and Newfoundland over their respective historic status within the British Empire. The Canadian and Newfoundland landfall theories actually shared common ideological underpinnings in British imperialism. In the Canadian case this was, in some part, an anti-American posture, and Cabot became, in some part, an anti-Columbian tradition. This was less relevant in Newfoundland, where the attractions of Cabot as a culture hero resembled those of Columbus in the United States, in his ability to transcend sectarian tensions.

A kind of nationalism has pervaded traditions about the European 'discovery' of America since the beginning, because 'discovery' is as much a political act as it is a geographical one. In this political sense Cabot discovered Atlantic Canada, whether or not he was preceded by generations of maritime hunter-gatherers or anonymous, unsponsored, and illiterate European fishermen, neither of whom could reveal their discovery to the world as he could. Cabot's landfall was a real historical event, once the subject of diplomatic negotiation over title to a continent. Subsequent competitive attempts to appropriate the meaning of the event should be no surprise, for the flag-planting was an intentionally symbolic act: a photo opportunity before its time, for which the tourism departments of several jurisdictions now vie to supply a caption.

This book is about the way subsequent ages have remembered Cabot and it therefore confronts an issue to which historians and sociologists and anthropologists have paid increasing attention in the twentieth century: how human beings remember their collective past. What you are reading is not, however, an attempt to stake out a new theoretical perspective on this interesting question. It is an attempt to describe and examine the significance of a specific 'memory perpetual,' a constructed tradition of a particular event, of interest to Canadians and Newfoundlanders because it happened here. In doing this I make choices in methodology, some of which reflect theoretical assumptions unexamined in this text. Occasionally the notes will guide the reader towards a larger and more profound literature, or at least the bits and pieces that have drifted into my limited view.

The theoretical apparatus at work is certainly not my own. Throughout what follows I place perceptions of the past in four categories, borrowed from the British anthropologist John Davis.[6] There may be more than four ways of recalling the past, but the four he proposes certainly suit my purposes: namely, *(auto)biography, precedent, myth*, and *history. Biography* is a cumulative account of the life and deeds of an individual. We will puzzle, as others have before, over the life of John Cabot and will ponder, at some length, the issues raised by the mendacious autobiography of his son Sebastian. *Precedent* abstracts events from their past context and presents them as examples of the way things ought to be. As we will see, Cabot's 'discovery' was invoked, for several centuries, as a precedent for British possession of North America. *Myth* offers a symbolically satisfying account of past events. The landfall of Cabot is, in my view, a myth designed to suit the symbolic requirements of an immigrant people and one that echoes, as we will see, other earlier myths. *History* is a discipline that attempts to give a more or less linear account of how things came to be as they more or less verifiably were. Or at least that is the kind of account I have tried to offer, as a basis for indexing the normative and symbolic content of the Cabot *tradition* – a term used here to summarize, roughly, what Davis defines as *myth* and *precedent*. Eric Hobsbawm's term *invention of tradition* is useful in parsing what francophone historians call *l'histoire de l'événement*: that is, the historiography of what we have collectively selected as turning points in national mythology.[7]

The opposition, taken for granted here, between invented tradition and objective history resembles the approach of the French sociologist Maurice Halbwachs, notably in *La mémoire collective*.[8] From this point of view, the discipline of *history* can provide access to an objective past because it is written with critical distance and attends to the genuine differences between past and present, while *tradition* (for Halbwachs, *memory*) invents in order to make emotionally satisfying connections between past and present. In this vein, the following chapter assumes, with positivistic naïveté, that we can begin our task of understanding traditions of John Cabot by reviewing the historical Cabot and, furthermore, that we can do this despite the fact that our public memories are collective constructs shaped by the social forces around us. According to Halbwachs these collective memories typically locate past events in specific settings. In other words, given that we wanted to remember Cabot's voyage, it was inevitable that we felt compelled to choose a landfall. Commemoration, of the sort organized in Canada and Newfoundland in 1897, prompts specific memories, Halbwachs would say, and strengthens the identification of remembered event and particular place: in this case, of discovery with landfall. Commemoration also serves to disguise the awkward fact that traditions evolve – as they must, if they are to misrepresent the past as like the present.

2
Everything We Know about John Cabot

Extensive preparations are being made at Bristol, England, in Canada, and in Newfoundland to commemorate, on the twenty-fourth of the present month [June 1897], the landing of John Cabot on the coast of the North-American continent. The intention is praiseworthy; but it is well to recollect that we do not know exactly when and where he first sighted the New World.

Henry Harrisse, *The Discovery of North America by John Cabot* (1897)[1]

THE DOCUMENTS WE LACK

Five hundred years is a long time. The handful of contemporary documents that shed light on the explorations of the man we remember as John Cabot are half a millennium old. A number of factors conspire to limit our historical access to his celebrated voyage of 1497. He was a peripatetic Venetian who arrived in England only a few years before his famous voyage in 1497. The fishermen who actually exploited the coasts that Cabot explored led unglamorous lives; they went about their business unnoticed and their affairs are, largely, forgotten. Mariners in this period were not, typically, literate and there were no legal requirements to keep ship's logs or journals. Much of the extant documentation is cartographic and subject to uncertain interpretation. Taking into account the navigational uncertainties of the period, distances given in the documents that have survived must be taken with a grain of salt. Cabot and his company did not actually encounter Native North Americans, and the peoples of the region he explored were, in any event, not literate and most of their oral traditions of early contact have been lost, through extinction and cultural upheaval.[2] John Cabot disappeared in a follow-up expedition to North America in 1498 and was survived by an influential and long-lived son, Sebastian, who systematically misappropriated his father's achievements as his own. That we know much about the elder Cabot at all is a testimony to the perseverance of a handful of scholars during the five centuries that have passed since his time.

The scant surviving documentation has not prevented the publication of many volumes of what might be called 'must-have-been' history.[3] Cabot must have been a Genoan. He must have known Columbus as a youth. He must have been a wealthy merchant. He must have been attracted to Bristol by its connections to the north. He must have named his ship, the Matthew, after his wife, Mattia. It must have been a caravel, or a balinger, or a bark. He must have left Ireland from this point or that. His course must have been affected by this rate of current or that degree of magnetic variation. Cabot must have landed here. He must have named that island. He must have coasted Greenland or Florida or Maine, because he must have been to Iceland or because he must have needed water or because he must have been in a hurry. A certain map must have been drawn with information from his voyage, another must have been a deliberate misrepresentation. It is difficult to say much about John Cabot without engaging in this kind of must-have-been. The years around the quadcentenary celebration of his voyage in 1897 saw the publication of reams of such material.

Those interested in Cabot today have one advantage over the scholars who pawed over the small grab bag of Cabotian documents available a century ago. The single most informative fifteenth-century report of John Cabot's transatlantic voyage of 1497 was not discovered until the middle of the twentieth century. This crucial document was identified in the Archive at Simancas, Spain, by Louis-André Vigneras and first published in English only in 1957.[4] It consists of an intelligence report written, circa 1497, by the London merchant John Day, addressed to the 'Grand Admiral' of Spain, probably Columbus himself. Day was a well-educated man from an influential family who had lived and worked in Bristol, under the alias 'Hugh Say,' following a business failure.[5] He was, in other words, well qualified to gather and to understand intelligence about Cabot's North American adventure. This is not the only document with this kind of information, but it does provide several very useful clues about the expedition missing from previously known contemporary accounts of the Cabots.

In order to understand how and why particular traditions have attached themselves to Cabot and his voyage, it would be useful to recount, in the first place, what we actually know about the famous mariner and his celebrated voyage of 1497. Like any historical narrative, this will involve a certain amount of implicit must-have-been: some sources will be taken seriously and others less so (since they must have been misinformed or mendacious or misunderstood). Those interested in such debates can ransack the endnotes. Those interested in what happened to John Cabot during his lifetime, as opposed to what happened to his memory after his death, can start with the following facts.[6]

CABOT

First of all, he wasn't John Cabot, of course. On the other hand, he wasn't Jean and he wasn't even Giovanni, as biographers like to call him.[7] He was Zuan Caboto.[8] Although a citizen of Venice, he was not born there but naturalized circa 1472. Aliens applying for naturalization in Venice were expected to have been resident for at least fifteen years, which in the case of Zuan Caboto would have been since sometime before 1457, making him at least twenty-seven when he married his Venetian wife, Mattia, circa 1484, and over forty when he made his successful North Atlantic exploration, in 1497.[9] A Spanish agent in London told King Ferdinand and Queen Isabella that Cabot was 'another Genoese like Columbus.'[10] On the other hand, someone known as 'Johan Caboto Montecalunya' had promoted a harbour development in

Valencia, on the Mediterranean coast of Spain, in 1492, and 'Montecalunya' sounds Catalan rather than Italian.[11] His contemporaries, in any event, normally referred to the mariner, Zuan, as a Venetian.

By 1496 Zuan had arrived in England, where, as 'John Cabotto,' he petitioned King Henry VII to grant letters patent authorizing a northern exploration.[12] A chronicle of the period called him 'very expert and cunning in knowledge of the circuite of the worlde and Ilandes of the same.'[13] Raimondo di Soncino, the Milanese ambassador in London, thought him 'a most expert mariner' and noted his facility at using charts and globes to explain his geographical ideas.[14] Whether or not Cabot promoted his project in imitation of Columbus's innovative westward route to the Indies, this was how the Spanish perceived his activities.[15] King Henry cautiously avoided overt competition with his allies Ferdinand and Isabella of Spain; the patent that he granted gave John and his three sons, Lewes, Sebastyn, and Soncio, and their heirs and deputies, carefully defined powers:

to sail to all parts, regions and coasts of the eastern, western and northern sea, under our banners, flags and ensigns, with five ships or vessels of whatsoever burden and quality they may be, and with so many and with such mariners and men as they may wish to take with them in the said ships, at their own proper costs and charges, to find, discover and investigate whatsoever islands, countries, regions or provinces of heathens and infidels, in whatsoever part of the world placed, which before this time were unknown to all Christians.[16]

The wording of the royal patent thus excluded the Caribbean islands already explored by Columbus, since they were in southern waters and known to Christians. King Henry invested nothing in the project, although he waived customs in perpetuity for goods imported by the Cabots from 'those places thus newly discovered,' in exchange for a promise of 20 per cent of net profits payable to the Crown. He did encourage his subjects to back the venture. This Cabot needed; he was not himself a wealthy man.[17]

BRISTOL EXPLORATIONS

King Henry's patent specifically assumed that Cabot would oper-
ate out of the port of Bristol and it appears that John Cabot was
able to mount a voyage of exploration there, in the summer of
1496. A terse summary of this abortive expedition survives in the
Day Letter. On this first voyage, Cabot 'went with one ship, his
crew confused him, he was short of supplies and ran into bad
weather, and he decided to turn back.' In passing, Day takes it for
granted that his correspondent knows that Bristol mariners were
already carrying out transatlantic exploration and had found land
which they called 'the island of Brazil.' Other documents independently confirm organized Atlantic exploration based in Bristol, as early as 1480, in the form of an unsuccessful exploration
backed by the wealthy merchant John Jay, under the command of
one Thloyde, 'the [most] knowledgeable seaman of the whole of
England.'[18] A year later, Thomas Croft, part owner of the *Trynitie*
and the *George*, loaded these small ships with forty bushels of salt
'not by cause of marchandise but to thentent to serch & fynde a
certain Isle called the Isle of Brazile.'[19]

The identities of the backers of Cabot's expeditions of the
1490s are uncertain. In the following century Robert Thorne, the
younger, claimed that his father, of the same name, and another
Bristol merchant, Hugh Elyot, were 'the discoverers of the New-
found Landes.'[20] The Elizabethan antiquarian polymath John
Dee also gave credit to Thorne and Elyot, dating the discovery
to 1494.[21] After 1497 the royal household paid rewards for
voyages 'towardes the new Ilande' to several men besides 'hym
that founde the new Isle,' that is, John Cabot himself. These
included Launcelot Thirkill of London, Thomas Bradley, John
Cair, William Thomas of Bristol, Edwarde le portingale (that is,
Edward the Portuguese), 'the merchauntes of bristoll that have
bene in the newe founde launde,' and others.[22] In 1501 King
Henry granted letters patent for northwestern explorations to
Richard Warde, Thomas Asshehurst, and John Thomas of Bristol, together with three experienced Azorean Portuguese pilots:
João Fernandes, Fransisco Fernandes, and João Gonsalves. The

King issued a further patent to Elyot, Asshehurst, Gonsalves, and F. Fernandes in 1502.[23] Which, if any, of these men were associated with Cabot in 1496–8 is uncertain, but all are candidates: Soncino reported that the 'leading men' in the enterprise of 1497 were based in Bristol.[24]

THE VOYAGE OF 1497

It is doubtful that Cabot had extensive financial backing for the voyage of 1497, since he again undertook his expedition with a single small vessel, the fifty-ton *Matthew*.[25] The crew of eighteen or so were 'practically all English and from Bristol,' although the company included a Burgundian associate of Cabot's and a Genoese 'barber,' that is, a surgeon.[26] John's son Sebastian later claimed to have been on the voyage. Indeed, in his dotage he told some acquaintances that his father had died and that he commanded the expedition himself.[27] On other occasions Sebastian claimed that he co-discovered North America with his father.[28] In fact, since his parents were married about 1484, he is not likely to have been much more than thirteen years old in 1497, and there is no independent evidence that he accompanied his father. It would not have been unusual for him to have done so, since among mariners this was how boys learned their fathers' trade. As for the vessel, a bark called the *Mathewe* of Bristol traded to Ireland, Bordeaux, and Spain, in 1503 and 1504, carrying goods for Hugh Elyot and William Thorne, among others.[29] The 20-metre reconstruction designed by Colin Mudie for the Bristol quincentenary celebrations in 1997 is as close a facsimile of the small three-masted ships of the period as we are likely to see, based on present research on late-medieval to early-modern naval architecture (figure 2.1).[30] The original *Matthew* set out from Bristol, with provisions for seven or eight months, about 20 May 1497.[31] Cabot took his little ship to the west of Ireland, then headed north before striking west again.[32]

This sounds like an attempt at latitude sailing, an important technique for transoceanic navigation, which became possible in the late fifteenth century with the development of reliable instru-

2.1 The 20-metre reconstruction of John Cabot's ship the *Matthew*, designed by Colin Mudie for the Bristol quincentenary celebrations in 1997. (© 1993 Colin Mudie, RDI)

ments for determining latitude at sea: the quadrant, the astrolabe, and the cross-staff.[33] Leaving aside, for the moment, the navigational technology of the period, it is enough to say here that latitude sailing involved observation of the altitude above the horizon of a celestial body, generally either Polaris (the North Star) or the sun, at its noon maximum. In the northern hemisphere the altitude of Polaris, with some correction for the time of night, equals terrestrial latitude. The altitude of the sun at noon is related to the observer's latitude in a more complex way, requiring adjustment for the time of year. The ability to make reasonably accurate observations of *altura* made it possible for pilots to make good estimates of their latitude or north/south position.[34] These pilots did not yet work with a numerical concept of latitude, but instead identified their north/south position by saying, for example, that Polaris had the same altitude as it did at such-and-such a point on the coast of Europe. Deducing the exact altitude actually required further skill in celestial navigation, since Polaris is just off the celestial North Pole and rotates in a tight circle around it every twenty-four hours. Its position relative to true north can be deduced from the position of the nearby stars in Ursa Minor, called by navigators 'the Guards,' and early modern pilots devised another simple instrument, the nocturnal, to do this. These innovations, together, were as useful in their way as the magnetic compass, which had already become a standard navigational instrument in the late Middle Ages.[35] The new celestial navigation made it possible to determine north/south position in strange waters. This technique of running down the latitude called for charts with a scale of latitude, and the first such charts date about 1500.[36]

The idea that the world was a globe was not, by any means, new in the era of Columbus and Cabot. The supposed medieval flat earth is a tradition invented by eighteenth-century apostles of progress to denigrate the Middle Ages and adopted by nineteenth-century writers, like Washington Irving, to glorify Columbus as a modern hero.[37] What was new, in the late fifteenth century, was a vivid sense of the physical implications of the fact that ships travel on the surface of a sphere. The early-sixteenth-century English man of letters John Rastell emphasized these novel links between navigation and celestial mechanics in *The Four Elements*, an entertainment written in 1517, about the time he himself commanded an abortive New World expedition, just twenty years after Cabot's voyage.[38] In this dialogue, Studious Desire asks Experience how he knows the earth is round, and is told:

Yes, that I can well prove.
You see the North Star in the sky;
Mark well, but you shall scarcely spy
That ever it doth remove.

But I assure you, if you go
Northward a hundred mile or two
You shall think it riseth,
And that it near approached
The point over the top of your head
Which is called your zenith.

Yet if you go the other way
Southward ten or twelve days' journey,
You shall then think anon
It is descended and come more nigh
The circle parting earth and sky
Which is called your horizon.
...
This proveth of necessity
That the earth must needs round be.[39]

Although experienced pilots like Cabot could thus estimate their position north or south, they had much more trouble estimating east/west position. The determination of longitude requires precise shipboard timekeeping, which had to await the invention of the marine chronometer in the eighteenth century.[40] Sebastian Cabot, among others, was to make premature claims for esoteric celestial and magnetic means of determining longitude.[41] On his deathbed he told his friend Richard Eden that he had 'the knowledge of the longitude ... by divine revelation.'[42] This technique was not, unfortunately, reproducible and early modern mariners continued to rely on dead reckoning and guesses about wind and current to estimate their easting or westing. It is the relative precision of north/south positions combined with the imprecision of east/west positions that gives the territories mapped on the best early charts their curious and charming combination of familiarity and otherness. It was this same intersection of precision and imprecision that led transatlantic pilots to the concept of latitude sailing. Since longitude was uncertain, it made sense to sail first, in known waters, north or south to the latitude of your intended landfall and then to head east or west, staying as close as possible to the chosen latitude so that the ship's position was known, at least in one dimension, somewhere on a particular east–west line.

The long and the short of all this is that we can take late-fifteenth-century indications of latitude seriously, perhaps within a degree or so, say 100 to 200 kilometres, whereas east/west distances given in contemporary reports of Cabot's voyage would have been based solely on his estimates of wind, current, and speed over the sea bottom and would therefore be subject to a much larger fudge factor, perhaps in the order of 20 to 30 per cent, that is, up to 900 kilometres in a 3000-kilometre crossing. This discrimination in our use of the sources is essential. The Day Letter has given us estimates of latitude, expressed in the typical style of the period, in the form of equivalence to a European location. Some other contemporary reports make estimates of transatlantic distances and distances coasted along the North American littoral explored. The latitude data in the Day Letter are much more likely to be accurate than these distance estimates; not because of the special virtues of that document but simply because these were a kind of data that were obtainable in the period, while exact distance figures were not. The fact that Day does not bother to mention distances, except in terms of days sailed, is a mark of his own navigational sophistication and of the navigational experience he assumes for his correspondent (Columbus?).[43]

The surviving reports of Cabot's voyage are not specific about where he chose to leave Europe and head west 'in order to sail to the east,' as the Milanese ambassador Soncino put it.[44] If Cabot was attempting latitude sailing and had no preference for any particular latitude, he would likely have departed Europe from one of the headlands on the west of Ireland; for if he sailed further north, out of sight of land, his position would have been less certain. On these assumptions he would have begun his transatlantic crossing somewhere between about 51 degrees and 55 degrees north. One maritime historian has argued that he must have departed from Dursey Head, at the southwestern extremity of Ireland, at about 51½ degrees north; others that he must have departed from Achill Head in western Connacht, at 54 degrees north.[45] These are reasonable speculations, but there is no reason Cabot might not have chosen the Kerry Peninsula, a little north of 52 degrees, or Slyne Head near Galway Bay, at about 53½ degrees north, or any other prominent Irish headland as his point of departure.[46] Western Ireland is a rocky coast, potentially treacherous in the prevailing onshore winds: good reason for any sailor to stand off from it as soon as convenient. Nevertheless, Soncino reported that Cabot sailed north 'some days' before putting 'the north on his right hand' and heading westward, timing that would favour a change of course at one of the northern headlands, like Slyne or Achill Head, or even farther north, beyond St Kilda and the Hebrides.[47]

There is a small clue in the Day Letter, not often remarked, that might tell us quite a lot about Cabot's itinerary. According to Day, Cabot ran before an east-northeasterly wind on his outward passage. This was a convenient but curious wind. If Cabot found a steady east-northeasterly off the west of Ireland in late May, or in fact at any other time of the year, then the prevailing Atlantic winds have changed since 1497.[48] In many months of the year sailors would have to run north to about 65 degrees north, the latitude of Iceland, to find prevailing easterlies. That is not necessary in May, when easterlies blow regularly at about 60 degrees north.[49] Medieval Norse traders venturing from Norway to Greenland certainly knew about this wind. The traditional course is given in the fourteenth-century *Hauksbók*: 'From Hernar in Norway sail due west for Hvarf in Greenland; and then will you sail north of Shetland so that you can just sight it in clear weather; but south of the Faroe Islands, so that the sea appears half-way up the mountain slopes; but steer south of Iceland so that you may have birds and whales therefrom.'[50] This itinerary for a voyage from southwest Norway to what we now call Cape Farewell at the southern tip of Greenland amounts to latitude sailing at 61 degrees north, right in the middle of the easterlies that can be expected in that part of the North Atlantic in the right season.[51] (Figure 2.2 is a map showing this traditional Norse itinerary with the winds prevailing in May.) We cannot be certain that Cabot followed in the wake of the Norse traders, but it would have been a sensible course and one that would certainly have been known in fifteenth-century Bristol, which traded with Iceland and Greenland and where many Icelanders lived. This clue does not, however, help us much with the itinerary west of Greenland. By June the winds there are confused westerlies.[52] A heading roughly southwest is probably the best the *Matthew* could have done on any one tack and would be a likely course, given that Cabot was looking for temperate Japan and not arctic Tartary.

Cabot made his landfall after thirty-five days at sea, which was not too bad for a western transatlantic passage, although it probably did not last as a record for very long.[53] The weather must have been reasonably clear, because he was able to check his compass against celestial observations and determine that it no longer pointed north but 'marked two rhumbs below,' or 22½ degrees west.[54] In their fifteenth-century ventures into the Atlantic, Portuguese mariners had noticed that in various locations compass needles misreported due north in varying degrees. In the first half of the sixteenth century they attempted to measure and tabulate this variation. An *oblique meridian*, which appears on some early charts of the northwest Atlantic, was an early attempt to allow for variation by showing a local adjusted scale of latitudes, oriented to account for the angular difference between true and magnetic north.[55] What Cabot had observed, in recording to what degree his compass 'failed,' was the largest magnetic variation observed to date. (Magnetic variation at any point on the earth's surface itself changes slowly over the years, but happens to be about the same in the northwest Atlantic in 1997 as it was five hundred years ago.) Again, it is the relatively recently discovered Day Letter that tells us that Cabot was aware of magnetic variation. Nineteenth-century scholars, not having the advantage of this document, spent gallons of ink on minute calculations of Cabot's likely course, given an unrecognized magnetic variation.[56] In fact,

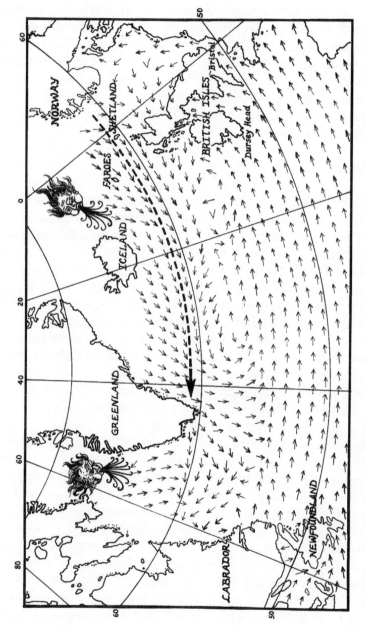

2.2 The North Atlantic, showing the traditional Norse itinerary for the Greenland trading voyage, with the winds prevailing in May.

Cabot could compensate for his compass variation once he had determined its extent. The sea was generally calm, although an early summer storm caught the *Matthew* just a few days before land appeared on the horizon. As he approached North America the storm and the effects of the Labrador current might have forced him somewhat south of his intended course, but he would have been able to re-establish his north/south position as soon as the weather was clearer.

THE LANDFALL

On 24 June 1497, Zuan Caboto and his companions made their North American landfall.[57] As Henry Harrisse pointed out a century ago, we do not know where this was. We would like to know but, unfortunately, we do not really know.[58] This is a circumstance that has opened up scope for us to invent what 'must have been,' according to our fundamental prejudices, particularly when we are more interested in biography, myth, or precedent than we are in a scrupulous and therefore intermittent history. This, in a nutshell, is the point of this book. To admit the point is not, however, to deny that we know anything about Cabot's landfall. By 1897 scholars knew enough for many volumes of 'must have been.' More to the point here, we know enough today to narrow the geographical range of possibilities, thanks largely to the Day Letter. (For a map, see figure 2.3).

Day reported that Cabot found a 'mainland' and some islands. One of these islands he identified as the Island of the Seven Cities, a common feature of late-medieval legendary Atlantic geography, often known as Antillia.[59] The southernmost part of this Island of the Seven Cities he found to be in the same latitude as the Bordeaux River.[60] Allowing a degree or so of possible error in celestial navigation, we might expect to find the southern part of Cabot's island between 44 degrees and 47 degrees north. In fact, the Strait of Canso, south of Cape Breton Island, lies at 45½ degrees north and Cape Pine, at the southern extremity of Newfoundland's Avalon Peninsula, lies at about 46½ degrees north. (The Avalon was usually misperceived as an island until the later

2.3 The northwest Atlantic, showing some of the places where John Cabot is supposed to have made his landfall, 24 June 1497.

sixteenth century.[61] According to the Day Letter, Cabot and his crew 'landed at only one spot of the mainland, near the place where land was first sighted.' The landfall, then, was not one of the islands discovered but some part of the 'mainland,' which means that Day's letter tells us what geography has always suggested: Cape Breton is an unlikely landfall for a westward expedition departing from Ireland. If the Island of the Seven Cities was Newfoundland's Avalon Peninsula rather than Cape Breton Island, then we must look even farther afield for a 'mainland.'

Where was Cabot's 'mainland'? The only other latitude information that has come down to us from the voyage of 1497 is also contained in the Day Letter, which reported that 'the cape nearest to Ireland is 1800 miles [*millas*] west of Dursey Head.' For the reasons already discussed, we have to take such distance information with a grain of salt, although the identification of a cape at the latitude of Dursey Head is easy enough: at 51½ degrees north, this would be the prominent Cape Dégrat, near Cape Bauld in the Strait of Belle Isle, at the northern end of Newfoundland's Great Northern Peninsula.[62] (Considering a possible navigational error of plus or minus a degree or two does not introduce another geographical candidate, in this case, assuming we treat Cape Bauld and Cape Dégrat as essentially one feature.) Cape Dégrat is, in fact, about 3000 kilometres from Dursey Head, very close to Cabot's estimated 1800 miles.[63] It is not, however, actually the cape closest to Ireland; this would be Cape Spear, the most eastern point of North America, just south of St John's. Pasqualigo thought Cabot's 'mainland' was '700 leagues away.'[64] As an estimate of distance from Bristol it was not a bad one, if Pasqualigo expressed himself in land leagues of three miles; if he used sea leagues of four miles, it was an overestimate.[65] At any rate, east/west inaccuracies are a predictable aspect of the navigational technology of the period.

Neither the 'Island of the Seven Cities' nor 'the cape nearest Ireland' are necessarily candidates for the landfall; indeed, the fact that they are mentioned but not specified as such rather argues against them. They do provide us with some sense of the coast explored by Cabot in 1497. He was, after all, an expert navigator and he thought he had been in the latitudes of the Strait of Belle Isle and of the south Avalon or Cape Breton Island. 'All along this coast,' John Day reported, 'they found many fish like those which in Iceland are dried in the open and sold in England and other countries, and ... called in English "stockfish"' (the late-medieval term for dried cod). Zuan Caboto himself told Soncino that the sea was 'swarming with fish, which can be taken not only with the net, but in baskets let down with a stone.'[66] Paradoxically, it looks very much as if Cabot's 'mainland' may have been, at least in part, the Island of Newfoundland, with or without the Avalon Peninsula.

On their single venture ashore, not far from their first sight of North America, Cabot's party found a landscape covered with trees, some smaller, some taller 'of the kind masts are made.' The latter could well have been black spruce, which were used for centuries as masts and spars by shipwrights in Nova Scotia, Newfoundland, and Labrador because they develop straight trunks with little taper and few large branches.[67] One fifteenth-century source describes the new land as 'excellent and temperate,' with potential not only for brazil wood but also silk.[68] This does not necessarily rule out Newfoundland: summer visitors of every era have been prone to overestimate its agricultural potential.

The description of the landfall area in a later source has a different and much more arctic flavour. This is the Eighth Legend on the margin of what is known as the Paris Map – a legend that describes the *prima terra vista* or land first seen by John Cabot and his son Sebastian. The only known copy of this very early printed map, published in 1544, was discovered in Germany in 1843, in the home of an obscure Bavarian curate, and soon purchased for the Bibliothèque Nationale in Paris, hence its name in Cabotian jargon.[69] The Paris Map also bears a legend asserting that Sebastian Cabot 'made this figure,' so this document specifically claims to contain an authentic report of the landfall.[70] The Eighth Legend describes the landfall region as 'very sterile' with 'many white bears, and very large stags like horses.' The latter sound more like moose than caribou, which would rule out a landfall south of the Strait of Belle Isle, since the former were not introduced to Newfoundland until the late nineteenth century. The colour of the bears also suggests a Labrador landfall, although even today individual polar bears occasionally turn up on Newfoundland's east coast as far as Renews, south of St John's.

The legend in question actually puts the landfall elsewhere and is probably not very good evidence about the terrain in the landfall area, since it seems to reflect a compilation of observations made by John Cabot in 1497 with later observations made by his son Sebastian in a voyage along the Labrador coast in 1508.[71] It is not likely that either Cabot *père* or Cabot *fils* distinguished between the Island of Newfoundland and coastal Labrador. That is to say, it appears that they treated the Strait of Belle Isle between Labrador and Newfoundland as a bay in a continuous 'mainland' coastline rather than as a body of water opening into the Gulf of St Lawrence, thus separating continental Labrador from insular Newfoundland. This is how Joannes Ruysch showed the area in his world map of 1508, and other early-sixteenth-century cartographers followed suit.[72] Indeed, the Basque whalers who exploited these waters in the mid-sixteenth century continued to refer to the Straits of Belle Isle as 'La Gran Baya.'

Wherever it was that the elder Cabot and his company came ashore in 1497, they found an inhabited world. They observed 'a trail that went inland, they saw a site where a fire had been made, they saw manure of animals they thought to be farm animals, and they saw a stick half a yard long pierced at both ends, carved and painted with brazil.'[73] Besides making these observations, Cabot brought back snares for game and a needle for making nets.[74] He was certainly wrong about the farm animals; the droppings must have been those of moose or caribou, for Native North Americans had no such domesticates. (The nearest large domesticates would have been the llamas of South America.) The rest of the cultural evidence matches what we know of Amerindian peoples of the northeast coast, including the ancestors of the Mi'kmaq in Nova Scotia, the now-extinct Beothuk of Newfoundland and the ancestors of the Labrador Innu, all of whom were adept woodworkers who used red ochre for decorative purposes, mistaken by Cabot's crew for 'brazil,' a more exotic and valuable dye.[75] This cultural datum would seem to rule out a landing in Labrador north of Hamilton Inlet, then a territory occupied by early Labrador Inuit, who are not known to have used red ochre to decorate their tools.[76] Cabot did not meet the people whose artifacts he collected, at least on this voyage, and he feared contact, given his small crew. 'Since he was with just a few people, he did not dare advance inland beyond the shooting distance of a crossbow,' as one report had it.[77] The fact that he landed only once speaks volumes.

Assuming Cabot followed the old Norse route westward along the 60 degree parallel towards Cape Farewell at the southern tip of Greenland, assuming he then headed as far west as he could into the prevailing winds on a southerly tack, and given the southward trend of the Labrador current during a storm in the days before he reached North America, it would seem most likely that he made his landfall somewhere between Sandwich Bay, Labrador, and White Bay, Newfoundland.[78] Latitude sailing from a departure point in western Ireland would result in a landfall in roughly the same latitudes, supposing Cabot was somehow favoured by a steady easterly so far south. The Paris Map of 1544 credits 'John Cabot, the Venetian and Sebastian Cabot his son' with naming the landfall area 'Prima Terra Vista' and a large island nearby 'Saint John,' in honour of the saint's day, June 24th. There are a number of insular candidates for this feature in the region, including the Grey Islands off Roddickton on Newfoundland's Great Northern Peninsula, Belle Isle in the Strait between Cape Bauld and Labrador, as well as various less prominent islands on the southeastern coast of Labrador – Great Caribou Island at Battle Harbour, for example. Most other supposed landfalls elsewhere in Newfoundland and Cape Breton lack a prominent large island nearby, as a possible Island of St John. Only Grates Cove, Newfoundland, can claim this kind of insular feature, in the shape of prominent Baccalieu Island. It is, however, too far south (at just over 48 degrees north) to fit an itinerary based on the latitude sailing. Located at the northern end of the Avalon Peninsula, Grates Cove is more likely to have been part of Cabot's Island of the Seven Cities than his landfall.[79]

Neither Cape Bonavista nor Cape North, the landfalls beloved by Newfoundland and Nova Scotian tradition, respectively, have much to recommend them, at least from the point of view of the early documents. There is absolutely no fifteenth- or sixteenth-century evidence that Bonavista was Cabot's landfall and it seems considerably less likely than the Strait of Belle Isle region, broadly conceived, for the reasons already considered. A landfall at Bonavista is reconsidered in chapter 4, relegated to the status of a tradition as opposed to a plausible historical scenario. Unlikely as a Cape Breton landfall at Cape North may be, on geographical grounds or on the basis of Day's information that it was the 'mainland' that Cabot first saw, there is at least some sixteenth-century evidence in its favour, in the form of the Paris Map of 1544, published under the authority of Sebastian Cabot.

A legend in the Gulf of St Lawrence on the body of the Paris Map is clearly intended to describe Cape Breton as the 'first land seen' (figure 2.4). At the same time, as we have noted, the Eighth Legend on the margin of the map describes the country near the landfall as 'a very sterile land,' with 'many white bears,' and so on. [80] The map is careless, and its many errors suggest that it was not produced under Sebastian's close supervision.[81] He almost certainly authorized publication, however, since he had contracted to produce such a *mappemonde*, since it was printed within the Habsburg Empire of his master Charles V, and since the Seventeenth Legend, in which Sebastian takes credit for the map, goes on at some length about one of his pet subjects: 'certain reasons for the variation which the needle of the compass makes with the north star.' Even if we read the Paris Map as an expression of what Sebastian had to say, in 1544, of the events of 1497, this does not mean we have privileged access to what actually happened. He was not averse to bending the truth when it suited his own purposes, as he did, for example, by claiming a responsible role on a voyage that took place when he was barely adolescent. In 1544 Sebastian was in the process of negotiating a return to English service after many years in Spain. Given Jacques Cartier's recent explorations and attempt at colonization in the Gulf of St Lawrence, between 1534 and 1541, and noting England's

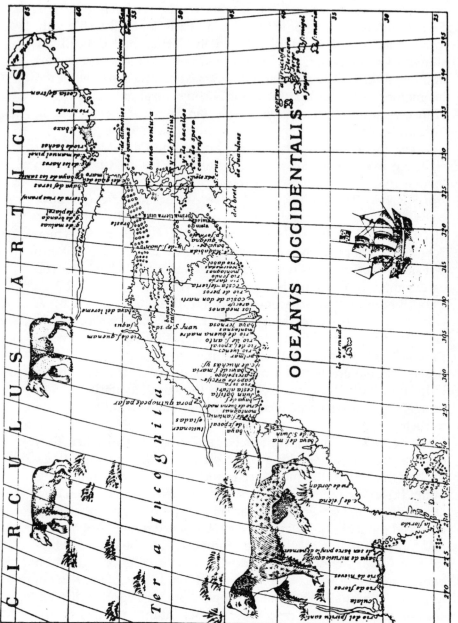

2.4 Northeastern North America as shown on Sebastian Cabot's Paris Map, 1544, according to J.G. Bourinot (1891).

state of war with France (1543–7), it would have been greatly in English interests to be able to claim an early landfall in the gulf, rather than on Newfoundland, which Cartier had definitively shown to be insular, Cape Breton then being understood as part of the mainland. The suspicion that Sebastian might have tailored his memories to suit his ambitions is conjectural but, as the great Franco-American cartographic historian Henry Harrisse put it, 'fort probable.'[82]

There are no strong reasons for giving the Paris Map greater standing than any other and, unfortunately for the Cape Breton theory, maps dating closer to the actual voyage tell a different story. Robert Thorne labelled the Newfoundland and Labrador coast 'The land here was first discovered by the English,' in a map of 1527, based on Spanish intelligence gleaned in Seville, where Sebastian Cabot was then *piloto mayor* (figure 2.5).[83] Diego Ribeiro put similar inscriptions on maps of 1529 and circa 1530.[84] An even earlier map, in the Kunstmann Atlas of circa 1514 to 1520, labels Cape Breton as 'land discovered by the Bretons' (figure 2.6). A later map, published by Jacopo Gastaldi in 1558, shows a cross on an inlet, just north of Cape Spear and well south of 'Bonne vista' (figure 2.7).[85] Was this intended as the cross John Cabot is supposed to have erected as a mark of discovery or is it simply an indication that Christians frequented the spacious harbour of St John's? The cartographic record is ambiguous when it is not contradictory.

We do at least know what Cabot and his men did when they came ashore, besides taking on fresh water: they planted flags. Each of the extant contemporary reports of the voyage makes this point. It is one of the few aspects of the expedition on which they all comment and on which they are in pretty close agreement. Soncino told the Duke of Milan that Cabot 'hoisted the royal standard, and took possession for the king.' John Day told the Grand Admiral that Cabot's crew 'disembarked ... with a crucifix and raised banners with the arms of the Holy Father and those of the King of England.' Pasqualigo's Venetian report puts a slightly different spin on the event: 'The discoverer of these things planted on the land which he has found a large cross with a banner of England

2.5 Northeastern North America as shown on Robert Thorne, *Orbis Universalis Descriptio*, 1527. The Latin legend northwards of Newfoundland (shown here as a peninsula) reads 'Land here first discovered by the English.'

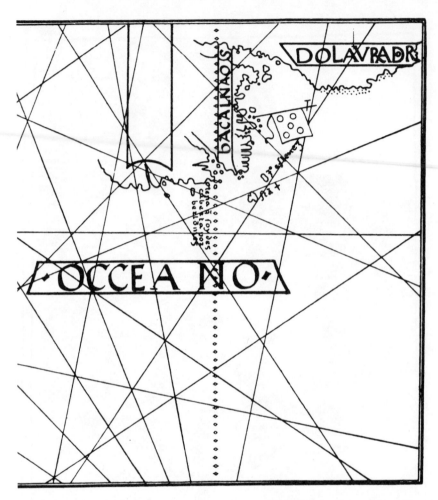

2.6 Atlantic Canada in the Kunstmann Atlas, ca. 1520, according to Henry Harrisse, 1900. Newfoundland is labelled 'bacalnaos'; the legend off northern Nova Scotia reads 'tera ã foy descuberta por bertõmes' (land discovered by Bretons).

and one of St Mark, as he is a Venetian, so that our flag has been hoisted very far afield.' It was, in effect, Cabot's job to make such symbolic gestures; his royal patent instructed him 'to set up our aforesaid banners and ensigns in any town, city, castle, island or mainland whatsoever, newly found.'[86] Let us leave aside, for the

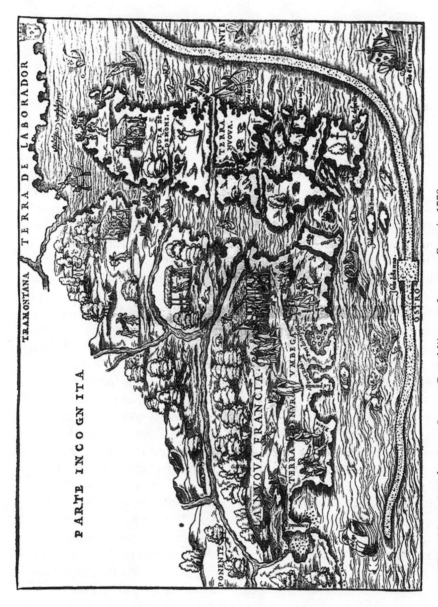

2.7 'Terra Nuova' as shown on Jacopo Gastaldi's map *La nuova Francia*, 1558.

moment, the question of what Cabot and King Henry intended by
such a ceremony, and attend to what followed.

AFTER THE LANDFALL

The latitude information given in the Day Letter provides a minimum indication of the North American littoral explored by Cabot
in 1497. If he was in the latitudes of the Strait of Belle Isle and of
Newfoundland's Avalon Peninsula and/or Cape Breton Island,
then he explored, at least, the coast between these latitudes, that
is, the east coast of Newfoundland from the Great Northern Peninsula to Trinity and Conception Bays.[87] Cartographic historians
have often credited the voyage of 1497 with exploration of Newfoundland's south coast as well, which would certainly make
sense, if the Island of the Seven Cities was Cape Breton Island.
This view of the voyage is usually supported with an analysis of
the la Cosa Map. Baron Walckenaer recovered this manuscript
map on oxhide from a Parisian bric-à-brac shop in 1832; his friend
the naturalist Alexander von Humboldt identified it in the
Baron's library; and it was sold to the Naval Museum in Madrid
in 1853, after appearing in Europe in various published versions.[88] In the twentieth century it has often been used by those
who argue that Cabot landed at Cape Breton, exploring Nova
Scotia and the south coast of Newfoundland before departing the
New World from Cape Race.[89] Juan de la Cosa's planisphere is
usually dated to about 1500 and, if the dating is correct, it incor-
porates the earliest depiction of northeastern North America. On
this map a very long stretch of east/west trending coastline is
shown on the Atlantic coast, marked with English flags and
labelled with a number of place names (figure 2.8). Proponents of
a Cape Breton landfall have argued that Cavo de Ynglaterra is
Cape Race and that the Cavo descubierto must be Cape Breton,
despite the fact that it is shown continuous with the supposed
Newfoundland coast. This requires us to accept that Cabot somehow missed the conspicuous strait between the former and the
latter, to which the British Admiralty would give his name in
1888.[90] There are other problems with the interpretation.

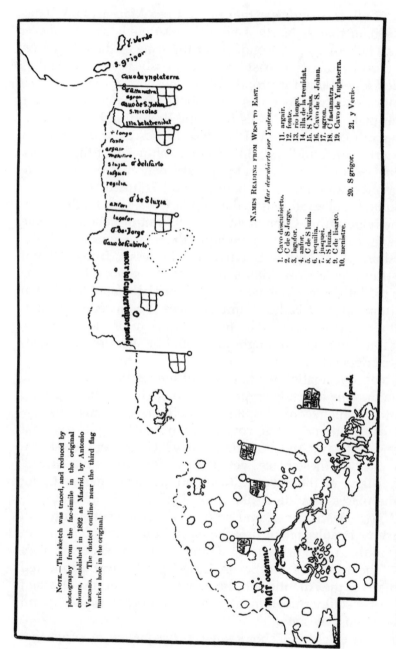

NOTE.—This sketch was traced, and reduced by photography from the fac-simile in the original colours, published in 1892 at Madrid, by Antonio Vascano. The dotted outline near the third flag marks a hole in the original.

NAMES READING FROM WEST TO EAST.

Mar descubierto por Yngleses.

1. Cavo descubierta.
2. C de S Jorge.
3. lagafor.
4. anfor.
5. C de S luzia.
6. requilin.
7. jusquei.
8. S luzia.
9. C de lisarte.
10. menistre.

11. argair.
12. fonte.
13. rio longo.
14. illa de la trenidat.
15. S Nicolas.
16. Cavo de S. Johan.
17. agron.
18. C f-actanatra.
19. Cavo de Ynglaterra.

20. S grigor.

21. y Verde.

Y. Verde
S. grigor
Cavo de ynglaterra
d'Altanatra
agron
Cavo de S. Johan
S. nicolas
illa latrenidat
+ longo
fonte
argair
menistre
S luzia d'delisarte
lufquei
requilia
anfort
lagofor d' de S luzia
d'de Jorge
Cavo de Kubierto

Mar oceano
Cuba

2.8 North American coastline as shown on Juan de la Cosa's *Mappemonde*, ca. 1500–8, according to Samuel Dawson (1894).

First of all, it is not clear that the la Cosa Map actually dates from 1500, or that its North American coastline is based only on Cabot's 1497 voyage.[91] Second, either the scale or the orientation of the North American coast must be grossly in error. This has provided a field day for proponents of various landfalls to trace mutually exclusive itineraries for Cabot. S.E. Dawson and W.F. Ganong make plausible cases for Cape Breton and Newfoundland's south coast; but G.W.F. Prowse makes a good argument for eastern Newfoundland; B.F. Hoffman shows that the la Cosa coastline resembles some contemporary concepts of the whole North American littoral; D.B. Quinn and J.T. Juricek each argue, with some topological twists, that the la Cosa Map might represent the region from Cape Breton to the Strait of Belle Isle; some nineteenth-century scholars thought the map represented the north shore of the Gulf of St Lawrence; Professor True of Miami argues that the la Cosa Map shows Cabot's voyage from Cape Breton to Florida; one ingenious geographer has Cabot fetch up in the Miramichi; and Father Campeau sees it as a representation of northeastern Eurasia.[92] The map appears to be able to prove almost anything and we might justifiably be wary of interpretations that depend upon it.

The only information we have about the territory coasted, the latitude minima apart, is cryptic. Historians have fallen back on the cartographic record, despite its ambiguities, because the few extant descriptions of the voyage do not make it clear what exactly Cabot saw. And how could they? There were few European names for these places yet; just legendary ones like 'Brasil' or the 'Island of the Seven Cities' and whatever names Cabot gave the places he visited, like the 'island of St John' and, perhaps, 'Cavo Descubierto,' and so on. Cabot's nomenclature did not survive in subsequent use; the early European toponomy of Newfoundland is Portuguese, dating from the sixteenth century.[93] 'The Island of the Seven Cities' gradually disappeared from maps of the Atlantic and the name 'Brazil' became attached to part of a southern continent, where Europeans finally found the dye-wood they sought.

As for the extent of Cabot's voyage, Pasqualigo reported that he coasted his 'mainland' for about 300 leagues, which would be 1400 to 1800 kilometres (900 to 1200 miles), depending on whether he was using English or Italian leagues and was thinking of land or sea distances. The Day Letter says, obscurely, that 'most of the land was discovered after turning back.' This can be taken as an indication that the landfall was near but not at one terminus of the littoral coasted and that Cabot went a little in one direction before making most of his explorations in the other. Alternatively, it might mean that he did more of an inshore exploration on his return trip, after a more rapid headland to headland survey following the landfall. He would have headed south from his landfall, or at least from any landfall in the latitudes of Ireland, since his intention was to find the fabled land of Cipango or Japan, described by Marco Polo, and he knew this to lie in more temperate climes.[94] Assuming a landfall somewhere in or near the Strait of Belle Isle, a southwards coastal voyage of '300 leagues' would have taken the *Matthew* at least as far as the southern Avalon Peninsula and possibly along Newfoundland's south coast to Cape Breton Island – if Cabot took his ship and crew from headland to headland and did not keep inshore.

It is possible that a description given by Sebastian to the Italian historian Peter Martyr relates, in part, to the 1497 voyage. In this account, Sebastian boasts of commanding an expedition of two ships to 55 degrees north, 'where he found the sea full of large masses of ice,' which forced him to turn back. Since there are no references to ice in the early descriptions of the 1497 voyage this almost certainly refers to Sebastian's later expedition of 1508. Martyr goes on to report that, after turning back, the younger Cabot was able to 'make his way along the coast which runs at first for a while in the southerly direction, [and] then turns west, and ... in that part he found great numbers of very large fish, which swim in shoals near the shores ... In this place and for the remainder of the voyage which he made back along this coast towards the west, he said that he always found the waters running westwards towards the gulf that, it had been reported, the said land makes.'[95] This sounds a lot like a voyage from a landfall in Labrador, southwards along the east coast of Newfoundland, following the Labrador current around Cape Race to the south coast of the island. Unfortunately, Sebastian's celebrated unreliability as a witness makes it impossible for us to be sure which voyage this itinerary summarizes. His father certainly had enough time to complete a voyage something like this. It is quite possible to sail from the Strait of Belle Isle along the east and south coasts of Newfoundland and back in a month, which is the time he spent on exploration in 1497.[96]

John Cabot left North America from Cape Dégrat: the Day Letter is explicit on the subject, in the sense that it gives specific latitude data. (If only the landfall could be so easily identified!) Running before favourable winds, the *Matthew* made a speedy return passage and was off the coast of northern France in fifteen days. Day told the Grand Admiral that Cabot made Brittany rather than the Bristol Channel 'because the sailors confused him, saying he was headed too far north.' Together they had made an error of a degree or so. Cabot was probably still grappling with the difficult problem of correcting for compass variation, a variation that would have slowly decreased as he recrossed the Atlantic. Under medieval maritime law, the Rule of Oléron, the crew were quite within their rights to expect that their opinion about the ship's course be taken into account.[97] At any rate, ship and company were back in Bristol by 10 August and, by 23 August, Zuan Caboto was in London, to report what he had found to the King.[98]

He was, one gathers, the toast of the town. Pasqualigo reported that he was paid vast honours and called 'the Great Admiral'; he dressed in silk and the English ran after him 'like mad.' He granted islands to his friends and considered himself 'at least a prince.'[99] Upon receiving news of the success of his voyage, the notoriously parsimonious King Henry gave him a reward of £10 and, later that year, granted Cabot an annual pension of £20, payable out of the Bristol customs receipts.[100] These were substantial amounts, in a period when Cabot could rent a house for £2 a year.[101] Master and men had different perspectives on what was the most valuable result of the voyage:

These same English, his companions, say that they could bring so many fish that this kingdom would have no further need of Iceland, from which place there comes a very great quantity of the fish called stockfish. But Messer Zoane has his mind set upon even greater things, because he proposes to keep along the coast from place at which he touched ... until he reaches an island which he calls Cipango [viz., Japan], situated in the equinoctal region, where he believes that all the spices of the world have their origin, as well as the jewels.[102]

Traditionally these things came to Europe by caravan from the east, from one hand to another. It would be possible to reach their eastern origin by travelling west, 'always assuming that the earth is round,' as Soncino commented.[103] Cabot made 'a description of the world in a map' and a globe as well to show where he had been.[104] As far as the Milanese ambassador was concerned, 'He tells all this in such a way, and makes everything so plain, that I also feel compelled to believe him.'

More to the point, King Henry believed Cabot, liked his ideas for turning London into 'a more important mart for spices than Alexandria,' and was willing to support further exploration. There was talk, in the heady days just after his successful return, of an expedition of ten or a dozen ships.[105] Pasqualigo observed that 'he can enlist as many ... as he pleases, and a number of our rogues as well.' Early the next year, King Henry granted new letters patent, authorizing Cabot to man a fleet of up to six ships of up to two hundred tons burthen in any English port.[106] In the end, he sailed again out of Bristol, with a vessel manned and victualled at royal expense, accompanied by three or four smaller ships. This time he had the backing of London merchants, as well as his Bristol principals. They freighted the ships with 'sleight and grosse merchandizes': coarse cloth, caps, laces, points (that is, decorative laces for tying one's hose to one's doublet) 'and other trifles.'[107] These were the very goods the English would trade to New World peoples for the next century or two, with the later addition of knives and hatchets. The goods shipped are one of several distinct indications in the documents of 1497/1498 that the court in London and the merchants, mostly in Bristol, perceived Cabot's voyages in different ways. In some respects it was parochial of the western adventurers to focus attention on fish and the possibilities of trade in small goods, presumably to a relatively unsophisticated market, instead of attending to the geopolitical possibilities of opening a new spice trade with the Orient. On the other hand, their limited horizons served them well. Cabot and Henry VII were still working under an illusion: the Venetian navigator had not reached Asia, let alone the advanced civilizations of China or Japan. Meanwhile, within five years, Bristol would be mounting fishing voyages to the new found land (although, to be sure, these early ventures were not sustained).[108]

At this point John Cabot sailed, as they say, into history. He did not return from the voyage of 1498 and he found new lands, as the historian Polydore Vergil cruelly put it, 'nowhere but on the very bottom of the ocean.'[109] One of his ships turned back and put into an Irish port; Cabot kept on and we remain unsure of what happened to him or the others.[110] According to Robert Fabyan's *Chronicle*, an English expedition of this period did return, with 'three savage men ... clothed in beasts skinnes.'[111] Although Hakluyt prints this immediately following an account of the voyage of 1498, it actually refers to the seventeenth year of the reign of Henry VII, that is, 1502.[112] There are, nevertheless, indications that at least some of the ships reached the New World and carried on further explorations. Gaspar Corte-Real's expedition of 1501 to the northwest Atlantic retrieved a broken Italian sword and a pair of Venetian silver earrings.[113] The new information about English discoveries on the early sixteenth-century la Cosa Map may reflect achievements of Cabot's third voyage.[114] Of Zuan Caboto, we hear nothing more. Bristol customs officials paid his pension in 1498, in his absence, presumably to Mattia.[115] There are no records of further payments. One of the great navigators of early modern Europe had disappeared at sea. Within a century he was virtually forgotten.

3

Legends of Sebastian

The stream of time has been dragged with humane perseverance, and many who, it was supposed, had sunk to rise no more, are made to reappear at the surface.

Richard Biddle, *A Memoir of Sebastian Cabot* (1831)[1]

THE CABOT THAT TIME FORGOT

For centuries, the name 'John Cabot' was obscure, forgotten in most chronicles, known to few historians and confused by most with his son Sebastian. This is not to say that his voyage was forgotten. Even if memories of the voyages of 1496, 1497, and 1498 were mixed up, one with another and with a voyage that Sebastian made to Labrador in 1508, the fact that a pilot named Cabot had mounted an early transatlantic expedition from Bristol was remembered.[2] What is more, this was remembered as a precedent: the basis of British claims to North America. The great eighteenth-century conservative Anglo-Irish writer Edmund Burke began the historical part of his *Account of the European Settlements in America*, with the following argument:

We derive our rights in America from the discovery of Sebastian Cabot, who first made the Northern continent in 1497. The fact is sufficiently certain to establish a right to our settlements in North America: but the particulars are not known distinctly enough to encourage me to enter into a detail of his voyage. The country was in general called Newfoundland, a name which is now appropriated solely to an island upon it's coast. It was a long time before we made any attempt to settle this country; though in this point we were no more backward than our neighbours, who probably did not abstain so long out of respect to our prior discovery.[3]

The argument was, doubtless, à propos in 1757, early in Britain's Seven Years' War with France, when Burke first published his *Account*; but neither the argument nor the historical misconceptions were new. The New England merchant Henry Gardener had expounded the same thesis and exhibited the same confusion in *New-Englands Vindication*, in 1660, and the pedigrees of both argument and misconception were even longer.[4]

John Dee, the Elizabethan cosmographer who first came up with the concept of a 'British Empire,' likewise credited the voyage of 1497 to Sebastian.[5] In 1578 he made notes regarding the lawful title of his sovereign lady, Queen Elizabeth, to North America. What is significant about this 'brief remembrance of sundry foreign Regions, discovered, inhabited and partly conquered by the Subjects of this Brytish Monarchie' is not simply the confusion of John Cabot's voyage of 1497 with Sebastian's voyage of 1508, but also the context in which Dee misremembered these events – a mix of what we now regard as myth, on the one hand, with the elusive, poorly documented history of proto-discovery, on the other. Dee lists the sixth-century Irish monk Brendan, the twelfth-century Welsh prince Madoc, besides Thorne and Elyot of Bristol, circa 1494, before he mentions the Cabot explorations: 'Circa An. 1497 ... Sebastian Caboto, sent by King Henry the seventh, did discover from Newfownd Land so far along and abowt the Coaste next to Laborador tyll he came to the Latitude of 67½. And styll fownd the Seas open before him.'[6] Dee was the most learned British scholar of his time, with a library of thousands of volumes at his home in Mortlake.[7] If he could not remember John Cabot, eighty years after his last voyage, who could?

The elder Cabot was, in fact, never quite forgotten, although often assigned a modest role in what the chroniclers remembered, essentially, as his son's achievements. The Elizabethan editor Richard Hakluyt spent decades compiling and publishing accounts of English exploration. Most of the Cabot materials he collected mention Sebastian alone but Hakluyt did recognize that John had some kind of role in the early voyages. He printed Henry VII's Letters Patent of 1496 to John and his sons. When he published the third volume of his famous *Principal Navigations* in 1600, he amended his 'Note of Sebastian Cabots first discoverie,' first published in the original *Divers Voyages* of 1582, so that Robert Fabyan's *Chronicle* mentioned the elder Cabot, as a kind of consultant.[8] But for every early modern account that alluded to John, there were several that celebrated Sebastian. Peter Martyr described the Bacallaos, that is, Newfoundland, as the discovery of Sebastian, in his influential *De Orbe Novo Decades* of 1516, as well as in the *Historia dell' Indie Occidentali* of 1534.[9] He was followed in this by Francisco Gomara in his *Historia General de las Indias* of 1552 and by André Thevet in his fanciful account of the Americas of 1558.[10] Martyr's *Decades* and Gomara's *Historia* were widely circulated works, in many editions in their original Latin and Spanish, as well as in French, German, and English translations.[11]

Often, as in Dee and Hakluyt, such accounts confused the son's 1508 voyage to northern Labrador with the father's 1497 voyage in the middle latitudes. Alonso de Santa Cruz laboured under this misunderstanding in a Spanish manuscript geography of 1541. Giovanni Ramusio presented a like account in his widely read *Navigationi et Viaggi* of 1550, which went through several editions and many printings, into the seventeenth century.[12] In 1563, two comparably confused accounts appeared in print, one by the Portuguese historian Antonio Galvano in his *Tratado* and one by the French pilot Jean Ribault.[13] Ribault's history of the European exploration of the Atlantic coast of North America appeared simultaneously in an English edition, later reprinted in *Divers Voyages* by Richard Hakluyt, who also published an English translation of Galvano in 1601.[14] By the late sixteenth century, Continental scholars had established a tradition that featured Sebastian as the European discoverer of North America. English scholars, generally following Hakluyt, kept the memory of John just barely alive, as a shadowy background figure in a similar narrative.

If the Cabots were mentioned at all by seventeenth- or early-eighteenth-century historians, it was Sebastian who was credited with discoveries in the northwest Atlantic. The 1624 edition of John Smith's *Generall Historie of Virginia* praises Sebastian and notes: 'For though *Cullumbus* had found certaine Isles, it was 1498 ere he saw the Continent, which was a yeare after *Cabot*.'[15] In his *Pilgrimes* of 1625, Samuel Purchas went so far as to argue that Sebastian was such 'a great Discoverer' that America should have been called 'Cabotiana.'[16] With blithe Euro-centrism he reported that John and Sebastian together 'discovered that land which no man before had attempted,' but went on to quote an account that emphasized Sebastian's participation to the exclusion of John.[17] In a book of 1635 on his own Arctic explorations, Luke Foxe recalled the elder Cabot but, deriving his narrative from Hakluyt, he celebrated Sebastian. So did Reverend William Hubbard in his manuscript history of New England (ca. 1682), calling Sebastian 'a famous Portuguez.'[18] In the 1660s, Gardener thought of the younger Cabot as the discoverer of North America, as did John Oldmixon in *The British Empire in America* (1708), Thomas Lediard in *The Naval History of England* (1735), and Thomas Prince in his *The Chronological History of New England* (1736).[19] Lediard quoted at length from a number of documents that mention John, like the royal patent, as well as from accounts that credit Sebastian independently. He puzzled over the apparent contradiction and ventured an explicit explanation, which others had, perhaps, tacitly assumed:

By what is said hitherto, it has the Appearance as if these Discoveries were made by *John Cabot*, and his Son, *Sebastian*, in Company: And it is certain, that the Commission was granted to both; And the License to *John Cabot* alone. But by a Piece which we find in *Hakluyt*, it would seem as if the voyage was made by *Sebastian* alone, and as we hear no more of his Father, after this Time, he may perhaps, have died, between the Interval of granting the License, and the departure of his little Fleet; or have staid at Home, and sent his Son alone.[20]

By the mid-eighteenth century, John Campbell had sorted these confusions out. In his *Lives of the Admirals*, first published in 1748, he distinguished carefully the achievements of the Cabots. Thus, Edmund Burke was a little behind the times, historiographically, in his 1757 account.[21] Campbell's treatment is quite traditional in the great credit it gives to Sebastian's abilities. The younger Cabot's reputation as an explorer seems to have outlived the historiographic basis on which it was originally founded, so that even for Campbell he was 'the most accomplished seaman who lived in his time ... whose memory deserves for his industry, penetration, and integrity to be transmitted to posterity.'[22] William Mavor's collection of *Voyages*, published in 1796, also credits Sebastian with great discoveries in the north in 1497, following a supposed discovery of Newfoundland by father and son the previous year.[23] John Forster's widely read late-eighteenth-century *History of the Voyages and Discoveries Made in the North* resolved the earlier confusions in yet a different way, by ascribing the 1497 voyage to John but doubting that he reached northern Labrador – that is, by rejecting the confusing early accounts, in Hakluyt for example, which actually pertain to Sebastian's subarctic voyage of 1508. Sebastian nevertheless remained for Forster a kind of nebulous hero.[24] In France, the mid-eighteenth-century *Histoire générale des voyages* stressed the uncertainties of the Cabot story and gave as much credit to Sebastian as to his father.[25] This grew into a French tradition that gave credit either to an unspecified 'Cabot,' as in Abbé Raynal's *History of British Settlements* of 1776, or to Sebastian, as in Alexander von Humboldt's *Examen critique de l'histoire de la géographie du nouveau continent* of 1836.[26]

The apotheosis of Sebastian came with the first important American publication on the subject, Richard Biddle's *Memoir of Sebastian Cabot*, published anonymously in Philadelphia, in 1831.[27] Biddle was aware of John but, after weighing the 'Comparative Agency of John and Sebastian Cabot,' credited the latter with command of the voyages of exploration.[28] He even attacked Hakluyt's 'perversion' of inserting John's name into Fabyan's *Chronicles*, flaying the Elizabethan scholar in print for 'his guilty deed.'[29] For the first time, effacement of John provoked serious argument, setting the tone for nineteenth-century debate on these topics.[30] The pattern was repeated in 1869, with the publication, in Bristol, of J.F. Nicholl's *Remarkable Life, Adventures and Discoveries of Sebastian Cabot*, which prompted this bleakly succinct review by an American scholar who was more impressed with the new wisdom:

Sebastian Cabot – John Cabot = 0.

It is difficult to think of the appropriate historical units in which to compare the significance of John and his son, but it is worthwhile considering carefully the centuries of confusion between them. Understanding the origins of this confusion will help to clarify its effects on the several Cabot traditions. Among other things, it will explain why a perfectly rational historian might claim that Sebastian Cabot amounted to nothing more than what he 'borrowed' from his father.[31]

THE ACHIEVEMENT OF SEBASTIAN CABOT

The idea that Sebastian Cabot was a historical non-entity is, on the face of it, absurd. Not only did he enjoy a long and distinguished career as a pilot and cartographic adviser to several European governments, his life was better documented than his father's, with the result that we know much more about him than we know about the elder Cabot.[32] This circumstance alone might promote misapplication of elements of Sebastian's biography to his relatively obscure father. Instead, with one notable exception, it is the converse that happened. With the hindsight of five centuries, it seems clear that Sebastian's considerable achievements were not enough for him and that he made repeated attempts to take credit for his father's North American explorations in 1497 and 1498 in addition to his own. As we have seen, he came close to succeeding in this fraud. When the deception was exposed, in the nineteenth century, Sebastian's reputation suffered a catastrophic collapse.[33] In this historiographic context it was possible to assess his historical significance as nil compared with that of his father John. This was understandable, but unjust; Sebastian himself was a man of considerable parts.

As already noted, it is unclear whether or not he actually accompanied his father John on the voyage of 1497.[34] A complaint of the London chartered companies in 1521, when Thomas Cardinal Wolsey proposed to put Sebastian in command of another expedition to Newfoundland, is thought-provoking: 'We think it were to sore aventour to jeopardize 5 shipps with men & goodes unto the said Iland uppon the singular trust of one man, callyd as we understond, Sebastyan, whiche Sebastyan, as we here say, was never in that land hym self, all if he makes reporte of many thinges as he hath heard his father and other men speke in tymes past.'[35]

There is, on the other hand, good evidence that Sebastian Cabot commanded an expedition up the coast of Labrador in 1508. Peter Martyr described Sebastian's explorations in several early-sixteenth-century editions of his *Decades* and the voyage was recalled, later in the century, by George Best, in his account of the 1576 expedition of Sir Martin Frobisher, the English explorer first known to have followed Sebastian to these northern waters.[36] The younger Cabot often claimed to have explored as far north as 55 degrees, and he told Ramusio that he reached 67½ degrees north, finding open water in what we now call Hudson Strait, between continental North America and Baffin Island.[37] The modern European toponymy of the region celebrates the exploits of the English pilots of the early seventeenth century, who explored the eastern Canadian Arctic about a century after Sebastian's voyage. Martyr, Ramusio, and Best were, by no means, the only sixteenth-century writers to credit the younger Cabot with an arctic or subarctic exploration.[38] It was, without much doubt, an early attempt to find a northwest passage and therefore has great intellectual significance, for it signals English recognition that the lands explored by John Cabot and subsequent Bristol expeditions in the first few years of the sixteenth century were not the northeast coast of Asia but part of a New World.[39]

Sebastian was himself an associate of the Bristol/Azorean syndicate that mounted transatlantic expeditions between 1503 and

1505, the Company Adventurers in to the New Fownde Ilondes.[40] Henry VII granted him an annual pension of £10 in 1505, for 'diligent service and attendaunce ... doon unto us in and aboute the fyndynge of the newe founde landes to our full good pleasure.'[41] It looks as if the rights of the Cabots, by the patents of 1496 and 1497, had at this point been merged with the rights of the syndicate of Thomas Asshehurst, Hugh Elyot, João Gonsalves, and Fransisco Fernandes, granted under a patent 'to discover unknown Land' in 1502.[42] Although there is no unambiguous evidence that Sebastian actually sailed on any of these expeditions, discrepancies in his various accounts of Labrador would be resolved if we assumed that he made two voyages there. He may well have participated in a voyage mounted by Elyot and another Bristol merchant, William Thorne, in 1504, to the 'Newe Found Iland.'[43] On the other hand, Sebastian's services for this earlier expedition may simply have consisted in the preparation of charts. We are more certain that he accompanied (and in fact commanded) the Labrador expedition of 1508. Sebastian would have found it difficult to promote further English exploration after his return from this voyage; by the time he arrived back in England his patron Henry VII had died, to be succeeded by his son Henry VIII, who was less forthcoming in support of exploration.[44]

Through the rest of his long and eventful life, Sebastian found employment more often as a cartographer than as a practising pilot. It was, in fact, as a map-maker that he arrived in the Basque country of northern Spain in June of 1512, as part of an English military expedition against France. He soon met with officials at Burgos, the commercial and administrative centre of the region, and by October he was in Spanish naval service. The following year he became a royal pilot.[45] Initially, this may have been with the intention of leading a Spanish expedition to the northwest Atlantic, but in 1518, two years after the death of King Ferdinand, Charles V made him *piloto mayor* of Spain. For thirty years Sebastian was entrusted with maintaining the accuracy of the *padrón real*, the evolving unpublished map of the world, kept in Seville and used by the Spanish to update their charts.[46] In this respect he was, in sixteenth-century terminology, a cosmographer as much as a cartographer. As *piloto mayor*, it was also Sebastian's job to instruct and examine the pilots of the 'House of Trade,' the Casa de Contratación de las Indias, in new cartographic realities as well as in navigational technique.[47]

Throughout his career, Sebastian sold his services to the highest bidder. In the 1520s and 1530s this happened to be Spain. Iberian governments, in this period, funded research in the new sciences of navigation and cartography, with the explicit intention of promoting the national commercial interest.[48] At various times Sebastian toyed with the idea of returning to his native Venice, to further a revival of its waning maritime capabilities.[49] In 1521, he was tempted to return to England to command a Newfoundland expedition proposed by Cardinal Wolsey and opposed by the London merchant companies who were expected to foot the bill.[50] After the death of Henry VIII Sebastian would, eventually, return to English service, but Wolsey's project came to nothing and, for the time being, he remained in Seville.

In 1526, the younger Cabot took command of his only known expedition in Spanish service, one that turned out to be a disaster of considerable proportions. He never gained the trust of the merchant backers of the venture, who conceived of it as a voyage to the 'Spice Islands' of southeast Asia. Sebastian, meanwhile, had secret royal instructions to seek a South American passage to the Pacific Ocean more accessible than the Straits Magellan had found in 1520.[51] After losing his flagship on the coast of Brazil, Sebastian met European settlers who told him stories of gold and silver to be found up the Rio de la Plata, which meets the Atlantic where Buenos Aires stands today. At this news he unilaterally changed the aims of the expedition and headed for the River Plate. Calamity followed calamity. Before he could explore the river he had to arrest and maroon his more recalcitrant officers; Native Amerindians ambushed and killed many of his men; he never found the treasures he sought; and he returned to Spain in 1530 with little but a cargo of slaves, purchased on the return voyage. He had added a little to European geographical knowledge, although the Portuguese pilot Juan Diaz de Solis, who would briefly precede him as *piloto mayor*, had already explored the Rio de la Plata in 1515.[52] Sebastian was charged and convicted of disobedience and, in effect, manslaughter. He paid heavy fines but seems never to have served a sentence of banishment to the Spanish colony in Morocco.

By 1532 Sebastian had resumed his duties as *piloto mayor*. He devoted much of the following decade to cartography. In 1533 he began drafting a new map of the world.[53] About 1540 he became embroiled in a series of professional disputes with the royal cosmographer, Alonso de Chaves, who would eventually succeed Sebastian as *piloto mayor*. The issues concerned, in part, Sebastian's profitable monopoly over the certification of charts and navigational instruments, but also the serious scientific question of how best to deal cartographically with the problem created by magnetic variation in certain parts of the world, particularly the northwest Atlantic, where the compass pointed west of north by 20 to 30 degrees. Sebastian and Diego Gutiérrez, a fellow cosmographer of the Casa de Contratación, suffered a serious professional setback about 1545. Gutiérrez and his family produced the charts that Sebastian so profitably certified and his technique of using local scales of latitude was rejected by the Spanish authorities because the results did not conform to the *padrón real*.[54]

Sebastian also became involved with a more public cartographic enterprise, the engraving and publication of maps. In March 1541 he contracted with a pair of German printers to produce an up-to-date world map.[55] Published maps were a complete novelty at the time, one that would revolutionize the chart trade and eventually have the profound effect of facilitating the scientific correction of geographical misconceptions.[56] This development also meant that geographical information, which previously had limited circulation, might become more widely known. The contents of the *padrón real* were not, however, secret.[57] It was normal for the *piloto mayor* and other royal pilots to prepare and sell charts based, on the *padrón real*. They were required to certify that these charts were so based, and one of the charges made against Sebastian and his ally Gutiérrez in the 1540s was that their charts did not conform to the *padrón* as they were supposed to.[58] It has been argued that Sebastian's published world map is a reflection of the state of the *padrón real* in this period, just as Gutiérrez's manuscript regional charts, produced for a limited, Spanish, professional market, were supposed to be.[59] The published map actually resembles other manuscript sources, for example, the 1541 world map drafted by Nicholas Desliens of Dieppe, an early record of Cartier's explorations.[60]

Sebastian's map was engraved on copper plate and published in 1544.[61] A single copy survives: the Paris Map, which gave nineteenth-century Cabot scholars much food for thought, with its legend implying a Cape Breton landfall by John and Sebastian at the surprisingly early date of 1494. The technique of engraving had not reached Spain in the 1540s and the image was probably cut in Antwerp, in the Spanish Netherlands.[62] This implies that Sebastian could not have had close editorial control over production of the map, which may account for some of its plentiful blunders. Comparison with a nearly contemporary manuscript world map executed by Sancho Gutiérrez of the Casa de Contratación suggests that the legends, at least, are based on information from the *padrón real*.[63] This does not, of course, prove that they are accurate, but it does suggest that they reflect the history of Atlantic exploration according to Sebastian Cabot or, more precisely, that they reflect the latter's autobiographical intentions. As we have already seen, they may also reflect a wish on Sebastian's part to win diplomatic favour with his former patrons in London.

In the later 1530s Sebastian had again put out feelers regarding the possibilities of a return to England. He spoke to the English ambassador to Spain in 1538, although nothing came of this contact at the time. Records of subsequent negotiations have not survived, but in 1547, shortly after the death of Henry VIII, the Privy Council budgeted £100 'for the transporting of one Shabot, a pilot, to come out of Hispain.'[64] The following year, Sebastian took a leave of five months from his duties in Seville, ostensibly to go to Germany. Instead, he returned to England, where Henry's successor King Edward VI granted the Venetian pilot an annuity of £166 13s 4d. This was not the odd sum it sounds but 250 marks, a unit often used for honourable emoluments. Sebastian's stock had risen considerably in the three and a half decades since he had abandoned Henry VII's annual pension of £10. Although in some part a reflection of inflation, which characterized the sixteenth century as it has the twentieth, this was also a measure of the valuable navigational and cartographic expertise that Cabot brought with him. English ships of the period were full of Venetian, Genoese, Breton, Norman, and other European mariners, because the English still lacked the navigational skills achieved by Continental pilots.[65] They would master this repertoire of techniques in the later sixteenth century and Sebastian Cabot was one of the vectors through which expertise in the new celestial navigation reached England. In this sense he was, as he has been called, 'the father of English navigation.'[66]

Sebastian's movements to and fro among several incipient modern European nations, had for some nineteenth-century scholars an air of treachery.[67] This is an anachronistic illusion. For much of the sixteenth century, England was, in effect, a client state of Spain. England's Queen Mary would share her throne with her husband, Philip of Spain, from her marriage in 1554 until her death in 1558, so that Philip was King of England before he became king of his own country, in 1556. Mary's death and the treaty of Cateau-Cambrésis between France and Spain in 1559 together mark an important turning point in European history. Until then European international relations were structured by the Habsburg/Valois struggle, pitting Spain against France, England being a peripheral ally of the former. After reconciliation of the two major Catholic powers, conflict emerged between Catholic, Mediterranean Spain and the newly Protestant north.[68] It is this later struggle, made vivid by public memories of the Armada of 1588 and the various Elizabethan sea-dogs who made their names attacking Spain, that we find easiest to remember when we think of the sixteenth century. Early Tudor England remained, however, a junior ally of Spain. In this diplomatic context, it is not so surprising that the English permitted Sebastian Cabot to pursue contacts with the Spanish court in 1512, or that he was able to return to London in 1520 to negotiate with Wolsey, or that the merchant investors in the Spanish expedition of 1526 included Robert Thorne of Bristol.[69] Although the Habsburg emperor, Charles V, would try to convince Sebastian to return to Spain and would make claims to the English government for his services, the peripatetic pilot's career was unlikely to cause an international incident, either in 1512, when he left English service, or in 1548, when he returned.[70] Besides, as Peter Martyr remarked, such mobility was 'the habit of ... Venetians, who in the pursuit of trade are the guests of all lands.'[71]

King Edward's decision to encourage Sebastian's return reflects renewed English interest in maritime expansion. This may have resulted, in part, from awareness of Cartier's explorations in the Gulf of St Lawrence between 1534 and 1542 and of Roberval's Canadian colony of 1541–3.[72] The 1550s saw the first renewal of serious English commitment to well-capitalized deep-sea trades since the Bristol expeditions of the early 1500s.[73] One of the first expressions of this renewal was the Willoughby-Chancellor expedition of 1553. It headed northeast to the White Sea rather than across the Atlantic, however, making a passage soon exploited by the Muscovy Company. The English thus avoided conflict with Spain, whose interests lay to the west and south. The distinguished governor of the 'mysterie and companie of the Marchants adventurers for the discoverie of Regions, Dominions, Islands and places unknown,' which opened up this trade, was the elderly Sebastian Cabot, who was then about seventy.

We have several late glimpses of Sebastian. He came down to the London quayside in April 1556 to wish success to another early northeastern expedition. The master, Steven Borough, recalled:

The 27 being Monday, the right Worshipfull Sebastian Cabota came aboord our Pinnasse at Gravesende, accompanied with divers Gentlemen, and Gentlewomen, who after that they had viewed our Pinesse, and tasted of such cheere as we could make them aboord, they went on shore, giving to our mariners right liberall rewards: and the good olde Gentleman Master Cabota gave to the poore most liberall almes, wishing them to pray for the good fortune, and prosperous successe of the *Serchthrift*, our Pinnesse. And then at the sign of the Christopher [a blessing], hee and his friends banketted [banqueted], and made me, and them that were in the company great cheere; and for the very joy that he had to see the towardnes of our intended discovery, he entred into the dance himself, among the rest of the young and lusty company: which being ended, hee and his friends departed most gently, commending us to the governace of almighty God.[74]

A year later, the good old gentleman was dead.

A contemporary portrait of Sebastian, in his later role of senior adviser to a new generation of English deep-sea mariners, survived into the nineteenth century. It had a convincing provenance and was probably the one Samuel Purchas saw hanging in a private gallery in the palace of Whitehall in the early seventeenth century. Two centuries later it was purchased for the very large sum of £500 by Richard Biddle, Sebastian's hagiographer, but was lost when Biddle's Pennsylvania mansion burned in the Pittsburgh fire of 1845. Fortunately, oil copies of the portrait and a number of engravings were made before its destruction, so that we can still contemplate Sebastian, in one version or another, with his globe and navigator's dividers, as he stares serenely past us, into space and time (figure 3.1). The inscription in a cartouche on the image begs a significant question: 'Portrait of Sebastian Cabot, Englishman, son of John Cabot, knight of Venice, First Discoverer of Newfoundland under Henry VII of England.'[75] Who was supposed, by the subject, the artist, and their mid-sixteenth-century audience to be the 'first discoverer of Newfoundland'? John Cabot, knight of Venice? Or Sebastian Cabot, Englishman, his son?

Sebastian was, in old age, a significant human link between two distinct periods in the development of British imperialism. In his youth, he participated in the first successful English transatlantic explorations between 1497 and 1508. There followed a kind of fallow period in which the English barely participated in the new European long-distance trades. (The Newfoundland fishery is a good case in point, where Bretons, Normans, Basques, and Portuguese fishermen greatly outnumbered England's Westcountrymen until the 1560s.) In the second half of the century, England began to develop overseas ambitions again. Although we tend to think of this reawakening as Elizabethan, it really began somewhat earlier, at mid-century, in the reign of Edward VI.[76] At the

SEBASTIAN CABOT.

From the original formerly in the possession of Charles Joseph Harford, Esq., of Stapleton, in the county of Gloucester. This painting afterwards became the property of Mr. Richard Biddle, of Pittsburg, Pennsylvania, and was destroyed by fire at his residence.

3.1 A nineteenth-century engraving based on an oil copy of the lost portrait of Sebastian Cabot, as reproduced in Charles Deane's 'The Legends of the Cabot Map of 1544' (1897). The inscription in the upper left-hand corner of the image reads 'Portrait of Sebastian Cabot, Englishman, son of John Cabot, knight of Venice, First Discoverer of Newfoundland under Henry VII of England.'

close of his career, Sebastian was a significant player in this English maritime renaissance, both as an administrator and as a technical expert. He thus linked two eras – but not in the way that he claimed.

SEBASTIAN CABOT LIED[77]

The engaging charm of Sebastian Cabot reaches across the centuries, so that he still has his defenders, who see him as misunderstood by others rather than as misrepresenting himself.[78] Such problems in communication are often the result of prevarication by the communicator, as much as of anything else, and this certainly seems to be the case here. The great American cartographic historian Henry Harrisse may have gone a bit too far when he called Sebastian an 'unmitigated charlatan, a liar and a traitor.'[79] We can at least say that the historical confusion between Sebastian and his father, John, not to mention other subsidiary chronological and geographical confusions, arose because the younger Cabot repeatedly and deliberately misrepresented his role in the voyage of 1497. Although it was probably not his intention, this had the result of virtually obliterating his own father from public memory for several centuries. Let us consider how Sebastian did this, why, and with what result.

A useful starting point might be the celebrated Eighth Legend of the published planisphere of 1544, now known as the Paris Map. The information can probably be ascribed to Sebastian, even if he did not draft every detail of the whole image or compose the printed Spanish and Latin texts himself. Here Sebastian took credit, with his father, for the original European discovery of North America, in a curiously confusing claim: 'This land was discovered by John Cabot the Venetian, and Sebastian Cabot his son, in the year of the birth of our Saviour Jesus Christ 1494, on the 24th of June in the morning, to which they gave the name First Land Seen [Prima Terra Vista] ...'[80] The legend goes on to provide details of the Native people of the region, although John Cabot actually avoided face-to-face encounters in 1497, and to describe the land as sterile with many white bears and so on, although the landfall is identified on the map as Cape Breton Island, a well-forested region where the bears are and were black, at least for the last few millennia.[81] The apparent error in the date of '1494' for '1497' has been explained as a misreading of 'iiii' for 'vii,' although several other early sources give the date 1494 for an early transatlantic exploration.[82] At least one late-twentieth-century scholar has revived the old claim that Sebastian actually made a voyage at this time, but the idea that he might have had a significant role in such an expedition, whether it took place in 1494 or 1497, is beyond belief, since he would have been about ten years old in the first case or thirteen in the second.[83]

Sebastian's claim to have taken part in finding 'the first land seen' had immense influence in England, because the map was recut and published again by Clement Adams in about 1549.[84] It hung 'in her Majesties privie gallerie at Westminster, and in many other ancient merchant houses,' according to Richard Hakluyt, who reprinted Adams's version of Sebastian's Legend in *The Principal Navigations* (1599–1600).[85] In Hakluyt's text the date is given as 1497, so it may be that the date was corrected on later versions of the map, none of which has survived, unfortunately.[86] Historians' squabbles over the confusion of 1494 and 1497 have been a sort of a red herring in Cabot studies.[87] The important question is whether Sebastian incorporated data from his Labrador expedition of 1508 into his various accounts of the first successful Cabot expedition of 1497. In the case of the Paris Map, it seems obvious that he did.

Sebastian consistently made two claims. Both may actually have been literally true, although he presented them together in such a way as to give a false impression. First, he claimed to have taken part in the expedition of 1497, thus participating in the landfall and what he saw as the original European discovery of North America. He may well have done so, as a cabin boy, but the carefully worded way he put this, for example in the Paris Map, with its implication that he held some kind of command, appears designed to deceive. Second, he claimed to have explored the coast of Labrador; sometimes to 55 or 56 degrees north, roughly the location of the present community of Makkovik, north of

Hamilton Inlet; sometimes as far as 67½ degrees north, the northern extremity of the Labrador Peninsula at Cape Chidley. In each case we have supporting evidence for the account, but Sebastian used this Labrador experience to mislead, to the extent that he supplied data from the voyage of 1508 (and possibly another of 1504) as an account of the voyage of 1497 (sometimes misdated to 1494 or 1496 or 1498).[88] The confused sixteenth-century accounts that concatenate the two (or three) voyages, as the Paris Map does, are as likely to have resulted from the way Sebastian chose to report what he had seen in the New World, as they are from any other failure of communication.

In certain very influential accounts of his northwestern explorations it is evident that Sebastian went even further and omitted his father from the narrative altogether. An elision of the voyages of 1497 and 1498 characterizes Sebastian's version of early North American exploration, as given to Peter Martyr, who published a summary narrative in various forms between 1516 and 1534.[89] Martyr knew Sebastian well, 'as a familiar friend and sometimes as a guest in my house.' In the first edition of his friend Martyr's *Decades*, Sebastian took credit for the discovery of Newfoundland and Labrador: 'Cabot himself called these lands the Baccalaos because in the adjacent sea he found so great a quantity of a certain kind of great fish like tunnies, called bacallaos.'[90] (The text goes on to say that these fish, i.e., cod, were called 'bacallaos' by the Native inhabitants of the region; but the word is actually much older, in several European languages.)[91]

Martyr's second account of 'the very prudent and practical navigator Sebastian Cabot the Venetian' is even more explicitly oblivious of the elder Cabot's achievements:

Sebastian ... when a child was taken to England by his father, and on the latter's death, being very rich and of an enterprising mind, thought that, as Christopher Columbus had done, so he too wished to discover some new part of the world. And at his own expense he equipped two ships and in the month of July set sail between the west and the north, and sailed so far that with the quadrant he observed the pole star to be elevated 55 degrees, where he found the sea full of large masses of ice ...

And by reason of the said ice he was obliged to turn back and make his way along the coast which runs at first for a while in the southerly direction, then turns west, and because in that part he found a great number of very large fish, which swim in shoals near the shores, and understood from the inhabitants that they called them Baccalai, he called this the Land of the Baccalai.[92]

The fact that Martyr never mentions John Cabot in connection with discovery is a strong indication that the historian was misled by his good friend, the prudent and practical navigator.[93] If John was the father and Sebastian the son, then Columbus was the Holy Ghost who inspired them and Peter Martyr the first apostle of the gospel according to Sebastian. Since Jean Ribault published a similar account in 1563, equally oblivious of John Cabot, and since Ribault had worked with Sebastian for some time in London in the early 1550s, it would seem that it was the latter's policy, during his twilight years, to take sole credit for the early voyages.[94] Richard Eden, another friend of Sebastian's in this later period, published an English translation of Martyr, as *Decades of the newe worlde or west India*, in 1555, adding a note to it but, likewise, showing no awareness of the role of the elder Cabot.[95]

Sebastian was even more economical with the truth in his conversation with a 'Mantuan Gentleman,' reported by Giovanni Ramusio in his seminal *Voyages* of 1550. Sebastian is quoted as having told the Mantuan that 'his father died at the time when news came that Signor Don Christophoro Columbo the Genoese had discovered the coast of the Indies.' As he had told Martyr, he was inspired by this example:

Whence there was born in me ... a great desire and eagerness of heart that I should do some signal deed also, and knowing by reason of the sphere that if I sailed by way of the north west I should have a shorter road to find the Indies, I at once communicated my thought to his majesty [Henry VII], who was very pleased and equipped for me two caravels with all things needful, and it was, I believe, in 1496 at the beginning of summer. And I began to sail towards the north-west thinking not to find land until I came to Cathay, and from thence to turn towards the Indies. But at the end of some days I discovered land, which ran to the north, which greatly displeased me; and then going along the coast to see if I could find some gulf which turned, it fell out that having gone as far as 56 degrees under our pole, seeing that there the land turned eastwards, and despairing of finding a gulf, I turned back to examine again the same coast from that region towards the equinoctial, always with the purpose of finding a passage to the Indies, and came as far as that part now called Florida. And my victuals being short, I decided to return to England, where, on my arrival, I found great disturbances, of the people in rebellion and of a war with Scotland.'[96]

King Henry put down Perkin Warbeck's rebellion in 1497, so there is not much doubt that what Sebastian was claiming here was the European rediscovery of North America, although this account, like others, may incorporate details of his later explorations in Labrador.

Eden appended this account by Ramusio to his 1555 translation of Martyr's *Decades*, thus putting Sebastian's most duplicitous version of the early voyages into circulation in England itself. Hakluyt reprinted a different, derivative, text of the Mantuan Gentleman's story in the *Principal Navigations*.[97] Since Hakluyt became the most widely used source for the early history of exploration throughout the English-speaking world, it is no wonder that Sebastian's account became the authorized version of the Cabot voyages for several centuries. As we have noted, Hakluyt did recover and preserve some references to John and even inserted one in Robert Fabyan's chronicle, thus eventually outraging Richard Biddle, in the course of clarifying for his own contemporaries the identity of the Venetian who originally proposed a transatlantic voyage to Henry VII. We can hardly blame historians and editors, from Hakluyt to Biddle, for getting their narratives confused. They had accepted the misrepresentations of the source that seemed to them most likely to be a reliable eyewitness.

Sebastian Cabot hardly wasted his life. He accomplished much and had interesting and responsible duties into old age. Why, to put it politely, did he fail to give credit to his own father for the voyages of the 1490s? Or why, to put it at its worst, did he misrepresent his father's achievements as his own? Sebastian seems to have made whatever claims would do him the most professional good, that he thought he could get away with. About 1516, just when he was angling for command of a Spanish expedition to the Baccalaos, he emphasized to Peter Martyr his own experience in charge of the Labrador expedition of 1508. Many of those involved in the expeditions of 1497 and 1498 would still have been alive and Sebastian did not claim to have been in charge of them. Later, in his conversation with the Mantuan Gentleman, he did claim the original European exploration of northeastern North America as his own. Internal evidence places this conversation sometime before 1548, when Sebastian was still *piloto mayor* in Seville. Almost half a century had passed since the original exploration of 1497 and there would have been few still alive, besides Sebastian, who remembered much about it. Perhaps it was more relevant that he was then angling for an English reappointment. It would have done him no harm to identify himself with the early expedition in this memorable, albeit simplistic, way. He was interested in professional self-promotion and his inflated claims may well have been, for him, just business. It was, besides, a family business. His father was long dead, after all, and stories of Zuan's exploits would not feed the grandchildren. It is doubtful if he usually thought of either himself or his father as a potential historical monument. Sebastian Cabot lied, in other words, not to mislead future historians, but to promote himself professionally among his own contemporaries.

The portrait is the one gesture that can only be construed as an attempt to leave a memorial. At one time it was taken for a Holbein.[98] Whether the original figure in oils was impressive enough to merit this misattribution we will never know, for the surviving copies differ one from another.[99] The inscription though, is a masterpiece of ambiguity and expresses exactly the kind of message the old navigator could live with. He was Sebastian Cabot, Englishman, son of John Cabot, knight of Venice, first discoverer of Newfoundland. It confirmed the miscon-

3.2 Newfoundland, John Cabot and Victoria Jubilee issue postage stamp (enlarged 4×), 1897, engraved 2-cent carmine lake: 'CABOT – "HYM THAT FOUND THE NEW ISLE."'

ceptions of those who credited him with the early voyages and, at the same time, it could not offend the very few who might remember the actual circumstances. By a curious twist of fate, during the quadcentennial of 1897 the Newfoundland government presented the portrait as an image of John. In a commemorative issue of postage stamps, the two-cent carmine lake is the portrait of Sebastian, ambiguously labelled 'CABOT' and 'HYM THAT FOUND THE NEW ISLE' (figure 3.2).[100] The confusion lives, in 1997, as this postal imagery is reproduced on notecards for the quincentennial celebration. In this case a little of our concept of Sebastian has become attached to his father Zuan. In the domain of the Cabots this is, however, an anomalous case. Until the last century, the curriculum vitae of the son cannibalized that of his father.

THE RESURRECTION OF JOHN

The mid-twentieth-century identification of John Day's crucial letter to the Grand Admiral was not the first document retrieved from the oblivion of the archives to upset received wisdom on the Cabots. Hakluyt, of course, had kept the memory of John alive, among other things by inserting his name in Fabyan's *Chronicle*. In his eighteenth-century *Lives of the Admirals*, Campbell used this piece of falsified evidence to support his entirely accurate conclusion that John had been in command of the early explorations. Some were convinced, as the late-eighteenth-century narratives of Forster and Mavor indicated. As Biddle's *Memoir of Sebastian* illustrated, however, it was still quite possible to use a different and more accessible set of documents to animate an alternative history. It was two obscure nineteenth-century scholars, Craven Ord and Rawdon Brown, who dragged the stream of time with humane perseverance in the archives of London, Venice, and Milan and recovered the body of evidence that brought John Cabot back to the surface of history.[101] Ord worked on Henry VII's Household books, in the Public Record Office, and found evidence for the success of the expedition of 1497 in the form of the reward paid 'to hym that founde the new Isle.'[102] It was, however, the recovery of Lorenzo Pasqualigo's letter to his brothers in Venice and of Raimondo de Soncino's letter to Milan that really brought the events of 1497 to life; the former dating to within a few weeks of John Cabot's return to London, the latter written later that year.[103] Brown published the Pasqualigo letter in 1837, in the original Italian, in an edition of a late-fifteenth-century Venetian diary, making a privately printed translation in 1855, summarized in the literary journal *Notes and Queries*, three years later. Soncino's dispatch to Milan was published in Italian in the *Annuario Scientifico del 1865*, by which time both the Soncino and the Pasqualigo documents had become accessible to English-speaking scholars with the publication in 1864 of Brown's translations in his *Calendar of State Papers* for Italy.[104]

The gradual documentation of the life and achievement of Zuan Cabot made it increasingly possible to argue that his son

Sebastian was a charlatan, a liar, and a traitor, to rehearse Harrisse's indictment. Meanwhile, the plentiful evidence planted by Sebastian himself, in the annals of his contemporaries, continued to provide sympathetic historians with the documentary basis for idolizing 'the father of English navigation' well into the nineteenth century. Since that time there have been, in effect, two schools among Cabot scholars: on the one hand, what we might call the Sebastiolators and, on the other hand, the Sebastiophobes. No one in the twentieth century has given Sebastian quite the acclaim bestowed by Biddle and no one has attacked Sebastian with quite the scholarly intensity of Harrisse. Still, to make some sense of the documents, the modern reader of the literature must face this issue and decide how far to trust Sebastian on the subject of the early explorations. We have seen a number of reasons why many scholars have concluded that it is not possible to trust his uncorroborated testimony very far.

The confusion Sebastian sowed in the histories of his time and the doubts historians now have about the legends that he created have had unfortunate interrelated effects on the history of early exploration to this day. Sebastian does not seem to have been the kind of compulsive systematic liar who never tells the truth; he lied only when it really mattered. Like a lover caught once in a crucial manipulation of the facts, such liars are no longer believed, precisely when it really matters. Hence Sebastian is not believed, even when he probably should be. This is too bad for the history of European discovery, because it would be very interesting to sort out the various early voyages of which Sebastian had first- or second-hand knowledge. Unfortunately, it is impossible to do this on internal evidence alone, because there is no single assertion of Sebastian's that is safe from a plausible accusation of distortion. This historiographic problem became apparent in the eighteenth century and it is unlikely to go away.

The way in which Sebastian's status as an authority first became a widely recognized issue is itself historically instructive. We hear again the imperial chord sounded by Edmund Burke in his 1757 *Account of the European Settlements*, with which we introduced the legend of Sebastian. It was at this time that negotiations between the French and British over their North American possessions broke down, resulting in the Seven Years' War. In 1753 the English commissioners to these negotiations had put forward a claim to possession of North America on the grounds of European discovery by John Cabot. The French commissioners used the plentiful evidence that appears to make Sebastian responsible for early English explorations to undermine the credibility of the British version of their history and therefore of their rights – an argument which they published, in 1757, in the proceedings of the negotiations, the *Mémoires des Commissaires*.[105] They argued that the documentary evidence showed only that John planned an expedition, in search of a northwest passage, which Sebastian carried out, landing only on Newfoundland, at an uncertain date, which might be as late as 1507.[106] Etienne Chompré reproduced these doubts in his *Histoire générale des voyages*, with historiographic implications summed up by the Cabot bibliographer George Parker Winship a century ago:

This argument by the French diplomatist is, chronologically and probably in fact, the beginning of the misunderstanding which for more than a century confused everyone who undertook to study the history of the Cabot discoveries. The English representatives in 1753 found no difficulties in arriving at what we now know to be the facts about what happened in 1497. Their opponents, acting well within their rights, applied the subtleties of controversial logic to the sources of information; and it has taken historical students a hundred and fifty years to unravel the resulting tangle. The theories advanced in this book quickly found their way into the standard French works of reference; the desire to refute these errors led Biddle to write his great work; the glorification of Sebastian, as by Nichols, was the natural outcome; as natural a reaction drove Mr. Harrisse to the extremities of his efforts to discredit Sebastian utterly; the present volume [Winship's *Cabot Bibliography*] is an effort to restore and set things right once more.[107]

The Cabots, sometimes in the guise of the father, sometimes in the guise of the son, became much more important to Britain after the mid-eighteenth century than they had been since the time of

Hakluyt. The argument for British precedence in North America could be made, of course, with Sebastian as well as with his father; although General Wolfe probably counted for more than either of them in terms of taking actual possession of the continent. An anonymous loyal subject emphasized the importance of precedent in a publication of 1773: *The History of the British Dominions in North America: from the First Discovery of the Vast Continent by Sebastian Cabot in 1497, to its Present Glorious Establishment as Confirmed by the Late Treaty of Peace in 1763.* By the time of the Cabot quadcentennial of 1897, scholars had resolved the biographical question of the identity of the navigator in command on that June day four hundred years earlier. Despite the copious confusions bequeathed them by Sebastian, they had also managed to sort out the relatively minor issue of inconsistency in dating, between 1494 and 1497.[108] There remained a question on which there was no consensus, a question confused (like so many others) by the legend of Sebastian Cabot, a mythic question pregnant with symbolism, which therefore invited the history of must-have-been. This was the question of the landfall.

4
The Many Landfalls

The bias of nationalism in the study of exploration would make an interesting study ... The vested interests of nationalism are concerned with
territorial rights, and perhaps more recently with the tourist trade. The
mayor of St John's, Newfoundland, once assured the writer that 'John
Cabot landed right out here in this bloody harbour.'

Harold Innis, *Canadian Historical Review* (1941)[1]

The limitations and ambiguities of the documents relating to John
Cabot's voyage of 1497 have provided ample opportunity for several centuries of scholarly quarrel. For almost four hundred years,
confusion reigned over the simple questions of who led the expedition and when, or even if, it took place. An early modern consensus about the coast explored fell apart in the late eighteenth
century, with the first claims for a specific landfall, that first
glimpse of North America that post-medieval Europe was supposed to have had. A century later, the 1897 quadcentenary
became the occasion for intense dispute about the landfall, particularly between the Newfoundland proponents of Bonavista and
the Canadian proponents of Cape Breton Island. The arguments,
scholarly and otherwise, echoed through most of the twentieth
century. There are five main schools of thought about the itinerary of this celebrated voyage, each grounded in an aspect of the
inconsistent historical record. Other even more imaginative interpretations depart significantly from the documentary evidence.
All exhibit, to some degree, the symptoms of one nationalist

ideology or another. Let us consider the five landfalls that have
had some kind of scholarly respectability, at one time or another,
in rough order of historiographic precedence. If we end up cataloguing in obsessive detail the controversial literature of another
era, this is with the intent of rediscovering the forgotten genesis of
some dearly held traditions. In any case, authors and titles can be
skimmed; it is tables of contents that really matter. A look at the
landfall literature should convince even those inclined to take traditions at face value that these debates have as much to do with
nationalism as with navigation. Often, what is in question here is
not so much the interpretation of history as the creation of myth,
of what 'must have been.'

NEWFOUNDLAND: BONAVISTA

As Edmund Burke observed in 1757, the name 'Newfoundland'
was once a general term for northeastern North America,
although by his time it had come to mean solely the great island
off the Gulf of St Lawrence.[2] In a deposition of 1597, a Basque
mariner referred to the Magdalen Islands as part of the 'Neue
found lande,' although the master of the English ship at issue
distinguished Cape Breton from Newfoundland.[3] The Romance
terms 'Terra Nova,' 'Terre Neuve,' and the revealing plural 'Terres
Neufves' included both Newfoundland and Nova Scotia, well
into the seventeenth century.[4] As late as 1618, the French adventurer Marc Lescarbot used 'terre-neuvier' to refer to a Nova
Scotia–based fishing master.[5] Caution is likewise necessary in
interpreting early uses of place names like 'Newfoundland,' as in
Henry VII's 1502 Household Book payment 'to the merchaunts of
bristoll that have bene in the newe founde lande' or 'to one that
brought haukes from the Newfounded Island' in 1503.[6] A range
of terms that sound like 'Newfoundland' or as if they might
denote Newfoundland were used in English records of the early
voyages, as in King Henry's 1497 payment of £10 'to hym that
founde the new Isle' and the 1498 payment of £20 to Lancelot
Thirkell 'apon a prest for his Shipp going towardes the new
Ilande.'[7] Some of these records almost certainly refer to what we

now call the Island of Newfoundland, but the early and continued use of such terms as 'Newfoundland,' 'Terra Nova' or 'the
Baccalaos' are not themselves conclusive evidence of the location
of the Cabots' early explorations, since these terms once had a
very broad geographical meaning.[8]

Burke apart, toponymic considerations rarely concerned historians who attempted to describe the early English voyages of
exploration. Until the nineteenth century most authors assumed
that the part of North America first seen and named by one or
another of the Cabots was Newfoundland.[9] This was true both of
the Continental tradition of Martyr and Ramusio, which credited
Sebastian Cabot with the discovery of the Baccalaos in the early
sixteenth century, and of the more complex English tradition that
John or Sebastian or both 'found the new isle' in 1497. The
sixteenth-century Elizabethan scholar Dee thought Sebastian 'did
discover from Newfownd Land so far along and abowt the
Coaste next to Labrador.'[10] Hakluyt hedged his bets with an
ambiguous marginal note of 'Cabots voyage from Bristol wherein
he discovered Newfoundland, & the Northerne parts of that
land.'[11] An early-seventeenth-century Bristol chronicle supposed
'newfowndland fownd by Bristol men' and this was also the view
of Purchas, who saw in the Cabot explorations 'New-found Land
discovered by English Ships, Mariners and jurisdiction.'[12] Lediard's *Naval History* of 1735 reported the Cabot explorations under
the marginal title 'The Discovery of *Newfoundland*, and the North-
East Parts of *America*' and Campbell's mid-eighteenth-century
Lives of the Admirals, the first history to clearly define John Cabot's
role in the early voyages, made him the discoverer of 'Baccaloes,
or Newfoundland.'[13] The sceptical eighteenth-century French tradition of Etienne Chompré and Abbé Raynal put the Cabots in
Newfoundland and a tradition of a vague Newfoundland voyage
survived into the late nineteenth century both in Anglo-Canadian
textbook histories of the 1870s and 1880s and a pompous *History
of the New World* by the Oxford don Edward Payne, published in
1892.[14]

By the late eighteenth century a specific landfall had appeared
in the Cabotian literature, the first of the many. The German

scholar Johann Reinhold Forster published a history of Atlantic exploration in Frankfurt in 1784, soon translated as a *History of the Voyages and Discoveries Made in the North*. His monograph put the Cabots in Newfoundland, as was the conventional wisdom of the period, but also offered the earliest discussion of the exact location of the 'land first seen.' For various reasons, Forster found the account of a Labrador voyage to 67½ or even 55 degrees north improbable. Recalling the observation of immense quantities of fish, in the accounts of the voyage to which he had access, he concluded: 'This inclines me to suppose, that *Prima Vista*, the first land discovered by Cabot, was the headland in Newfoundland, which is still called *Cape Bonavista* and this conjuncture is still farther confirmed by the situation of the island of *Baccalaos*, which lies not far from thence.'[15]

Lewis Amadeus Anspach was rather more assertive about a Bonavista landfall, in his *History of the Island of Newfoundland* of 1819.[16] As a Conception Bay magistrate and missionary, Reverend Anspach has the distinction of being the first long-time resident of the Island to have recorded what he knew of its history. In fact he proposed two landfalls: Labrador in 1496 and Bonavista in 1497. The argument resembles that put forward in Forster's influential book, which the Swiss-born Anspach read either in the original German or in the Dublin translation of 1786.[17] The Newfoundland author cites Forster on various matters and follows him in crediting command of the expedition to John rather than Sebastian Cabot, celebrating the day when 'he had, at last, on the 24th of June, a sight of land, to which he gave the name of Prima, or Bonavista, (first or pleasing sight) a Cape still so called on the eastern coast of Newfoundland.'[18] Rev. Philip Tocque made a very similar argument in *Newfoundland: As It Was and as It Is in 1877*, although Charles Pedley's 1869 *History of Newfoundland* put the landfall in the Strait of Belle Isle (and credited it to Sebastian).[19] In the early 1890s the Roman Catholic cleric Michael Howley recorded his own complicated navigational arguments for a Bonavista landfall, which had not yet become a Newfoundland convention. Curiously enough, during the 1897 quadcentenary Howley defended a more northerly landfall at Cape St John, on similar navigational grounds, and would, with the passing years, change his conclusions again, if not his arguments.[20] Meanwhile another prominent Newfoundland nationalist had taken up the case for Bonavista.

Daniel W. Prowse (1834–1914) was the son of an English West Country merchant who had settled in Conception Bay, north of St John's. After being called to the Newfoundland bar in 1858 he served as a Conservative member of the House of Assembly, taking a pro-confederate position during debates about the creation of a Dominion of Canada. He became a district magistrate in 1869, in which capacity he served until 1898. The appointment required travel but also gave him time to hunt and to write – a *Justice's Manual* in 1877, his great *History of Newfoundland* in 1895, and hundreds of newspaper articles. He was a tireless local booster and later in life wrote a *Newfoundland Guide Book*.[21] In his justly celebrated *History*, in a separate pamphlet printed for the Cabot quadcentenary, and in newspaper controversies, Judge Prowse put forward an assertive case for Bonavista, displaying his lawyer's skills as much as those of a historian.

Prowse argued that in Newfoundland itself 'an unbroken tradition' pointed to Cape Bonavista as the landfall of 1497. He supported this claim with an inscription near Bonavista on John Mason's Newfoundland map of 1625 that reads 'a Caboto primum reperta,' that is, 'first reported by Cabot' or, in Prowse's version, 'First found by Cabot.'[22] (See figure 4.1.) Prowse also cites a French map by Dupont, of the same period, with a similar inscription. Although both maps postdate Cabot's voyage by over a century, the eminent jurist strode purposefully to a curious conclusion: 'These two maps make it clear that little more than one hundred years after the event, and when men were alive who had known Cabot and his companions, the tradition and belief common to both English and French sailors was in Cape Bonavista as Cabot's landfall.'[23] Since English settlement in Newfoundland dates from 1610, local tradition cannot effectively establish the point in question, no matter how long-lived were sixteenth-century mariners or how accurate their tales. 'If, indeed, there were any one in Newfoundland old enough to remember

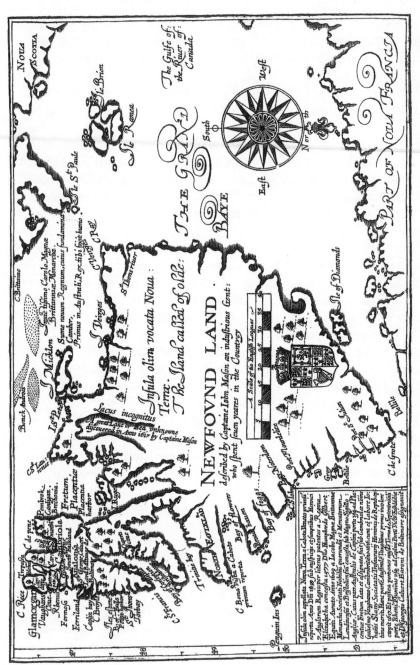

4.1 John Mason, *Newfound Land*, 1625. Note the legend off North Faulkland: 'C Bona Vista a Caboto primum reperta' (Cape Bonavista first found by Cabot). North is down on this map.

having seen John Cabot land at Bonavista, such an argument might be satisfactory,' as Prowse's Canadian opponent Samuel Dawson put it, in 1897.[24] Prowse used the names of two nearby harbours, Keels and King's Cove to buttress the argument imaginatively. His idea that Keels must be a place where boats first came ashore and that King's Cove must have been so named because Cabot raised Henry's royal standard there convinced neither Bishop Howley nor his other critics.[25] As for the map, the caption itself is ambiguous and may not intend to specify Bonavista as the landfall. There are, besides, a number of much earlier maps that suggest other landfalls, among them Sebastian Cabot's map of 1544, the ultimate documentary source for the story that Cabot called the landfall 'Prima Vista.'

Logic aside, the quadcentennial celebrations in 1897 gave Judge Prowse a platform, so to speak, from which to promote the Bonavista theory.[26] His arguments reached an international audience when Lord Dufferin adopted them for a patriotic address in Bristol and an elaborate article for the American magazine *Scribner's*.[27] G.R.F. Prowse, who had helped his father with his research, also published on the topic of the Cabots and in the early twentieth century presented a version of the cartographic argument for Bonavista to an international geographic congress in Washington.[28] This was to be the first of his many papers on the subject, which preoccupied or even obsessed him after his exile to an insurance office in Winnipeg. Through the first half of the twentieth century the interested reader could send a dollar or two to the younger Prowse and obtain freshly mimeographed reiterations of the argument under such compelling titles as 'Sebastian Cabot Lied.'[29] W.A. Munn recalled and expanded Judge Prowse's conclusions in the 1930s in the pages of the *Newfoundland Quarterly* and the St John's *Evening Telegram* reprinted the article as part of its 'John Cabot Supplement, 1497–1947' under the banner headline 'Establishes Proof Newfoundland Cabot's Landfall.'[30] The *Telegram* disposed of competing theories in a separate article, 'What the Historians Say' by 'Investigator.' This four-hundred-and-fiftieth anniversary special supplement is a rich mine of Cabotian folklore, awaiting McLuhanesque deconstruction.[31] Publicity for Tooton's, one of the original Kodak franchises in North America, set the tone: 'We Are Sorry That We Were Not There ... When John Cabot first sighted Cape Bonavista in 1497, to bring you a photographic record of that historic occasion which took place some 450 years ago.'

In Newfoundland, regional historians still defend Bonavista, with nationalistic fervour or with the limited evidence extant.[32] Bonavista is the officially sanctioned landfall site for the province's five-hundredth anniversary celebrations.[33] This vision of the past is promoted by the same tourism spokespersons who assert, in the face of all evidence, that St John's is 'the oldest city in North America.' (Mexico had cities a thousand years ago, St Augustine, Florida, was founded in 1565 and Quebec City in 1608, while there is no evidence for over-wintering at St John's until about 1620.) In both cases it is pretty obvious that what is in question is national myth rather than history. The tenacity of the Bonavista landfall tradition in Newfoundland requires explanation and we will return to this question. For the moment, let us simply observe that in 1997 the Newfoundland government will not hear of other landfalls, as the current mayor of St John's discovered when, in the best local tradition, he recently tried to promote his own city to this status. The desire to claim that 'John Cabot landed right out here,' in the words of a former incumbent of that office, reflects a long civic tradition that probably originates in Bishop Michael Howley's conversion on the landfall question, after the quadcentenary, from Cape St John, on the northeast coast, to the City of St John's, on the Avalon Peninsula.[34] In the run-up to the Cabot 500 celebration, Newfoundland's bureaucrats have acted decisively to promote commitment to the myth of a Bonavista landfall, requesting, for example, that a 'landfall debate' at a sponsored symposium on Cabot be renamed a 'discussion.'[35]

Local boosters have occasionally proposed other specific landfalls. Tradition of a rock at Grates Cove inscribed 'IO CABOTO SANCCIUS SAINMALIA' would provide a kind of evidence for a landfall there – that is, if the rock could be found. William Cormack put this tradition into print with his 1856 *Narrative of a Jour-*

ney Across the Island of Newfoundland, an account of his expedition of 1822, at that time 'the only one ever performed by a European.' He had no doubts about the landfall: 'The Point of Grates is the part of North America first discovered by Europeans. Sebastian Cabot landed here in 1496, and took possession of *The Newfoundland*, which he discovered in the name of his employer, Henry VII, of England. He recorded the event by cutting an inscription, still perfectly legible, on a large block of rock that stands on the shore.'[36] Cormack would be a more convincing historical authority if he had not preceded this claim with a completely confused account of the early seventeenth-century English settlement of Newfoundland, crediting Sir George Calvert (who actually founded Ferryland) with a colony at Port de Grave (near another early colony at Cupids) before being 'lost at sea' (although he actually died at home). In a government tourism publication of the 1950s, the curator of the Newfoundland Museum gave the reading quoted above and claimed that the inscription was 'still partly discernible.'[37] Photographs and transcriptions made at this time by more level-headed visitors to Grates Cove suggest that one side of the rock was in fact covered with inscriptions, but that these were along the lines of 'IS 1669' and 'RH 1713,' with faint engravings of a house and flag.[38] Similar grafitti are known elsewhere on the coast of Newfoundland, where for centuries fishing crews have had to sit out stretches of bad weather.[39] These inscriptions were probably the genuine record of the otherwise-anonymous seventeenth- and eighteenth-century fishermen who harvested Newfoundland's inshore cod stocks rather than evidence for a landing by the man who first brought back clear sailing directions to these fishing grounds.[40] The Grates Cove inscriptions are gone, according to local legend taken by the Newfoundland Museum, Memorial University, or the Canadian Broadcasting Corporation, more likely simply fallen into the sea, for the Grates Cove rock was already badly cracked in 1955.[41]

There are other theories of a Newfoundland landfall. British scholars have occasionally proposed Cape Race, at the southeastern vertex of Newfoundland.[42] This has not given rise to a local tradition, probably because for years no one has lived at or near Cape Race, except the lighthouse keeper and he has, of course, been replaced by a bank of silicon chips (in the interests of global competitiveness). In the 1970s one local booster elaborated a landfall at Flatrock, a scenic community a few miles north of St John's and a truly difficult place to land, as anyone who has sailed there knows.[43] In this imaginative chronicle, Cabot's Irish crew befriend the Beothuks and admire the beautiful Native women in their tight-fitting fur garments, expressing surprise that the Indians are so 'well clad and respectably covered.' Flatrock has refrained from making much of this scenario, preferring to take it in the imaginative spirit in which it was offered. St John's, Grates Cove, and Cape Race remain minority views 'on the rock'; most Newfoundlanders now take the Bonavista landfall for granted.

LABRADOR

In his late-eighteenth-century dictionary of *American Biography,* Jeremy Belknap admitted that the land discovered by John and Sebastian Cabot was generally supposed to be part of Newfoundland. He cited Forster's Bonavista theory but favoured a competing interpretation, based on a reading of John Stow's *Chronicle,* of 1580, which would put the landfall on the 'north side of Terra de Labrador.'[44] In 1831, Richard Biddle challenged the conventional wisdom of a Newfoundland landfall and argued that the discovery of 1497 actually related to Labrador.[45] Biddle's *Memoir of Sebastian* epitomizes the long historiographic tradition that conflated the achievements of John and his son, confusing the voyage of 1497 with that of 1508. No one working within this tradition had ever shown much interest in the 'land first seen' and Biddle was reacting, as he makes plain, to the English tradition of a Newfoundland landfall by John.

The influential American historian George Bancroft adopted Biddle's interpretation of the Cabot itinerary in his *History of the United States,* which appeared in several editions between 1834 and 1883.[46] Bancroft's *imprimatur* on the Labrador theory gave it scholarly credibility and his article on the Cabots in *Appleton's New American Encyclopedia,* in the editions of 1859 and 1873, gave it wide circulation in the United States.[47] The Labrador landfall had become American conventional wisdom. This explained, no doubt, why J.G. Kohl stood by the theory in 1869 in his *History of the Discovery of Maine*, despite the fact that he was one of the first English-speaking scholars to note 'recently found' evidence to the contrary, in the form of the Prima Vista legend, just off Cape Breton, on the surviving copy of Sebastian Cabot's 1544 world map. Kohl did not think very highly of this document and used then better-known sources to argue for a Labrador voyage in 1497, followed by a Newfoundland voyage in 1498.[48]

Another American-trained scholar, Henry Harrisse, also distrusted Sebastian's testimony and sometimes expressed doubts about the possibility of establishing John Cabot's landfall at all.[49] Harrisse (1829–1910) came as a young man to the United States, where he turned to the law, developing an international American clientele, which enabled him to return to France after the publication in 1866 of his *Bibliotheca Americana*, a description of publications on America between 1492 and 1557.[50] Harrisse became an internationally respected expert in the early cartography of North America and published many books and papers on the Cabots in the 1880s and 1890s, several of which became standard reference works, including particularly *Jean et Sébastien Cabot* (1882) and *The Discovery of North America* (1892). For those with an interest in early Canadian history, his scholarly monument remains the *Découverte et évolution cartographique de Terre-Neuve et des pays circonvoisins*, which he published in 1900.[51] By 1897 Harrisse had been doing research on early European exploration for decades. Whether or not they agreed with him, Harrisse's opponents Dawson and Prowse had to take him seriously.[52]

Harrisse was sceptical about the authenticity of Sebastian's map of 1544, the sole source for the landfall date of 24 June, and, in particular, about the value of the legend locating the landfall in Cape Breton.[53] He came to favour the theory of a Labrador landfall and in several publications suggested the area near the present community of Domino, south of Sandwich Bay, on the part of the Labrador coast that bulges farthest out towards Europe.[54] He argued that the Soncino letter of December 1497 reported that Cabot departed Europe from Ireland and that he altered a generally westward course northwards – an itinerary which would have brought him to Labrador. Furthermore, he observed that early Spanish maps of North America locate British discoveries in the Labrador region. Harrisse was, however, the greatest of Sebastiophobes and was not willing to believe in the possibility of early-sixteenth-century voyages to Labrador by the younger Cabot. This led the American scholar to fit Sebastian's account of voyages to 55 or 67½ degrees north into an itinerary for his father's voyage of 1497. It was not true, as Dawson the Canadian champion of Cape Breton suggested, that Harrisse ever actually proposed Cape Chidley, at the northern tip of Labrador, as a landfall; although another late-nineteenth-century American scholar made this case, in the pages of the *Transactions of the Royal Society of Canada*, and Harrisse did suggest Cape Chidley as one limit of the coast explored by Cabot.[55] In the 1950s, the publication of the Day Letter would cast serious doubts on such an itinerary. What Day told the Grand Admiral suggests that Cabot coasted at least the region between the Strait of Belle Isle and the southern Avalon Peninsula of Newfoundland, if not Cape Breton Island.[56] In the single month he spent off the coasts of North America, this would not have left him time to visit Cape Chidley, almost 1000 kilometres north of Belle Isle.[57] We have, besides, a plausible explanation for Sebastian's tales of northern Labrador, in the form of one or more later voyages to the region by the younger Cabot.

The idea of a 1497 landfall in southern Labrador remains plausible and has had other proponents, in Harrisse's time and since. The Labrador landfall appealed to Québécois historians, such as the Abbés Ferland and Laverdière, who each published histories of Canada in the 1860s.[58] The prominent Newfoundland geologist James P. Howley, brother of Bishop Michael Howley, drew like conclusions in the 1880s, also published in Quebec.[59] Similar interpretations have been revived occasionally in the twentieth century. The growing awareness of the historical basis for the Norse sagas and of the close commercial ties between Bristol and Iceland in the late Middle Ages made plausible the suggestion that John Cabot followed the old Norse circum-Atlantic route via Iceland to Greenland to Labrador, an idea that continues to interest some scholars.[60] Using the alternative hypothesis of latitude sailing and assuming a European departure from Achill Head in northwestern Ireland, one mid-twentieth-century American maritime historian has made an argument for a landfall at Cape St Lewis, near the present community of Fox Harbour, just a little south of Harrisse's proposed landfall.[61] If a landfall in southern Labrador has had only a few intermittent proponents since the nineteenth century, a cynic might suspect that this has less to do with the considerable merits of the case than with the relative lack of influence of the region in political and academic circles, compared at least to insular Newfoundland and Cape Breton Island.

CAPE BRETON ISLAND

Cape Breton Island did not become a candidate for the Cabot landfall until the late nineteenth century. In 1794, Jeremy Belknap had observed that Thomas Prince's *Chronological History* of 1736 implied a landfall in Nova Scotia.[62] This was based on Prince's erroneous report of a landfall by Sebastian Cabot at 45 degrees north (rather than the 55 degrees Sebastian actually claimed in the accounts of Martyr and Ramusio). In 1829, the Nova Scotian writer Thomas Haliburton also recognized the implications of the latitude given by Prince, but relegated the possibility of a local landfall to a note. His *Historical Account of Nova Scotia* puts John and Sebastian off Bonavista not Cape Breton.[63] Nineteenth-century Canadian history texts simply reproduced the original vague English theory of landfalls in Newfoundland or Labrador.[64] There was no local tradition, in Cape Breton, of a Cabot landfall until after the quadcentenary. Dawson, the major proponent of the theory at that time, observed that 'the people who live there have not now, or at any previous time, manifested the slightest interest in this question.'[65] As late as 1869, Richard Brown's *History of the Island of Cape Breton* argued for a coasting voyage by Cabot as far south as Cape Sable, in southeastern Nova Scotia, but assumed a landfall in the Strait of Belle Isle.[66] In 1879 James Hannay drew the same conclusions in his *History of Acadia*.[67] Both were aware of the famous Eighth Legend, describing the landfall area, polar bears, and so on, on the world map attributed to Sebastian Cabot. Like all scholars before this period, they knew only Hakluyt's quotation of the legend, from the lost English version of the map. Thus, they did not know that the legend was associated on the original map with the Island of Cape Breton.

The sole surviving impression of the copper-engraved first edition, published in 1544, now in Paris at the Bibliothèque Nationale, was not discovered until 1843. M.A.P. d'Avezac-Macaya described the Paris Map in an 1857 article, but this was largely devoted to Sebastian Cabot's South American explorations.[68] A second article by d'Avezac on the map, in 1869, reprinted by J.G. Kohl in his contemporary *Discovery of Maine*, was much more concerned with the landfall date of 1494, in the original edition of the Eighth Legend, than with the obvious implications of the 'Prima Terra Vista' legend on the body of the map.[69] This was also true of another early discussion of the Paris Map, by the New England scholar Charles Deane.[70] It was as if American and European writers at first found the Cape Breton landfall so implausible that they did not think this aspect of the Paris Map worth comment. Kohl himself favoured a Labrador landfall, as we have seen. Sebastian's map would soon reach a wider scholarly audience, nonetheless. In 1862, French scholars published a facsimile.[71] The relevant part of the map appeared in 1868, in an American article by J. Carson Brevoort on 'Early Voyages from Europe,' and the Bristol city librarian J.F. Nicholls printed a small re-engraved copy of the Gulf of St Lawrence portion in his *Remarkable Life of Sebastian Cabot* in 1869.[72] This part of the map appeared, at a much more comprehensible scale, in the United States, as one of the cartographic supplements to Henry Stevens's contemporary book on *The Earliest Discoveries in America*.[73]

Even before Deane donated photographic facsimiles to a dozen major American libraries, in 1882, and well before the Public Archives of Canada obtained their copies, in 1897, the Paris Map was being used to support claims of a Cape Breton landfall.[74] In his 1868 article, Brevoort made the interesting suggestion that

John Cabot landed in Cape Breton because he deliberately avoided Newfoundland and its fishing grounds, of which he was already aware. The Bristol writer Nicholls proposed a landfall at Cape North, on Cape Breton island, in his homage to the younger Cabot. His vociferous American critic Stevens, who took such a dim view of Sebastian and his enthusiasts, also accepted the Cape North landfall.[75] In 1874 Frederic Kidder told the Maine Historical Society that the landfall was Cape Breton proper, 'near the eastern point of the present island,' again on the basis of the Paris Map.[76] The vice-president of the Massachusetts Historical Society, Deane, explained that the Paris Map proved the case for Cape North, in a chapter on the Cabots in Justin Winsor's widely cited *Narrative and Critical History of America* of 1884.[77] The argument became part of a history of Cape Breton, published in 1891 by a native son, J.G. Bourinot, in the *Transactions of the Royal Society of Canada*.[78] The prolific British geographer Sir Clements Markham instructed the members of the Hakluyt Society who read his 1893 edition of the *Journal of Christopher Columbus* to the same effect, although he would change his mind, in favour of Bonavista, in time for the quadcentenary.[79]

The Cape Breton landfall first received intensive scholarly attention in the years immediately preceding the Cabot quadcentenary of 1897, with the publication of a series of articles by Samuel Edward Dawson in the receptive pages of the *Transactions of the Royal Society of Canada*.[80] Dawson's conclusions and argument differed somewhat from most earlier versions of the Cape Breton theory.[81] He suggested a landfall not at Cape North, but at Cape Breton itself, somewhat to the east. Dawson's interpretation rested, in part, on the Paris Map of 1544, the discovery of which had originally given life to the Cape Breton Island theory, but the heart of his argument was an interpretation of the mysterious la Cosa Map, which he dated to about 1500.[82] Like the Paris Map, the la Cosa planisphere had been identified earlier in the nineteenth century but was not published, except in reduced extracts, until 1862, in Jomard's *Monuments de la géographie*. It became more accessible to scholars in England and North America when Stevens published relevant parts of the map in 1869, in his book

on *Earliest Discoveries*.[83] It has remained central to subsequent
interpretations that take Cabot to have landed on Cape Breton
and to have explored the Nova Scotia coast and then the south
coast of Newfoundland, departing from Cape Race.[84] Dawson
and later proponents of a Cape Breton landfall give great weight
to the long stretch of east/west-trending coastline shown on the
la Cosa map, marked with English flags and labelled with place
names, interpreting Cavo de Ynglaterra as Cape Race and Cavo
descubierto as Cape Breton.[85] The interpretation remains uncon-
vincing, insofar as it depends on the unsupported assumption
that the la Cosa Map reflects only the geography of the Cabot
voyage of 1497, insofar as it conflicts with the latitude data in the
Day Letter, and insofar as the ambiguities of scale and of orientation of the North American coast have permitted scholars to
draw very different and very contradictory conclusions from the
map.

Nevertheless, by 1897 the Cape North/Cape Breton theory had
international standing. Despite Dawson's arguments, the published Paris Map of 1544 rather than the earlier but more vaguely
dated la Cosa manuscript remained, for many scholars, the conclusive evidence for a Cape Breton Island landfall. These included
the American Cabot bibliographer George Parker Winship, as
well as the Dominion Archivist for Canada, Douglas Brymner.[86]
The Reverend Moses Harvey, author of *Newfoundland, the Oldest
British Colony* (1883), introduced the Cape North landfall to Newfoundland readers in the revised (and retitled) 1890 edition of his
history and explained his conversion from the Bonavista theory,
on the evidence of the Paris Map, to the Nova Scotia Historical
Society in 1893.[87] The American Cabot scholar Deane edited the
legends of the Paris Map for the Massachusetts Historical Society,
and the Royal Society of Canada reprinted his transcripts in its
Transactions for 1897.[88] In a pair of articles, the president of the
Royal Society of Canada, the Roman Catholic Archbishop of Halifax Cornelius O'Brien, expounded on the Cape North landfall
and on his identification of Prince Edward Island as the 'Island of
St John.' With intellectual arrogance and deep self-satisfaction he
heaped scorn on those who doubted either the Paris Map or his

own insights: 'Minds are variously constituted: dearly hugged theories die hard; and certain, often unconscious, prejudices are difficult to shake off ... Small wonder that a geographical conclusion of mine, at variance with received ideas, should be looked at askance. In the end, however, it will prevail.'[89] The archbishop appears to have been in error, at least in his certainty that his theories would stand. On the other hand, a landfall on Cape Breton Island became received wisdom in Canada for half a century.

Many Canadian anglophone scholars of the turn of the century embraced the idea that John Cabot made a periplus or tour of the Gulf of St Lawrence, entering the St Lawrence at Cape Breton and exiting by the Strait of Belle Isle, almost forty years before Jacques Cartier's exploration of 1534.[90] The Americans Brevoort, Kidder, and Stevens and the Bristol librarian Nicholls were first to discuss the gulf periplus, although Haliburton, in his tentative note of 1829, had suggested that such an itinerary was a corollary of a Nova Scotian landfall. The idea that Cabot had explored the Gulf of St Lawrence delighted the Italian scholar Franceso Tarducci, who defended it in his 1892 biography of John and Sebastian.[91] The gulf periplus even won a francophone convert, in the person of Abbé Beaudouin, who published conciliatory reflections on the issue in both French and English in the 1880s and 1890s.[92] Predictably, however, the idea that Cabot did in 1497 what Cartier was generally credited with accomplishing in 1534 was opposed vociferously in Quebec, notably by the nationalist intellectual N.-E. Dionne. The myth constructed by anglophone Canadians about Cabot impinged on francophone traditions about Cartier: a collision of nationalisms to which we will return in the following chapter.

Although they abandoned the idea that John Cabot had made a circuit of the gulf, twentieth-century Canadian scholars from H.P. Biggar to W.F. Ganong took the landfall at Cape North as an article of faith.[93] In the 1940s, one of the few dissenters, Harold Innis, the eminent historian of the cod fishery, observed that Canadian scholars stressed the landfall on Cape Breton 'exhaustively,' although the less widely discussed evidence for Newfoundland was better.[94] The landfall legend on the Paris Map certainly provided a prima facie case for a Nova Scotian *prima vista* but even by 1897 serious doubts about that evidence had been clearly spelled out, by the American cartographic expert Harrisse in particular.[95] Within the Dominion of the North, however, doubters like Innis were spitting into the wind. In the 1930s, the Nova Scotian government attached Cabot's name to a new tourist trail around Cape North.[96] As late as 1957 L.-A. Vigneras took the landfall for granted, in the pages of the *Canadian Historical Review*, when he published John Day's letter – a document that itself clearly called for reassessment of the issue.[97] When scholars did reconsider the evidence for the Cabot landfall, in the second half of the twentieth century, two new theories emerged, one very much a minority view and one that has become the new scholarly wisdom. Even in these products of late-twentieth-century scholarship, the bias of nationalism is evident.

MAINE OR SOUTHERN NOVA SCOTIA

Two respected British scholars have suggested that a landfall in Maine or southern Nova Scotia makes best sense of the evidence. This view is developed at length in the standard documentary history of the Cabots, by the editor J.A. Williamson and by R.A. Skelton, a keeper of cartographic materials in the British Library.[98] On the face of it, this is a difficult position, since the supposed landfall lies outside the latitudes for Cabot's exploration mentioned in the Day Letter, a document both experts take seriously. These scholars identify Cavo de Yngleterra on the la Cosa Map with Cape Race and assume that this is the Day Letter's 'cape nearest Ireland' and therefore the point from which Cabot departed for home. They cite Pasqualigo's letter to Venice, to the effect that Cabot coasted for 300 leagues (at least 900 miles or 1400 km).[99] Tracing this distance southwestward, they find the landfall in Maine. The interpretation depends crucially on a particular reading of the la Cosa Map. It also ignores the implication in the Day Letter that the landfall was not on the 'Island of the Seven Cities,' an island in the latitude of Cape Breton or the Avalon Peninsula, but on the 'mainland' to the north, somewhere towards a cape in the latitude of the Strait of Belle Isle. Faced with this difficulty, Williamson uses rhetorical sleight of hand to make the southern region identified in the Day Letter 'the south-western end of Nova Scotia, somewhere near Cape Sable.'[100] In the end, the British scholars treat the southern latitude given by Day as somewhat inaccurate and the northen latitude as wildly so. The la Cosa Map is, however, too ambiguous a source, too vaguely dated, and too uncertainly related to the Cabot explora-tion of 1497 to be the basis for discarding information clearly stated in the Day Letter – a signed contemporary document ex-plicitly related to the voyage.

The southern landfall theory has no historiographic precedents, unless we count the murmurings of Belknap and Haliburton about Nova Scotia based on the apparent latitude error in Prince's early-eighteenth-century *Chronological History*.[101] One might think that the idea of a Cabotian landfall in the territory of the present northeastern United States would appeal to American scholars, but even Kohl's 1869 *Discovery of Maine* sticks with the American convention of a Labrador landfall.[102] We have here, arguably, an example of the power of myth, in this case the myth of Columbus. In the mythic story of the United States of America Columbus is a founder hero. It does not make sense, mythically speaking, for another discoverer to approach American waters as early or as close as he did. Obeying the logic of myth, Americans have gener-ally preferred to remember Cabot as a northern mariner. By and large, it is the British to whom an American landfall has appealed. David Quinn, for example, the distinguished Professor Emeritus of History at Liverpool, sometimes inclines to this interpretation, and a pair of recent popular books by another English writer promote a similarly unlikely landfall on Cape Cod.[103] Canadian scholars have shown little interest in the theory, despite the Brit-ish scholar Skelton's presentation of the case in his entry on John Cabot in the *Dictionary of Canadian Biography*.[104] After 1949 and confederation with Newfoundland, there were several landfalls Canadian historians could choose from, without leaving the country, including a new alternative to the threadbare theories of Bonavista and Cape Breton.

THE STRAIT OF BELLE ISLE

To the extent that there is a current Canadian scholarly consensus about John Cabot's landfall, it is that he landed near the Strait of Belle Isle and then coasted down the eastern shore of Newfoundland at least as far as Cape Race, perhaps along the south coast, possibly as far as Cape Breton, returning by the same route.[105] This is, in effect, a Canadian compromise between the very old British tradition of an unspecified Newfoundland landfall and the nineteenth-century American theory of a landfall in southern Labrador.[106] It was, in fact, the grand old man of American maritime history, the biographer of Christopher Columbus, Admiral Samuel Eliot Morison, who put this theory back on the map.[107] He maintained that the Day Letter and other documents suggest that Cabot headed west from Dursey Head in Ireland, that the Venetian navigator was perfectly capable of maintaining a generally westward course, and that he probably attempted to do so, which would have brought him to Cape Bauld in the Strait of Belle Isle.[108] (The alert reader will recognize the gist of the argument.) Belle Isle itself can be plausibly identified with the large island that Cabot named 'St John,' to commemorate the landfall on the saint's day, 24 June, leaving Cabot plenty of time to coast the eastern shore of Newfoundland as far as Cape Race or even farther.

The interpretation remains uncertain. As one of the best ethnohistories of Cabot's time puts it, the sources are sufficient to locate his landfall in the region of Newfoundland, but attempts at further specification are speculation.[109] And, indeed, there are difficulties even with the Strait of Belle Isle landfall. One is that accounts of the 1497 voyage do not mention either pack ice or icebergs, both of which might be expected in the Strait of Belle Isle in June. Still, this is negative evidence and there are years when the pack ice is gone from the Straits by this time and when there are few icebergs inshore. The main apparent difficulty is an issue raised by the Day Letter.[110] Most scholars have taken the latitude data given in this source as the northern and southern limits of the littoral coasted by Cabot.[111] Day notes that 'most of the land was discovered after turning back,' which Quinn and others read as suggesting that the landfall was not quite at either terminus of the latitudes coasted, which in turn would rule out the Strait of Belle Isle as the landfall area, since it lies in the northern latitudes given.[112] In fact, the Day Letter does not actually give the latitude data as limits but simply as information about the location of two places explored: the Island of the Seven Cities and the cape nearest Ireland. Hence, the difficulty with a Strait of Belle Isle landfall is more apparent than real. The cape nearest Ireland could be Cape Bauld, in the Strait of Belle Isle; the landfall could have been in the area; and Cabot could have explored somewhat farther north, then turned back and investigated eastern Newfoundland, before returning to Cape Bauld for the voyage home. All this is plausible and, arguably, more plausible than any of the competing landfall scenarios. To raise it to certainty, on the other hand, is to enter the mythic realm of 'must-have-been,' a region extensively explored by Canadian and Newfoundland scholars during the Cabot quadcentenary observations of the 1890s.

Given the limited evidence available for any landfall, it might reasonably be asked how Cape Breton Island became, for the first half of the twentieth century, Canadian conventional wisdom. We might wonder, likewise, how Newfoundland attained such certainty about Bonavista that it has been able to convert Canada, or at least federal-government heritage agencies, on the landfall question, in the period since Confederation in 1949. Innis's suspicion that the 'bias of nationalism' came into play is doubtless well founded. As successive mayors of St John's have reminded us, such local enthusiasms have come to reflect concern for the tourist trade as much as for the territorial precedents defended by John Dee, Edmund Burke, and the plenipotentiaries of George II and Louis XIV. Scholarly nationalisms are not, however, confined to these issues. In the cases of both the Cape North and the Bonavista landfall theories, it is arguable that wider cultural issues are at stake. These issues were displayed colourfully during the quadcentennial debates between Newfoundland and Canadian enthusiasts of the Cabots, to which we will therefore return, as an instructive episode in the invention of national myth.

5
Traditions of Invention, 1897: Columbus, Cartier, and Cabot

If then, Columbus' great discovery merits a centenary celebration, should not the Cabots be accorded befitting honours? ... Surely the northern people will not permit the year 1897 to pass without some worthy celebration in grateful recollection of the man who first opened Northern America to European civilization.

Rev. Moses Harvey, 'Voyages of the Cabots' (1893)[1]

THE INVENTION OF TRADITION

The ideological additives in John Cabot's centennial birthday cakes make the literature on his voyage hard to digest, especially in the large servings common around 1897. This literature is, nevertheless, worth sampling, if only the better to understand public memory of this event. Besides helping us to deal with the flummery that has come our way during the five-hundredth anniversary, the origin of public myth about the many landfalls may teach us as much about the construction of our national identities as the event itself.[2] Eric Hobsbawm's concept of 'invention of tradition' is particularly relevant to such cases when, as he puts it, what enters the national story 'is not what has actually been preserved in popular memory, but what has been selected, written, pictured, popularized and institutionalized.'[3] At the close of the twentieth century it is fashionable to observe that the latter is the norm. What follows is a late-nineteenth-century illustration of this cynical generalization.

The staking of claims for the Cabot landfall, during the quad-centennial celebrations of 1897, amounted to the invention of competing national myths by Canadian and Newfoundland intellectuals. At this time, recently rediscovered sixteenth-century maps offered new evidence for a Cape Breton landfall. In the pages of the *Transactions of the Royal Society of Canada*, the Canadian writer Samuel E. Dawson, and others, promoted this theory and took up the cudgels against Daniel F. Prowse, the eminent Newfoundland jurist and historian, who had become the most vociferous proponent of a Bonavista landfall. Both had to contend with the erudite and sceptical American scholar Henry Harrisse, who could easily muster the disparate scraps of historical evidence that cast doubt on both theories. There was some ill-expressed truth in an American jibe about the quadcentennial celebrations at Bristol, Halifax, and St John's: 'If the Eskimos, of whom Lieutenant Peary has been telling us so much lately, had only attained a higher degree of civilization, they would no doubt be on hand these days ready to prove their claims, and to set up a memorial to Cabot on their rock-bound coast somewhere near latitude 60 degrees.'[4] It will be argued here that the Cape Breton theory in Canada, or at least English Canada, was not simply a way of competing with the separate and self-governing dominion of Newfoundland for some kind of historical precedence in the annals of British imperialism, it was also a product of internal cultural tensions. Between 1884 and 1892, anglophone Canadians had watched the three-hundred-and-fiftieth anniversary of Jacques Cartier's voyages from the sidelines, and by 1897 the moment was ripe for them to claim their own founder-hero. In Newfoundland, the Cabot mythology served the purposes of a growing nationalism in a different way, although usually draped in familiar colours, for Canadian and Newfoundland landfall myths borrowed similar themes from the ideological storehouse of British imperialism.

Let us amplify the notion of 'invention of tradition' and distinguish between the invention of historical tradition by what we might call historical artisans and state-sponsored mass production of tradition.[5] A single individual might engage in both facets of production of tradition, as the career of Judge Prowse illustrates nicely. Prowse was an accomplished regional historian, whose *History of Newfoundland* of 1895 represents an immense amount of serious and dedicated work in 'the English, Colonial and Foreign Records.'[6] He was also the driving force behind the construction of Cabot Tower on Signal Hill in St John's as a suitable memorial of the voyage of 1497.[7] Prowse's *History* is, clearly, a different kind of cultural artifact than Cabot Tower. Each commemorates the past but in a different way, the latter serving as a physical memorial and celebration of a barely documented event picked out by the former from the continuum of early European exploitation and exploration. Both phases involve the invention of tradition. In the first phase of the invention of tradition events are selected and history is written and pictured. In a subsequent phase of mass production, these new historical traditions are popularized and institutionalized, often with the intention of establishing or symbolizing the social cohesion of communities.[8]

The late nineteenth century was, par excellence, the great era for the mass production of tradition, that is to say for institutionalizing particular understandings of the past in ceremonies, holidays, souvenirs, monuments, and so on. The very idea of celebrating centenary anniversaries in public ceremony was an innovation of the period.[9] This was an expression of a late phase in the evolution of the nation state. It was, in fact, in this period that the very term 'nationalism' was put to its modern use.[10] Aspects of the Cabotian tradition were mass produced for nationalist purposes, both in 1897 and in the following century. As a way of sampling the mass production of such traditions over time we will turn in this chapter, briefly, to philately and consider the use of commemorative postage stamps in the propagation of national myth.

Most of the scholars who have dealt with the Cabot landfall have exhibited distinct national biases. In the first century of their republic, the Americans, from Belknap in 1794, through Biddle, Bancroft, and Kohl, traditionally put Cabot in the north, in Labrador or close to it – and as far away from 'Columbia' as possible. Although late-nineteenth-century American scholars helped lay the groundwork for the turn-of-the-century consensus in favour of a Cape Breton Island landfall, in the twentieth century Admiral Morison and fellow Americans have rejoined Henry Harrisse on or near the coast of Labrador.[11] Twentieth-century British historians like Williamson, Skelton, and Quinn have tended to put their man Cabot in Nova Scotia or Maine, as far south as possible, as near to the heart of 'Columbia' as the evidence will bear. Newfoundlanders and Canadians have other traditions to defend (or invent), of course.

The Canadian scholar Dawson, in his quadcentennial papers for the Royal Society of Canada, became intensely involved in a debate with Newfoundland's Bishop Howley and Judge Prowse, who offended his sensibilities with their *ad hominem* arguments.[12] These Newfoundlanders had been sidetracked by what Dawson called the dangerous snare of national feeling.[13] Such sentiments should be irrelevant to historical investigations, Dawson maintained. At the same time, he himself argued that Canadians were especially suited to analysis of the Cabot voyages, by their 'intimate local knowledge' of 'seas and coasts familiar to them from boyhood,' which the learned of other nations could not possess.[14] Others could at least share his mode of reasoning. For Bishop Howley, Dawson's idea that Cabot might have missed Newfoundland en route to Cape Breton 'may appear quite reasonable to the ordinary reader looking without professional skills on the map; but, to people born with the 'nautical sense,' as we are here in Newfoundland, it is at once obviously absurd and impossible.'[15] Participants on both sides of the debate made repeated appeals to the snare of national feeling.

For Samuel Edward Dawson, Cabot's landing was 'the primal event in Canadian history.'[16] The emotions of Canadian nationalism, as Dawson expressed them, suggest that the location of the Cabot landfall was not simply a question of Canadian versus Newfoundland nationalism but a question that bore on competing Canadian nationalisms. His attention had been drawn to the subject when, as local secretary to the British Association for the Advancement of Science, he was asked to prepare a *Handbook for the Dominion of Canada*, for a conference in Montreal in 1884.[17]

The Nova Scotia–born Dawson (1833–1916) was a partner in Dawson Brothers, the Montreal English-language publishers of his 300-page *Handbook*. The firm had already published his pseudonymous political pamphlet 'The Northern Kingdom,' another booklet on episcopal elections, his lecture on copyright law, and his study of Tennyson.[18] In 1891 Dawson was appointed Queen's printer in Ottawa and he played an active role in the Royal Society of Canada, serving as secretary in 1894 and as president in 1907. He was also the most active member of the committee set up by the society in 1895 to coordinate 'commemoration of the discovery of the mainland of North America by John Cabot.[19] The result of Dawson's research on the history of Canada for the British Association and for the Royal Society was predictable enough, given his Anglophilia: 'Upon that easternmost point of this Nova Scotian land of our common country John Cabot planted the banner of St George on June 24, 1497, more than one year before Columbus set foot upon the main continent of America, and now, after almost four hundred years, despite all the chances and changes of this western world, that banner is floating there, a witness to our existing union with our distant mother land across the ocean.'[20]

COLUMBUS IN AMERICA, 1892

It is not too difficult to find evidence that the British North Americans who sought to celebrate Cabot in 1897 were, at least in part, reacting to the apotheosis of Columbus south of the border, and elsewhere, earlier in the decade.[21] In retrospect, Henry Harrisse could not refrain from making the comparison:

It cannot be said that the four-hundredth anniversary of the discovery of the American continent by Jean Cabot was celebrated with as much enthusiasm as that of the West Indies by Columbus. A good test is the number of historical and literary productions published on these two occasions. For the achievement of the great Genoese, we know of six hundred and fifty books and pamphlets printed in 1891 and 1892, in nearly all the languages of Europe, in prose and verse. Concerning

Cabot's discovery, we have heard of only two or three volumes, a dozen review and newspaper articles, three memoirs, an address, four speeches, two medleys of barefaced plagiarism, the one fabricated in Bristol, the other, quite recently, in London, and no poem at all.[22]

Harrisse was wrong about the lack of verse: William Wilfred Campbell read a poem to the 1897 Halifax meeting of the Royal Society of Canada, and in St John's at least two odes to Cabot saw print, besides Johnny Burke's satire.[23] Harrisse even underestimates the quantity of Cabotian prose, but he was right in principle. Whether we confine ourselves to the textual tradition or whether we cast our net wider and consider the mass production of popular tradition in public ceremonies, memorials, and ephemera, in 1897 neither Canada nor Newfoundland came near to matching the American celebration of Columbus five years before.

   The United States of America had outdone themselves in nationwide commemorations that saw 'the Admiral enthroned' in 1892. Chicago organized the Columbian World's Fair, by far the largest to date, to glorify American progress. New York celebrated for five days, culminating in a public holiday and parade which drew a million visitors into the city. Congregations of all denominations honoured Columbus for American freedom of religion and President Benjamin Harrison proclaimed a school holiday, the forerunner of the annual 12 October Columbus day, declared a national holiday by his successor Franklin Roosevelt in 1934. The Knights of Columbus, founded in 1881, numbered forty thousand by 1899 and much was made of the founder hero, in this period, as a Catholic leader symbolizing a shared Americanism that superseded ethnic background. For the quadcentennial in New York, the financial aristocracy installed a bronze statue by a Spanish artist in Central Park, while Catholic ethnic associations outdid them with an eighty-four-foot monument by an Italian sculptor in Columbus Circle, which came to serve 'as a secular shrine for immigrants trying to find their place in the New World.'[24]

   For many British North American intellectuals, the American commemoration of Columbus in 1892 formed a sort of model on which plans for Cabot celebrations might be based.[25] In the end, however, the Cabot commemorations that actually took place in 1897 were modest compared to the preceding Columbus extravaganza. The small size and great impoverishment of Newfoundland put economic limits on commemoration there. In Canada, observation of the Cabot quadcentenary was limited, essentially, to ceremonies in Halifax, organized by the Royal Society of Canada. The small scale of the Cabot memorials created in British North America circa 1897 was not for lack of early planning. Reverend Harvey had suggested public observance of the Cabot quadcentenary as early as 1874 and made the public proposal prefacing this chapter to the Nova Scotia Historical Society in 1893, following this up in 1894 with a letter to the secretary of the Royal Society of Canada, Dawson.[26] Moses Harvey (1820–1901) was a prolific man of letters and had very good contacts, both in his adopted country of Newfoundland, where he was minister of St Andrew's Free Presbyterian Church in St John's, and also in Canada, where he published regularly in the Montreal *Gazette*. In 1891 he received an honorary LL.D. from McGill and was elected to the Royal Society of Canada, then a remarkable honour for a Newfoundlander.[27] His proposals for a Cabot commemoration were adopted by the society and its propaganda on the subject probably influenced government efforts to get British cooperation in a Canadian celebration. This was one of the purposes of an informal trip to England by Sir Sanford Fleming and Sir Mackenzie Bowell, in the winter of 1895–6.[28] Harvey's proposals for a public commemoration of Cabot's voyage eventually had an effect at home in St John's as well, where Reverend A.G. Bayly organized a meeting of local notables, including Judge Prowse and Bishop Howley, to form a committee to organize the celebration of the Cabot quadcentennial. Bayly himself missed the meeting in late September 1896 in order to return as Anglican rector to his native Bonavista. The St John's committee carried on and, in the end, managed to promote both celebrations and a memorial on a scale that considerably surpassed anything accomplished in the much larger and wealthier Dominion of Canada.[29]

Invention of tradition about Cabot was a century or so behind what had developed around the founder hero of the United

States. Columbus had emerged from obscurity in the early years of the young republic and had become the subject of commemoration by 1792.[30] This might be partly explained by the accessibility and positive tone of early accounts of Columbus's voyages. He celebrated himself in the journal of his first expedition, published in 1493 by Bartolomé de las Casas, who later wrote a generally positive biography, as did Columbus's son Ferdinand. The mists in which John Cabot was shrouded by his son's ambiguous accounts of the early voyages doubtless had an effect on the invention of tradition about the Cabot landfall, if only by facilitating a kind of historiographic regatta in which memories of father and son were blown alternately hither and yon by each fresh gust from the archives and every shift in the prevailing winds of historical fashion. All this may well have been less significant than the political fact that it was not until the British dominions started to define their own relationships to the motherland that they had much use for their own founder-hero. In 1797, neither Newfoundland nor Canada needed John Cabot in the way that they were beginning to need him in 1897. Whether or not John Cabot was, as Harrisse put it, more to the people of England and the United States in actual historical deed than Christopher Columbus, it would seem that in 1897 Canada, as a whole, was still not prepared to embrace Cabot in the same way that America had embraced Columbus after the American War of Independence. Newfoundland nationalism was, for several reasons, more open to the myth of Cabot.

CABOT IN CANADA, 1897

The tale of Canada's Cabot celebrations in 1897 reads like a mock epic. With considerable fanfare, the intellectuals managed to invent a tradition, but their attempts at mass production fell flat. In a series of articles for the *Canadian Magazine* Oliver Howland, son of a former federal cabinet minister and himself an Ontario MPP, promoted the idea of a Canadian Historical Exhibition, to take place in Toronto in 1897. Howland found the 1892 Columbus Exhibition in Chicago flawed, to the extent that 'the historical was less

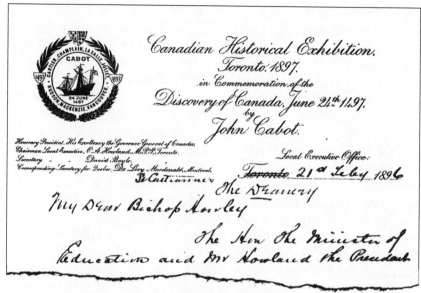

5.1 Letterhead of the Canadian Historical Exhibition.

attended to than the industrial,' and he wanted to rectify a shameful fact: 'in the whole length of Canada, whose existence and whose British nationality may be ascribed to John Cabot, there is not to be found the most insignificant monument erected to commemorate the fact or to honour his adventurous memory.'[31] The primary object of the proposed exhibition was 'to duly celebrate the memory of that enterprising discoverer.' It would also present the culture of Native peoples, 'the palimpsest upon which European colonization has written the later histories.' Next would follow portraits, relics, and records of 'the discoverers'; then pictures, clothing, and weapons of early European settlers, culled from public and family collections throughout the Dominion. In October 1895, an executive committee chaired by Howland drew up a kind of prospectus, with a budget of $15,000.[32] Letters went out, soliciting subscriptions and a public meeting in February 1896 attracted the moral support of public figures, including the governor-general, Lord Aberdeen.[33] (See figure 5.1 for the exhibition letterhead.) Howland then proposed that the Dominion, Ontario, and Toronto governments guarantee $75,000 in debentures to finance the exhibition.[34] The whole idea was justified by the mythic Cape Breton landfall, as Howland made explicit in his preamble to the original text of the bill incorporating the exhibition.[35]

In any event, the organizers did not get the backing they were looking for. French Canadians found the proposal offensive and it is not surprising that federal assistance was not forthcoming. Meanwhile, provincial assistance does not seem to have amounted to much. When the First Canadian Historical Exhibition finally opened its doors at Victoria College in Toronto, 14 June 1899, it paid much more attention to General Isaac Brock than to the Cabots, who were acknowledged only in erroneous notes to a picture of the Old Merchant Venturers' Hall in Bristol.[36] The exhibition did absorb the balance of the 'Cabot Celebration Fund,' to the tune of a paltry $265.[37] The plan to commemorate Cabot in a Canadian Historical Exhibition in 1897 had come to virtually nothing.[38] In June 1897 the Toronto *Globe* covered Queen Victoria's Diamond Jubilee in great detail, but referred to Cabot commemorations only in a short notice of the meetings of the Royal Society of Canada in Halifax on the twenty-fourth and in a page-six single column the following day, reporting the 'Unveiling of the Tablet to Sebastian Cabot.'[39] The Montreal *Gazette* and the Winnipeg *Free Press* gave similar coverage; in Shediac, New Brunswick, *Le Moniteur Acadien* ignored the whole business. In Canada, public celebration of the quadcentenary of Cabot's landfall was restricted to the ceremonies in Halifax.

The trajectory of the Canadian Historical Exhibition is captured nicely, in miniature as it were, in the story of a dinner service of the period, painted on Doulton porcelain by Canadian women artists from Ontario, Quebec, and Nova Scotia. In 1896 the Woman's Art Association of Canada commissioned this two-hundred-piece state dinner service for twenty-four, as 'The Cabot Commemorative State Set,' in observance of the quadcentennial. The association chose historical scenes for the soup and dinner plates; the artists painted the rest of the set with Canadian game, fish, ferns, fruit, birds, and flowers. The historical scenes depicted, contributed by two Toronto women, resembled those eventually displayed at the First Canadian Historical Exhibition in 1899, running to views of Canadian forts and battle grounds, seasoned with the occasional church or Indian village. With the exception of a logo of the *Matthew* used on the bottoms of these vessels, the Cabots are conspicuous by their absence, and by 1898 the china had become 'The Canadian Historical Dinner Service.' The government of the day declined to purchase the set for Rideau Hall, as the Art Association had hoped. Instead, individual members of the House of Commons and Senate underwrote the costs, as a farewell gift to Lady Aberdeen, on the retirement of her husband as governor-general in 1898. She accepted the service graciously, and took it with her back to Scotland, where it was tastefully housed in custom cabinets, at the family seat.[40] It has remained at Haddo House, Aberdeenshire, until 1997, when the Canadian Museum of Civilization put it on display, in observance of the Cabot quincentennial.

The Royal Society of Canada had originally planned to erect a Cabot memorial on Cape Breton itself, but abandoned this idea in 1896. Archbishop O'Brien complained to Dawson: 'Perhaps Cabot landed in Cape Breton, but if so I am inclined to think no one has landed there since – or been there. [A] well informed gentleman who has lived half a lifetime on the Island ... actually did not know that there was a *Cape* Breton! Hence it will be altogether impracticable to set up any stone there.'[41] For the time being the society agreed to spend at least $1000 on a stone memorial in Sydney, the only real town in Cape Breton.[42] In the end they decided a memorial in Halifax would be simpler. A generous Haligonian offered to contribute $4000 towards the erection of a Cabot statue to be erected in the Grand Parade, if the city council would vote $2000 in matching funds. 'With characteristic stupidity,' in the words of a contemporary report, the city fathers let the opportunity pass.[43]

The Royal Society dedicated a smaller Cabot Memorial with some ceremony on 24 June 1897. The list of dignitaries was impressive, including not only the governor-general of Canada, the premier of Nova Scotia, and the mayor of Halifax, but also a resplendent collection of British military officers, two ex-mayors

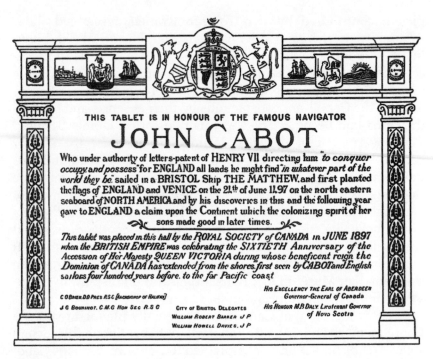

THIS TABLET IS IN HONOUR OF THE FAMOUS NAVIGATOR

JOHN CABOT

Who under authority of letters-patent of HENRY VII directing him *to conquer occupy and possess* for ENGLAND all lands he might find *in whatever part of the world they be.* sailed in a BRISTOL Ship THE MATTHEW and first planted the flags *of* ENGLAND and VENICE on the 21.ᵗʰ of June 1197 on the north eastern seaboard *of* NORTH AMERICA and by his discoveries in this and the following year gave to ENGLAND a claim upon the Continent which the colonizing spirit of her sons made good in later times.

This tablet was placed in this hall by the ROYAL SOCIETY of CANADA in JUNE 1897 when the BRITISH EMPIRE was celebrating the SIXTIETH Anniversary of the Accession of Her Majesty QUEEN VICTORIA during whose beneficent reign the Dominion of CANADA has extended from the shores first seen by CABOT and English sailors four hundred years before. to the far Pacific coast

C O BRIGER DD PRES R.S C. [ARCHBISHOP OF HALIFAX]

J G BOURINOT, C.M.G HON SEC R.S.C

His EXCELLENCY THE EARL OF ABERDEEN
Governor-General of Canada

CITY OF BRISTOL DELEGATES

WILLIAM ROBERT BARKER J P

WILLIAM HOWELL DAVIES. J P

His HONOUR M.B DALY Lieutenant Governor
of Nova Scotia

5.2 Brass plaque commemorating John Cabot's landfall, erected by the Royal Society of Canada in Halifax, 24 June 1897.

of Bristol and the Italian consul-general in Montreal. The military band of HMS *Crescent* marched to and fro, Archbishop O'Brien made a speech, as president of the Royal Society, and with some fanfare the governor-general pulled a Union Jack aside – to reveal a small brass tablet (figure 5.2). Even in the official account of the ceremony one can sense that it did not achieve the popular impact of the Columbus celebrations in Chicago and New York: 'The unveiling proceedings lasted more than an hour, and were exceedingly interesting, even to those on the noisy thoroughfare beyond the reach of the speakers' voices.'[44]

CABOT IN NEWFOUNDLAND, 1897

Newfoundland made much more of Cabot in 1897. A coalition of

THE CABOT SIGNAL STATION, ST. JOHN'S,
NEWFOUNDLAND.

Designed by Bishop Howley. The central tower is
to be adorned with a figure representing John
Cabot pointing to a globe with his left hand,
while in his right he holds aloft a cross-staff
bearing an electric light, which will be visible
to mariners far out at sea.

5.3 Original design for Cabot Tower, in St John's, by Bishop Michael Howley.

St John's merchants struggled to raise money for the Cabot
Memorial on Signal Hill. The observation tower eventually constructed was, to be sure, a reduced and simplified version of the
larger and more ornate edifice originally envisaged by Bishop
Michael Howley (figures 5.3 and 5.4). It was, nonetheless, a considerable project for the island polity. The promoters managed to

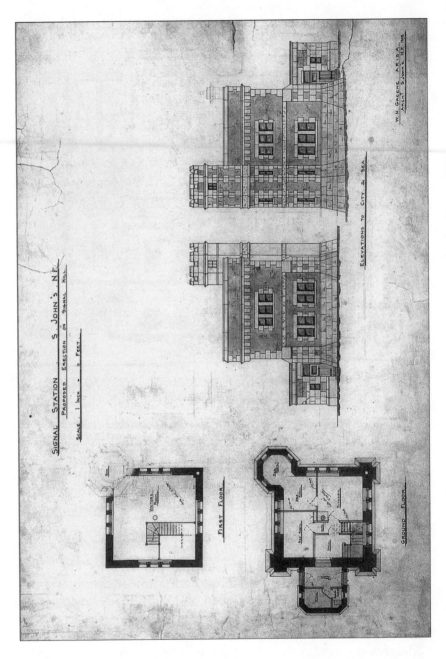

5.4 W.H. Greene, 'Signal Station, St. John's N.F.': plans and elevations of Cabot Tower, 1898.

get the memorial under way in time for the quadcentennial, although it was not opened until June 1900. The British themselves were no further ahead: on 24 June 1897, Lord Dufferin laid the cornerstone of a planned hundred-foot Cabot Memorial Tower, in the city of Bristol, but a public subscription for celebration of the discovery in Britain was an 'utter failure.'[45] In Newfoundland, on the other hand, there was strong local interest in and support for the anniversary festivities. The best modern account of the local celebrations concludes that Cabot fever swept Newfoundland in 1897, citing a landfall billiards tournament at the Mechanics' Hall, Burke's landfall ballad, James P. Howley's public challenge to Judge Prowse for a public debate on the topic, a Cabot calendar, as well as a special issue of stamps to celebrate the Cabot voyage and the scenic and industrial attractions of Newfoundland.[46] Bishop Howley gave a public lecture, attacking the Cape Breton arguments of 'the young Dr Dawson' and Judge Prowse published his case for the Bonavista landfall in the *Royal Gazette*.[47] (Dawson was actually a decade older than Howley.) The June celebrations in St John's attracted a popular audience and a crowd of 5000 people assembled on Signal Hill for the dedication of Cabot Tower. Local dignitaries made speeches, officials welcomed officers of the French and British naval vessels in port, and the internationally renowned diva Madame Toulinguet (Georgina Sterling) sang 'God Save the Queen.'[48] Prowse and Bishop Howley spoke eloquently, while a fellow Presbyterian clergyman read a paper by the ailing Moses Harvey, expressing 'the admiration we owe to one who did a great work for our race and nation.'[49] The publishers Devine and O'Mara printed a *Cabot Souvenir Number*, 'at the request of a number of sporting gentlemen and friends generally,' containing a report of the commemorations, as well as poems and stories.[50]

The Cabot celebrations in St John's were longer, larger, and locally much more significant than the official ceremony in Canada. They came nowhere near the scale of the Columbian hoopla in the United States, but given the population of Newfoundland, the 5000 people who attended the dedication of Cabot Tower in St John's were proportionate, in relative terms, to the million who were supposed to have attended the 1892 Columbus celebrations in New York. This was particularly remarkable because Newfoundland had suffered severely in the general trade depression of the 1890s. Five years after the great fire of 1892, and three years after the bank crash, St John's was not a prosperous city. As a correspondent pointed out to readers of the *Evening Telegram* in March 1897, building a memorial tower was a bit like putting 'a silk hat on the head of a man who had not a decent pair of boots to keep him warm.'[51] (Of course a silk hat is sometimes more useful than decent boots.)

Another factor that limited the scale of the Cabot celebrations throughout British North America was Queen Victoria's Diamond Jubilee. Because it coincided with the Cabot quadcentenary in 1897, it deflected national sentiment in an imperial direction, both in Canada and Newfoundland. Anglophone Canadian British North American nationalists invented their own Cabot tradition but, with the minor exception of the Halifax plaque, they did not manage to make this a public tradition in 1897. Indeed, when the *Globe* and the *Free Press* noted the Halifax ceremony they misunderstood it as a tribute to Sebastian. Only the Halifax papers gave the Cabot quadcentenary the kind of coverage in illustrations and special sections that the popular press throughout English Canada accorded the Victoria Jubilee.

In St John's, fund-raising for Cabot Tower as a combined signal station, observatory, and memorial conflicted with fund-raising for a new Victoria Wing on the General Hospital.[52] Prowse's pet project did not quite fit imperial conceptions of an appropriate Jubilee memorial, for these were supposed to be of social benefit. His argument that in stormy weather the signal tower would in fact serve as a work of mercy fell on deaf ears. When it came time to dedicate Cabot Tower, on Jubilee Day, 22 June 1897, Governor Murray refused to lay the foundation stone, officially on grounds that it was 'not in accordance with her Majesty's expressed wishes as to the method in which her Jubilee is to be celebrated.'[53] Privately he wrote the British Colonial Secretary Joseph Chamberlain that 'it would be out of place for me to take part in a ceremony by which Her Majesty's fame was to be celebrated in conjunction with

that of a foreign adventurer.'[54] Despite this conflict of commemorations, Newfoundlanders who saw themselves as British North
Americans did manage to mass-produce their Cabot mythology.

There was, at the same time, another strain of nationalism at
work in Newfoundland. In his discourse on Cabot, the Roman
Catholic Bishop of St John's, Michael Howley, had little to say
about British imperial destiny, instead making an appeal to a specifically Newfoundland national sentiment. Howley (1843–1914)
was one of thirteen children of Irish immigrants, several of whom
distinguished themselves in Newfoundland public life. When the
Holy See made him bishop of St George's, that is, of the west
coast of the Island, he became the first Native-born Newfoundland bishop. He published his *Ecclesiastical History* in 1888, in
1895 was installed as bishop of St John's, and, when Newfoundland became an Ecclesiastical Province in 1904, became archbishop. He was well known through his many contributions to
the local press, particularly for a patriotic song 'Fling Out the
Flag,' which became an unofficial national anthem, for some at
least.[55] His vision of the Cabot Memorial on Signal Hill calls to
mind a surreal combination of the Statue of Liberty and the huge
monument in Columbus Circle, erected by the Catholics of New
York: 'a colossal statue of Cabot, our discoverer and our patron,
who would stretch out his protecting arm over our city and our
coast; while from his brow should radiate a beacon bright, whose
electric rays would flash across the bosom of the ocean, would be
a guiding star to the approaching ship ... and at the same time
would enlighten the hearts of our people with noble aspirations,
and fill with sentiments of patriotism and national pride, the
minds of our countrymen for centuries to come.'[56]

Bishop Howley's views of the desirable form of the Cabot tradition resemble American traditions about Columbus more than
they do the imperialism of the British North American nationalists. Howley stressed Cabot's Italian origin and concluded that he
was born in Genoa about 1440: 'that is to say about the same time
as Columbus, of whom he was a fellow-citizen and probably a
companion and school-fellow.'[57] Cabot was an ideal candidate
to become a national Newfoundland founder-hero, for he could

transcend the colony's serious sectarian tensions. These had been just barely contained politically in the second half of the nineteenth century. The standard history of politics in Newfoundland observes that 'the denominational compromise of the 1860s had crystallized into an established principle of government and denominational segregation had become an unwritten law of social organization.'[58] Cabot was Italian and therefore an acceptable 'patron' for Newfoundland's ethnics, that is the Irish, but he sailed in the service of an English king. John Cabot lived and died before Henry VIII broke with Rome, so he was Catholic but no more Catholic than any other servant of the English crown in the period, so in that sense he was acceptably 'Anglican.' Cabot was potentially a pan-denominational hero. (The Canadian *Catholic Register* picked up this theme in its coverage of the proposed Canadian Historical Exhibition, citing 'the consoling assurance that the Celt and the Saxon are fast fusing into a solidified body, to be known as the Canadian people.'[59]

Bishop Howley had other nationalist ideas for Newfoundland. His stirring anthem honoured the old Newfoundland nationalist flag, which resembled the present Irish tricolour, substituting pink for orange to accompany the white and the green. This was based on an earlier 'Native' flag meant to celebrate the unity of the English and Irish inhabitants of the island. These banners appealed more to the latter than to the former, as the pink-white-and-green still does, and in 1904 London approved instead the regulation imperial red ensign, with badge, as a flag for Newfoundland. (The badge featured Mercury, the god of Commerce, presenting to Britannia a kneeling fisherman, who offers his catch.) At the same time the Newfoundland government of the day adopted Governor Cavendish Boyle's salute to Nature, 'The Ode to Newfoundland,' as an anthem. This is a beautiful song dedicated to a beautiful place, but it remains politically aseptic compared to Howley's anthem, or even 'The Maple Leaf, Our Emblem Dear.' The bishop was not much more successful in putting his mark on the officially adopted tradition of John Cabot, which was shaped instead by the British North American nationalism of Judge Prowse.[60]

For Prowse, Cabot's voyage was one of the great events in world history. If Newfoundland had not been discovered by Cabot it might have fallen into Spanish hands. What then, he wondered, might have become its fate: 'with chronic revolutions, disordered finances, pronunciamentos, half-breeds, and fusillades'?[61] Instead, Cabot's landfall 'gave North America to the English by an indefeasible title – the right of discovery – and above all, it afforded an outlet for the pent-up energy of a great insular people. The first rill of that great stream of maritime enterprise and mighty commerce which now overspreads the world began to flow in the Newfoundland trade and fishery.'[62] With precedents like this at stake, it was no wonder that it mattered intensely to Prowse, as it did to Dawson and Harvey, where 'in the New World England's flag first floated.'[63]

The underlying issue was the familiar one: rightful possession of a continent. One of the American delegates to the Halifax meeting of the Royal Society of Canada, in 1897, spelled this out. Territory, he explained, could be claimed by discovery, conquest, or purchase. Defining discovery as something Europeans do, he proceeded to celebrate the appropriation of North America as a case in point, considering Canadians and Americans 'part owners of the fairest domain on all the earth.' The voyages of the Cabots mattered historically, because '[w]hen we study the first westward sailings of hardy English navigators we are only reading the title deeds to our own beloved countries.' He went on to observe, in a memorable phrase, that there were several places contending 'for the honour of first receiving the feet of the English discoverers.'[64] If the question of a landfall was, for this reason, a sensitive issue for Newfoundlanders and anglophone Canadians, it was an even more difficult question for francophone Canadians.

CABOT VERSUS CARTIER

By this time nationalism was a crucial motive in the debate about the Cabot landfall, even if participants were prone to deny this coyly. This was, however, nationalism of a curious sort, in both Canada and Newfoundland, for it was generally expressed in imperialist terms. British North American nationalists identified with the imperial motherland so as to define the nation, whether English Canada or Newfoundland, against something not entirely British, whether the United States, French Canada, or, in the case of Newfoundland, mainland North America in general. What lurked in back of the minds of these nationalists was a kind of imperialist racism. Their British identity was a pressing matter for these British North American nationalists, whether they were Canadians, Newfoundlanders, or, as in the case of Reverend Harvey, a kind of hybrid. In his proposal for Cabot quadcentennial celebrations, Reverend Harvey argued:

The Cabots were the real discoverers of North America. In virtue of their discoveries, England established her claims to the sovereignty of a large portion of these northern lands ... Other nations, such as France, came to share in the spoils, but were finally compelled to retire from the field. That North America is now almost entirely occupied by an English speaking population, with all their vast energies and accumulated wealth, has been largely owing to the daring genius of the Cabots ... As truly as Columbus pioneered the way in the south, did the Cabots open a pathway for a far nobler civilization in the north.'[65]

By 1897 Harvey was prepared to say that 'by conquering a new world for England' Cabot epitomized 'the energy and enterprise of the English-speaking race' and set a precedent for its 'approaching supremacy.'[66]

The Canadian nationalist Samuel Dawson took a similar view of the issue; but the expression of his loyalties raises some issues usually obscured by the imperialist rhetoric: 'Solely upon the discoveries of the Cabots have always rested the original claims of the English race to a foothold upon this continent ... Canadians should not quietly resign Cabot into other hands, for he is more to them than Columbus is to the people of the United States. Cabot sailed in the service of the British crown and he landed in a territory which still owes allegiance to the queen of England.'[67] The logic here is curious. After all, the Union Jack still flew in Bonavista. Why was Cabot more crucial to Canadian identity than Columbus to America or, more to the point, Cabot to New-foundland? Essentially because there existed a competitor for the honour of being the founder-hero of Canada and this competitor was not British, even by adoption. This debate can be and was seen as a contest of British versus French-Canadian nationalism, or of Cabot versus Cartier, as Dawson demurely put it.[68]

The cult of Jacques Cartier as the founder of Quebec dates from the 1830s, the tercentenary of his voyages. In a pair of fascinating and complementary essays, Jacques Robert and Jacques Mathieu have recounted how Cartier was almost completely forgotten in the seventeenth and eighteenth centuries, to be rediscovered in the warehouse of memory and transformed by Québécois into the symbol of French presence in North America in the early nine-teenth century, just when the cities of Quebec and Montreal became predominantly anglophone.[69] Calls at this time by Georges Barthélemy Faribault and others for a monument to the Breton mariner resulted in a variety of curious designs, although nothing was actually built. Faribault, the clerk of the Quebec assembly, did manage to locate a painting of Cartier in Saint-Malo. No one worried that the portrait dated only to 1839. It was lithographed by Théophile Hamel, distributed in the thousands, and the rest is history. The bearded visage, still familiar to Cana-dians, became a national icon in Quebec, despite its lack of histor-ical authenticity. In 1843, the Société littéraire et historique published a new edition of the *Voyages*, the first since 1598. A few years later François-Xavier Garneau's *Histoire du Canada* glorified Cartier and the city of Montreal changed the name of its market square from Place Wellington to Place Jacques Cartier. Three-hundred-and-fiftieth anniversary celebrations followed in 1884–5 and, by 1890, Cartier was celebrated with a monument in Quebec City, in Ernest Myrand's historical novel *Une fête de Noël sous Jacques Cartier*, and in a long essay from the pen of N.-E. Dionne, the legislative librarian of the Assemblée Nationale. A former *premier ministre* summed up Cartier's role in the new national mythology: our people, he wrote, 'take Jacques Cartier for their first hero, they date our history from him; for them no figure, even that of Champlain ... stands as tall before posterity.'[70]

Cartier's significance to late-twentieth-century Quebec resides largely in his observations on natural history and ethnography, but in the nineteenth century he remained the founder-hero of a distinct and Catholic society. His popularity as the personal symbol of discovery and occupation of the St Lawrence valley by France peaked with the four-hundredth anniversary of his first voyage, in 1934. These celebrations provoked a renewed interest in John Cabot on the part of anglophones and Montreal's relatively new Italian community.[71] The Italians erected a statue, had Atwater Park renamed in Cabot's honour, and began to commemorate the Venetian navigator in annual ceremonies.[72] This was not, however, the first time that Cartier provoked invention of tradition about Cabot. The intense francophone cult constructed around the former in the late 1880s and early 1890s is a very relevant context in which to locate Samuel Dawson's interest in the Cabots, for he was an active member of Montreal's anglophone intelligentsia.

The Canadian anglophone scholars liked to pretend that the Cabot tradition they were inventing was not designed to diminish other, competing, traditions. In his 1896 paper Dawson disingenuously makes this point, while the Royal Society of Canada itself claimed that by honouring the Venetian navigator, 'there is no thought of detracting in the slightest degree from the fame of the intrepid sailor of St Malo, who was assuredly the first to enter the great valley of the St Lawrence, and see the ancient villages of Canada on the banks of the great river, which he followed to Hochelaga. But all historians agree that John Cabot discovered the continent of North America.'[73] In fact, the articles published on the Cabot voyages in the society's *Transactions* between 1894 and 1897 belie these sentiments. The president of the Royal Society, Archbishop O'Brien, himself identified Cabot's 'Island of St John' with Prince Edward Island and was insistent that Cabot had explored the Gulf of St Lawrence decades before Cartier. Even if Dawson refrained from accepting such an itinerary, which almost seems designed to diminish the achievements of Cartier, it attracted the enthusiasm of many late-nineteenth-century advocates of the Cape Breton school, from Brevoort to Tarducci. In this context, it is not surprising that the simple idea of a Cape Breton landfall, even when hedged with disclaimers of penetration of the Gulf, drew the wrath not only of French-Canadian nationalists but even of conservative federalists.

Howland's call for a Canadian Historical Exhibition built around the theme of John Cabot's discovery of North America triggered an impassioned response by the nationalist historian Narcisse-Eutrope Dionne.[74] In 1896 the erudite Dionne published a series of articles in the *Journal des Campagnes*, a weekly supplement to the Quebec City daily *Courrier du Canada*, which Dionne had edited before his appointment to the legislative library. The publisher Léger Brousseau designed the *Journal* to spread the clerical-nationalist ideology of the daily *Courrier* to the countryside.[75] Dionne's articles, entitled 'Cartier vs Cabot,' took an essentially defensive stance, arguing, 'If we do not put ourselves on guard, we will soon see the name of Jacques Cartier disappear as *Discoverer* of Canada.'[76] The francophone bibliographer and author of works on Champlain and Cartier was disturbed by a 'strange document,' namely the 1897 exhibition prospectus circulated by Howland, particularly by its assumption that Cabot had landed on Cape Breton. This Dionne read as an egregious error, which he proceeded to refute with a careful compilation of historical and cartographic evidence.

Joseph Pope, a key federal civil servant of the period, had exactly the same reaction as Dionne. Pope had francophone connections (his wife Henrietta was daughter of the Hon. H.T. Taschereau of the Quebec Supreme Court), but impeccable conservative credentials too, as Sir John A. Macdonald's private secretary and biographer. Pope's incisive reply to Howland, in the pages of the *Canadian Magazine*, debunks the Canadian anglophone Cabot mythology. He points out that received opinion based on school histories and guidebooks is not authoritative and, furthermore, that 'to speak of the man who first landed on the shores of Cape Breton as having thereby discovered Canada betrays an inexactness of thought which is not easy to parallel, even by way of illustration.'[77] He went on to lampoon Howland's cocksureness and the unhistorical tendency of Dawson and Harvey to project an essentially mythic connection between Cabot's landfall and eventual British possession of the continent: 'Why should we vainly strive to pierce the gloom which shrouds the name of Cabot, when we can point to Wolfe, or, rather, to that long doubtful conflict which, beginning with the seizure of Quebec in 1629, was destined, a hundred and thirty years later, to close in triumph on the Heights of Abraham?' Pope thought it quite understandable that French Canadians might offer 'a word of protest' to the bills proposed by Howland and his ilk to the Ontario Legislature and the Parliament of Canada. Emphasizing his own British North American imperialism and his own appreciation of strong ties with the 'Motherland,' Pope admits it would be gratifying to believe that 'first of white men' Cabot circumnavigated the Gulf and penetrated the St Lawrence. 'Truth however,' he concludes, 'compels us to acknowledge that the man who did these things was not English, or rather Italian, but French. He was not named Cabot, but Cartier.' As for John Cabot, he was a brave and skilful navigator: 'We would fain know more about him – why he did so much an no more – just where he landed – how long he remained ... and why his enterprise came to naught. Unhappily all this is oblivion.' The fact that someone has to say this every hundred years suggests that Cabot's voyage has considerable value as myth or precedent, however intermittent his biography and however conjectural the history that 'must have been.'

Competing Canadian national myths, crafted in the nineteenth century, reverberated publicly through the twentieth. The Cabot versus Cartier issue was surely not entirely irrelevant to Father Lucien Campeau's argument of 1960, in the pages of Abbé Groulx's nationalist *Revue d'histoire de l'Amérique française*, that John Cabot was a fraudulent failure.[78] Campeau makes much of Soncino's statement that Cabot explored the territory past the 'Tanais,' the medieval Don River. By reading the flagged coast on the la Cosa Map as a depiction of northeastern Eurasia and by ignoring the fact that the world is round, that it is possible to reach 'the East' by sailing west, and that Cabot knew this, Campeau makes the mythically convenient argument that the Italian navigator never came within seven hundred leagues of North America, let alone setting foot on it. About the same time another Québécois writer argued that the Portuguese captain Corte-Real was the real discoverer of Newfoundland and Labrador, in 1500, and that Henry VII's failure to refute Portuguese claims based on this voyage casts doubt on whether Cabot reached these shores.[79]

To return the discussion to the clash of traditions in 1897, it is worth noting that the gentleman scholars of the Royal Society of Canada took a tone of condescension to Newfoundland at the unveiling of the memorial plaque at the Halifax meeting of the society in 1897, just as they condescended to Quebec. An American observer thought: 'Most if not all of its members now accept Cape Breton island, although unable as yet to agree upon the exact spot ... But no one will grudge the plucky Newfoundlanders their right to appropriate as much of Cabot as they please. If the latest learning does not sustain their cherished traditions, they may say in reply that they are still prepared to argue.[80] And, in fact, the proponents of Bonavista and the alternative Newfoundland landfalls felt compelled to engage Dawson, and the other Canadians, wholeheartedly in a debate about these traditions. We can, surely, locate the florescence of the Bonavista tradition, as well as the British North American nationalist mythology of Cape Breton and Quebec's Cartier cult, within a wider historiographic context.

THE CONTEST OF TRADITIONS

A commitment to public history or national myth had become normal, in Europe and America.[81] The English, Welsh, and Scots had been redefining their historical identities with invented traditions for at least a century: the English making a fetish of the monarchy with deliberately archaizing cermonials, the Welsh reimagining the Celtic druids and bards of a remote past, and the Scots adopting an English cloth manufacturer's invented fiction of differentiated clan tartans, to cite some classic examples from Hobsbawm and Ranger's survey of the topic.[82] Paradoxically, others were at work forging the Protestant and imperialist tradi-

tions of the encompassing nation of Great Britain.[83] The commemoration of the 1792 tercentenary of Columbus's voyage in the
new United States of America and the spectacular celebration of
the quadcentenary in 1892 suggest that Americans were equally
adept at the public uses of tradition. United Empire Loyalists
put different traditions to similar uses in late-nineteenth-century
Ontario, developing a myth of the War of 1812 that celebrated
General Brock's victory at Queenston Heights, the better to forget
the Loyalist defeat of 1783.[84] The 1880s and 1890s seem to have
been a golden age for local history. Carl Berger tells us that fifteen
local historical societies appeared in Ontario between 1882 and
1896 and over eighty such organizations in the United States in
the 1880s. These societies were not founded to promote the dis-
interested study of the past but to promote nationalist agendas.
Canadian nationalists of this period turned anniversaries into
focal points for reminding other Canadians of their British heritage: besides the Cabot quadcentenary, they observed the Loyalist
centennial in 1884 and the one-hundredth anniversary of the Con-
stitutional Act in 1891.[85] It should be no surprise that Newfoundland nationalists did the same and, what is more, often used the
same imperialist language to do so.[86] This was the period when
local boosters began to speak of Newfoundland as 'The Oldest
British Colony' or 'England's Oldest Colony,' subtitles of the 1883
and 1890 editions of Reverend Harvey's book on Newfoundland.
(One would think that Ireland or Wales would have best claim to
this distinction.)[87]

The Canada-Newfoundland landfall contest of 1897 ended in a
draw – a split decision which was possible because these traditions were elaborated, largely, in separate venues. Samuel Dawson, Bishop O'Brien, and Reverend Harvey made their elaborate
cases for a Cape Breton landfall in the scholarly arena, in the
pages of the *Transactions of the Royal Society of Canada*. Dawson
and others would later translate these scholarly abstractions into
popular tradition.[88] It was only in the twentieth century that
Nova Scotia put these tradition to work with the development of
'The Cabot Trail' around Cape Breton in the 1930s.[89] The only
Canadian attempt at the mass production of a popular tradition

in 1897, Howland's Historical Exhibition, ran out of steam. Meanwhile, Judge Prowse and Bishop Howley put their cases for a Newfoundland landfall in the public arena, in commemorative lectures, pamphlets, and newspaper articles and, finally, gave Cabot a very visible physical memorial in the form of Cabot Tower.[90] It was therefore possible, paradoxically, for both sides to win. The scholarly victory of Dawson and Bishop O'Brien in Canada is not surprising; this fight was fixed. Just because the Royal Society refrained from taking an official position on the landfall when it erected a commemorative plaque in Halifax does not mean it did not take sides in the scholarly debate. An editorial fix in the *Proceedings* for 1897 is indicative. When the Royal Society reprinted coverage of the Halifax ceremony from the *Halifax Herald* of 25 June, they deleted parenthetical doubts about the Cape Breton landfall.[91] Of the approximately 350 pages in the *Transactions* devoted to the question of the Cabot voyages in the decade between 1894 and 1903, 87 per cent were written by Canadian authors convinced of a Cape Breton landfall; two American proponents of Labrador wrote about 10 per cent of the material and a single argument for Newfoundland (Bishop Howley's, in 1903) accounted for the remaining 3 per cent. It is hard to refrain from observing that Dawson and O'Brien, the declared champions in this one-sided contest, are now little read and no longer in print, while the major works of their opponents, Harrisse and Prowse, are well thumbed in recent editions.

Whatever Dawson's immediate success within the Canadian academy, Prowse and Bishop Howley won their battle to create a public tradition in their own country. Here the fight was fairer, in a sense, for several landfall theories had outspoken local proponents: Reverend Harvey for Cape Breton, James Howley for Labrador, Judge Prowse for Bonavista, and Bishop Howley for whatever part of Newfoundland his latest navigational computations had led him to. However, only Reverend Harvey and Bishop Howley carried on sustained research on the landfall; and neither was likely to win many converts in Newfoundland. Harvey accepted the Cape Breton landfall and Howley's evolving conclusions must have confused his public audience. The public likes a story it can remember and Daniel Prowse provided that. In the end, Prowse won the landfall debate, in Newfoundland, because he stuck with his 'must-have-been,' making the best of the limited evidence in favour of his case and doing his best, like any good barrister, to draw the jury's attention away from conflicting evidence.[92]

In a long article written for the Halifax *Morning Chronicle* in 1897, Prowse made an astounding admission: 'The real landfall of Cabot in North America must forever remain among the things that are unknown and unknowable.' He immediately added: 'One thing, however, is quite certain, the claim of Cape Breton as the first land found by the Great Italian navigator is utterly untenable, opposed alike to common sense, reason and all the contemporary records.'[93] For Prowse, the theory of a Bonavista landfall was a means to an end: protecting the tradition of a Newfoundland landfall.[94] He was doubly successful. He actually made international converts to the Bonavista theory, in the persons of the president of the Royal Geographical Society, Sir Clements Markham, and the former governor-general of Canada and dilettante man of letters Lord Dufferin.[95] Proud as Prowse was of swaying such prominent jurors in the courtroom of history, his success in making the Bonavista landfall a public tradition in Newfoundland was an achievement of greater consequence. Daniel Prowse was wonderfully prolific of Newfoundland traditions. He left his country an exemplary *History* and he created a national symbol by promoting the construction of Cabot Tower on Signal Hill in St John's as a suitable memorial of the events of 1497. Finally, he promoted the myth of a Bonavista landfall from one of a number of competing historical must-have-beens to the status of a national shibboleth – literally, a concept that can be used to detect (and thereby reject) strangers. As in the case of other emotional symbols, whether clan tartans, monarchical fetishes, or icons of Cartier, the crucial element was creation of a token of membership.[96] The place of the Bonavista landfall in Newfoundland popular tradition today is no less Prowse's achievement than Cabot's monument on Signal Hill.

Memorials like Cabot Tower are not built every year (nor, it would seem, even every century). The mass production of tradition is more efficiently achieved in media more cheaply obtained than granite. The competing Newfoundland and Canadian Cabot landfall myths were written by 1897. Let us turn our attention to one of the most common ways that such historical traditions, once invented, have been reproduced and given popular distribution in the last century or so. This may cast some light on what, if anything, is new about invention of tradition in the nineteenth and twentieth centuries.

PHILATELIC COMMEMORATIVES

Nineteenth-century nationalists devised many means for the mass production of tradition, not only through the ceremonial consecration of permanent memorials, like the towers erected in Bristol and St John's, but also with song-sheets and other ephemeral bits and pieces of material culture. Commemorative medallions and ceramic pieces had been used this way for a century or more, while paintings, like Benjamin West's *Death of General Wolfe*, served a similar function in reifying national myth.[97] In this connection, Hobsbawm makes an interesting analysis of the earliest historically commemorative postage stamps, as one of his contributions to the study of the invention of tradition. Thirteen European nations issued stamps of this type in the years between 1890 and 1914, although they had not issued such stamps earlier, despite the fact that most had been issuing stamps since the 1850s and 1860s. (Great Britain had introduced the use of postage stamps, with the famous penny black in the 1840s, but it did not issue historical commemoratives in the nineteenth century.) The first European commemorative stamp was Portuguese, issued in 1894 to salute the five-hundredth anniversary of Prince Henry the Navigator.[98] Thus, Newfoundland's 1897 Cabot commemorative issue was an early and typical example of such re-inforcement of tradition by European standards: besides Portugal only Greece (in 1896) issued historical commemoratives before Newfoundland.[99] Judge Prowse himself suggested the Cabot issue, which included the *Matthew*, a view of Cape Bonavista (figure 5.5), and

5.5 Newfoundland, John Cabot and Victoria Jubilee issue postage stamp (enlarged 4×), 1897, engraved 3-cent blue, 'CAPE BONAVISTA.'

Sebastian, ambiguously labelled 'Cabot,' standing in for his father (figure 3.2).[100]

The Quebec Cartier cult, with its attendant imagery, is another, and even earlier, example of the mass production of tradition. If we take historical postage stamps seriously as indicators that mass production of tradition was under way, then it is significant that Canada's first issue of stamps, of 1851–8, included a historical commemorative: the ten-pence blue 'Jacques Cartier' of 1855, re-issued at seventeen cents in 1859.[101] Canada issued no further historical commemoratives until the 1908 Quebec tercentennial set, which included joint portraits of Cartier and Champlain. Only a few other commemoratives preceded the 1934 Jacques Cartier, which had the distinction of being the largest postage stamp yet produced in the country (figure 5.6). Canada did not recognize Cabot until 1949, when Newfoundland's entry into confederation was marked appropriately by a commemorative of the *Matthew* (figure 5.7). Curiously enough, Newfoundland's valedictory postal issue of June 1947 had consisted of a handsome view from the deck of the *Matthew* 'off Cape Bonavista' (figure 5.8).

Canada's postal salute to Cartier in 1855 does not, however,

5.6 Canada, four-hundredth anniversary of Jacques Cartier, postage stamp (enlarged 4×), 1934, engraved 3-cent blue.

have the distinction of being the world's first historical commemorative, although it comes close. The Americans began issuing postage stamps in 1847. Their first standard issue consisted of two historical commemoratives: the five-cent brown Franklin and the ten-cent black Washington. What is more, the United States did not issue a postage stamp with a non-historical subject until the two-cent post rider and the three-cent locomotive of 1869, an issue which also included the Americans' first two-colour stamp: the blue and brown 'Landing of Columbus.' A whole set of six-

" Industry and Courage "
for a Better Canada
and a
Greater Newfoundland

Commemorative Cover

5.7 Canada, Confederation with Newfoundland, postage stamp, 1949, engraved 4-cent green, 'CABOT'S "MATTHEW" NEWFOUNDLAND' / 'LE "MATTHEW" DE CABOT TERRE-NEUVE,' on an envelope commemorating the day of issue.

5.8 Newfoundland, four-hundred-and-fiftieth anniversary of Cabot's landfall, postage stamp (enlarged 4×), 1947, engraved 5-cent purple, 'CABOT IN THE "MATTHEW" OFF CAPE BONAVISTA 1497.'

teen different designs devoted to 'Columbus' Discovery of America' followed in the 1890s. If the *Santa Maria* on the three-cent green looks familiar to Newfoundland's philatelists, it should: the American Bank Note Company recycled the American 1892 ship image for Newfoundland's *Matthew* in 1897.[102] (Compare figures 5.9 and 5.10).

It is no exaggeration to say that the normal American postage stamp of the nineteenth century had a historical subject, usually an early president; in fact, by 1980 the United States had issued seventy-four stamps honouring Washington.[103] Philatelists do not call these 'commemoratives' but they are, in the sense that they celebrate an aspect of the past. The postage of South America in the nineteenth century falls somewhere between the Canadian and the American patterns. That is to say, postal imagery was not predominantly historical, but historical images were well represented from an early date. Argentina, for example, commemorated Rivadavia and General Belgrano in the 1860s; Bolivia and Venezuela, Simon Bolivar, in the 1860s and 1870s. Brazil exhibited a European pattern, much like Newfoundland's, confining postal imagery to landscapes, decorative numerals, and the bust of Dom Pedro II, until the first historical imagery appeared in 1900 to

5.9 United States, four-hundredth anniversary of Columbus' voyage, postage stamp (enlarged 4×), 1892 engraved 3-cent green, 'FLAG SHIP OF COLUMBUS.'

5.10 Newfoundland, John Cabot and Victoria Jubilee issue postage stamp (enlarged 4×), 1897, engraved 10-cent black-brown, 'CABOT'S SHIP THE "MATTHEW" LEAVING THE AVON.' Compare with figure 5.9: both were printed by the American Bank Note Company.

commemorate the four-hundredth anniversary of discovery. What might we conclude about traditions of discovery from the evidence of such ephemera? New World postal history suggests that it was mass-producing traditions before the Old World, at least in this medium. Perhaps state-sponsored invention of tradition is most urgent in newer nation states, where vernacular national tradition is weak. The relatively recent expansion of this kind of mass production of national mythologies does not, however, mean that the nineteenth century invented the invention of tradition. In fact, inventing tradition was a traditional part of what students of the past did.

6

The History of Discovery

The island ... was uninhabited except for a few giants. It was, however, most attractive because of the delightful situation of its various regions, its forests and the great number of rivers, which teemed with fish ... When they had explored the different districts, they drove the giants whom they had discovered into caves in the mountains. With the approval of their leader they divided the land among themselves. They began to cultivate the fields and to build houses, so that in a short time you would have thought that the land had always been inhabited.

Geoffrey of Monmouth, *The History of the Kings of Britain* (ca. 1136)[1]

THE LEGENDARY HISTORY OF BRITAIN

The modern mass nation state that emerged in the eighteenth century differs profoundly from earlier states. Modern nationalism, the identification of the citizen with the state, facilitates social control and replaces, in a sense, the patriarchal authority that once gave order to a society based on rank and deference. Benedict Anderson argues that modern nationalism arose first in the invented 'creole' communities of the New World and that the nationalism of the French Revolution, for example, was an echo of the more original nationalism of the American Revolution.[2] But Linda Colley traces the gradual construction of modern British nationalism from the early eighteenth century, as Britons defined themselves as Protestants at war.[3] It is even possible to find incipient nationalisms in pre-modern Europe, as Colette Beaune has done in her study of the origins of the myth of the nation in late-medieval France.⁴ Although modern nationalism may well have such roots in the distant past, this does not therefore make it safe to assume that national identities are natural, primary, or permanent. As Eric Hobsbawm puts it, nationality is a historical construct.⁵

This is not to say that nationalism sprang fully fledged from the head of Liberty in 1688 or 1776 or 1789. Nations, in Anderson's sense of self-consciously invented communities, have been defining themselves for centuries and for centuries students of the past have invented myths that have helped them to do so. There is, in fact, a tradition of invention on these matters. As the great sceptic Ernest Renan put it, in the 1880s: 'Omission and even historical error are essential factors in shaping a nation.'⁶ As a case in point, with some relevance to the mythology of the Cabot landfall, we might recall the legendary origins of the British themselves, a favourite topic of late-medieval English history and a tale which illuminates a key conclusion of this study. Nationalism has not simply been imposed upon Cabot's landfall by those who have shaped traditions about it, because the original event was itself structured by national mythology.

One of the most influential examples of national invention in the British tradition is the story of Brutus, devised originally by Geoffrey of Monmouth in his *History of the Kings of Britain*. Geoffrey's text, written around 1136, became a major authority for early English history, throughout the Middle Ages and well into early modern times.⁷ What Geoffrey devised was a foundation legend not only for British kings but for the British themselves. In brief, his story was that Britain had been founded by an Italian hero named Brutus, the great-grandson of Aeneas. In this legend Brutus is exiled first to Troy and then, with other Trojans, to a series of wanderings until he seeks the wisdom of Diana. The goddess tells him: 'Brutus, beyond the setting of the sun, past the realms of Gaul, there lies an island in the sea, once occupied by giants. Now it is empty and ready for your folk. Down the years this will prove an abode suited to you and your people; and for your descendants it will be a second Troy. A race of kings will be born there from your stock and the round circle of the whole earth will be subject to them.' To cut a very long story short, Brutus follows up this lead: 'With the approval of his men Brutus returned to his fleet. He loaded his ships with all the riches which he had acquired and went on board. So, with the winds behind him, he sought the promised island, and came ashore at Totnes.' The 'promised island' turns out to be rather attractive, so Brutus and his tribe drive the few semi-human inhabitants into the mountains and make the landscape their own, with cultivated fields and houses.[8] The British are British because they are descended from Brutus and his people.

Geoffrey invented a tradition that most subsequent chroniclers regarded unquestioningly as authentic and incorporated into their own histories as sober fact.[9] There is little doubt that Geoffrey fabricated much of this story out of whole cloth, although he acknowledges a debt to an otherwise undocumented Walter of Oxford for providing 'a certain very ancient book written in the British language' and, in a rhetorical master stroke, closes his work by warning other historians not to discuss the Kings of the Britons, seeing that they do not have in their possession the book that Walter brought from Wales.[10] He intended the legendary settlement of Britain by Brutus and his followers to provide the British with a glorious heroic past, on a par with classical peoples.[11] The tradition of The Brut, as it was called in late-medieval times, helped to subdue prevalent social animosities among Bretons, Anglo-Saxons, and Normans, because the legend drew them together into a single nation.[12] A recent study of racial myth in English history observes that 'Geoffrey's success can be measured by the gradual acceptance of his account as a great national myth supporting a developing people moving toward nationhood.'[13]

Although Geoffrey had his doubters, from the beginning, he was still taken seriously at the time of the Cabot voyages. The Brutus legend was first questioned by John of Whethamstede, about 1440, but his criticisms were widely circulated only in William Camden's Britannia, published in 1586.[14] The Plantagenets used Geoffrey's invented tradition to support their place on the throne and it continued to served as a prop to both the house of

Tudor and the house of Stuart.[15] The tradition flourished in late-fifteenth-century England. There were thirteen editions of *The Brut* in print by 1528. Although the chronicle grew to cover the years up to 1479, the landfall of Brutus invented by Geoffrey remained an important part of the text.[16] When William Caxton published *The Description of Britain* in 1480 he gave the story of the founding of a civilized community by a supposed Trojan discoverer even wider circulation, in a simpler form.[17] The tradition would even live on into the sixteenth century: Hakluyt's much-debated editorial emendation to an account of Cabot's voyage of 1497 was exposed by the survival of a parallel version in John Stow's *Chronicles of England from Brute unto this Present Yeare* (1580).

The theme of Trojan foundations was widespread in medieval Europe, in France, Germany, and Italy, as well as in Britain.[18] Curiously enough, there is an emerging synthesis among pre-historians and linguists that a wave of Indo-European-speaking farmers advanced into Europe from Anatolia, in what is now Turkey, about 8000 years ago.[19] Whether or not some distant folk tradition of these migrations underlay the invented tradition of founder heroes supposed to come from precisely this region, the Trojans became national symbols in several Western European countries because they could be remembered as civilizing heroes.[20] Each nation, ostensibly so founded, learned from the inventors of its tradition how it had received special historic virtues. Beaune's recent study of the origins of the xenophobic ideology of late-medieval France observes that national sentiment there arose from the conjunction of a given people and a given countryside, but concludes that this national ideology did not simply happen but 'was consciously constructed by successive generations.'[21] The same, surely, can be said for England, if not Britain. And it might be said that the blueprints for the conscious construction of the British tradition were drawn by Geoffrey of Monmouth.

It should be obvious at this point that it would very difficult to defend the proposition that the invention of tradition was something novel in the eighteenth or nineteenth centuries. Even the uses to which invented traditions were put then were not entirely new, as the legend of the founder hero Brutus suggests. A comparison of accounts of the landfall of Brutus and accounts of the landfall of Cabot even suggests an astonishing similarity of content in the invented traditions of circa 1497 and circa 1897. It is therefore tempting to argue that it was the mass production of tradition, that is reproduction and popular distribution, that was the most distinctive feature of l'histoire de l'événement in the later period. Yet even this limited claim must be advanced very cautiously, for legends of king and nation could reach a wide audience in late-medieval times through church decorations, cheap prints, or pamphlets and, most pervasively, through the imagery that appeared on national coinage.[22] The literate élite, of course, could simply read the book. John Cabot's enactment of his landfall suggests that either he or his patron Henry VII had done so. The British North American nationalists of the late nineteenth century imagined, anachronistically, that when the intrepid Venetian navigator first set foot on North American soil he was looking forward to the British Empire. His behaviour suggests, on the contrary, that he had at least one eye on the past.

BEFORE HISTORY

The history of discovery is a paradigm of personalization. It was not enough for Geoffrey of Monmouth to say, quite accurately, that Britain had been found and settled by humans from elsewhere; he preferred the historical fiction that Britain was found and settled by the Trojan Brutus. Modern histories of North America are written in the same mode, if on a somewhat more factual basis. Whether they celebrate or revile him, accounts of the 'discoverer' Columbus agree that he explored several Caribbean Islands, including Cuba, in 1492, but reached the coast of Venezuela only in 1498 and did not visit the North American region of Honduras and Nicaragua until 1502–4, several years after English and Portuguese expeditions reached the coasts of Newfoundland and Labrador and half a millennium after Norse Greenlanders had briefly explored the same territory.[23] Columbus is, nevertheless, so revered as the discoverer of America that when Yale University tactlessly published a map of Norse Vinland on Columbus Day, 1965, American politicians rallied against the book, questioning not the debatable merits of the map, but the very idea that some other European might have preceded the accepted founder-hero. 'To say Columbus didn't discover America is as absurd as saying DiMaggio doesn't know anything about baseball or that Toscanini and Caruso weren't great musicians,' they argued.[24]

When we think about the human past we like to think about particular people. We personalize history; we even personalize pre-history. Archaeologists are rarely more pleased with their evidence than when it permits conclusions about an individual, if anonymous, representative of the otherwise faceless cultures they usually study: a three-million-year-old ancestor becomes 'Lucy,' the alpine remains of a neolithic traveller, 'the Iceman.' Historical archaeologists attempt a self-consciously anthropological approach to their sites but, if only for funding purposes, they look for Leif's camp, Frobisher's mine, Guy's colony, Champlain's tomb, or Baltimore's Mansion House. Even if we start from the premise that classes or nations or technologies are the real actors on the stage of the past we illuminate the script with a supporting cast of human faces. General Wolfe stands for the British soldiers who fell with him, General Montcalm for *les braves*. The conventional opening for an essay in the abstractions of social history is anecdotal, exemplary, and personal: 'Young Dan Vickers had never been to sea when he climbed the gangplank of the *Fisher* one cold October morning ...'[25] We personalize the past even though we know that biography is not a substitute for history.

In this chapter we will personalize history in this sense. Remember, nevertheless, that Zuan Caboto stands for something more; his achievements are not his alone. This is not so simply in the sense that we might 'thank the little people': the court of Henry VII, the investors, Cabot's crew, his wife, and even perhaps his son. Cabot is a symbol of others in another sense, for there were other voyages of exploration to the northwest Atlantic in the 1480s and 1490s and early 1500s and some were successful. To the extent that Cabot symbolizes the European discovery of the northern half of the New World, he takes on mythic charisma, despite the lacunae and ambiguities in an obscure historical record. As one student of the Cabotian literature recently put it: 'That he was an exceptional man, there can be no doubt. Why else would so many of us write so much about one of whom we know so little?'[26] If we can manage to set aside the myths of the landfall, the precedent of discovery, and centuries of biographical debate, we are still left with questions about the past. Why and how do we write John Cabot into history?

We remember Cabot because it was he who first made Europe aware of another continent. Native North Americans preceded him to the 'New World' by millennia, of course, and the Norse by centuries. Cabot and his backers foresaw that the lands he sought would be populated, which raises the question of what they meant when they spoke of his 'discovery' and what he intended by planting an English banner, wherever he planted it. Whatever words we choose to name the arrival of Europeans in America, this was a momentous human event, for it brought previously separated societies into regular contact with one another.[27] At a minimum, it marks a cultural discovery of the other.[28] The fact that this appears to have happened at least twice in the northwest Atlantic, once around 1000 and again about 1497, raises the obvious question of whether the northern tradition of Vinland was a significant element in Cabot's conception of Atlantic geography. The explorations of Cabot, his son, and their associates had outcomes very different from the medieval voyages of Leif Ericksson and his kin, and we might well ask in what respects Europe of the year 1500 was better prepared to exploit 'rediscovery' than Europe of the year 1000. This is a useful line of thought, for it also serves to elucidate the fundamental differences between Native North American societies and the early-modern European societies that reached across the Atlantic and profoundly changed things, for all concerned. These differences suggest that there is some sense in the currently politically incorrect term 'discover,' a sense worth rescuing from the half-baked notion of 'rediscover,' with its strategic ambiguity about whether the associated mythic charisma should be glimpsed first in the east or in the west.

Little as we know about Zuan Caboto, we know even less about the people who actually first found North America. At least 15,000 years ago hunting bands spread slowly across a Bering land-bridge between Siberia and Alaska, exposed when sea levels fell after a significant part of the world's water froze in Arctic wastes during a series of ice ages. By 11,000 years ago the Palaeo-Indian descendants of these immigrants were hunting caribou and sea mammals in what is now Nova Scotia.[29] The Native coastal people of the Canadian maritime provinces, now called Mi'kmaq, may be their distant progeny.[30] Modern tribal groups in the northeast as a whole may be best understood as realignments, following the epidemics and wars of the early seventeenth century.[31] The people that the English called 'Micmac' in the eighteenth century were known during the seventeenth-century French regime as 'Souriquois,' the name given them by sixteenth-century Basque fishermen.[32]

Whatever name they took, the people who became the Mi'kmaq share with the Innu and Inuit of Labrador a role that distinguishes them from many other Native peoples, for several reasons. They were among the first North American peoples to have regular contact with Europeans; for several centuries, they were not conquered but coexisted with the European newcomers; and they remain, to this day, largely within their ancestral home-lands.[33] The Mi'kmaq are an Algonkian people, speaking a language more closely related to those of the coastal woodlands to their south than to the northern Algonkian languages spoken by the historic Montagnais-Naskapi (now Innu) and Beothuk peoples who lived north of the St Lawrence. The question of the ultimate origins of these peoples is debatable, but an archaeological consensus exists that the adaptations recorded in the sixteenth century had developed *in situ* well before European contact. The lack of clarity about earlier ethnic relationships is not peculiar to Mi'kmaq prehistory: as a result of methodological difficulties, continuity of historically documented Native peoples has rarely been definitively established further back than about a millennium.[34]

As the North American climate warmed slowly at the close of

the Wisconsinan ice age, ten thousand years ago, some early maritime hunting bands followed the retreating glacier north. Europeans were doing the same thing and were then in the process of resettling what would become the British Isles, as sea levels continued to rise. Maritime Archaic Amerindians were exploiting the coastal resources of southern Labrador 9000 years ago and about 6000 years ago they reached northern Labrador.[35] This intricate maritime culture flourished on the northern and western coasts of the Island of Newfoundland as well. It must have been a very great surprise for the most northerly Maritime Archaic bands in Labrador when, about 4000 years ago, another people intruded into their hunting grounds – from the north. These Early Palaeo-Eskimo people had spread in a few centuries from Alaska across the Arctic.[36] Within another few hundred years they had displaced the Maritime Archaic bands of northern Labrador, a process that would be repeated with the later arrival of Groswater and Dorset Palaeo-Eskimo peoples, who spread southwards and reached the Island of Newfoundland about 3000 years ago. The Dorset were replaced, in their turn, by Thule Eskimos, the immediate ancestors of the present Inuit people of northern Canada, who reached northern Labrador by 1400 (our era) and were probably making seasonal forays as far south as the Strait of Belle Isle by 1500. Neither the Dorset nor their successors the Thule completely displaced Amerindian cultures from coastal Labrador or insular Newfoundland. The archaeologically defined Amerindian Point Revenge people of Labrador may be descendants of the Maritime Archaic and may also be closely related to the historic Montagnais-Naskapi, that is, the present-day Innu.[37] A similar ancestry probably holds for the pre-contact Little Passage people of Newfoundland, who are likely antecedents of the historic, but now extinct, Beothuk people of the Island. These Amerindian peoples of Newfoundland and Labrador were closely related. Cultural distance between the historic Beothuk and the Montagnais of the Quebec North Shore may well be a result of the intrusion of Inuit and Europeans in early-modern times into the crucial communication link of the Strait of Belle Isle.[38]

When Leif Ericksson and his kin reached Markland and Vinland around 1000 CE they found these lands occupied by people described in the Norse sagas with the pejorative term 'skraeling.' If the Norse encountered Native people in Newfoundland south of the exploration base camp that they built at L'Anse aux Meadows, in northern Newfoundland, these were probably the ancestors of the Beothuks who inhabited the Island when Cabot explored the coasts of Newfoundland in 1497. In southern Labrador they might have encountered the ancestors of the Montagnais of later times. Like the Mi'kmaq, both Montagnais and Beothuk were predominantly coastal peoples who used the resources of the interior as part of their annual round, but who would normally have frequented salt water each summer, exactly when Europeans could reach their territories.[39] The recovery of butternuts, which do not grow north of the St Lawrence, from archaeological excavations at L'Anse aux Meadows suggests that the Norse exploration of Vinland took them at least as far south as the north shore of New Brunswick, in which case the term 'skraelings' was likely also applied to the ancestors of the Mi'kmaq.[40] The Native peoples with whom the Norse traded and squabbled in the Arctic were Thule Eskimos; in coastal Labrador they might have crossed paths with vestigial groups of Dorset Palaeo-Eskimos.

The Norse encounter with these New World cultures was a significant moment in world history, for it marked the closure of human settlement in the northern hemisphere. It had taken something over 100,000 years for physically modern human beings to spread from Africa around the world. Whatever their routes, several human societies would now have to come to terms with what has been called 'the catastrophic process of bringing one-half of the planet to the attention of the other half.'[41] The Norse withdrew from any effort to colonize North America, at least in part because of conflict with 'skraelings.'[42] With some intermittent lapses, Norse livestock farmers and Thule hunters managed to share Greenland's limited resources for several centuries, so that the issues raised by the closure of human settlement did not arise in a serious way in the North Atlantic until the late-fifteenth-century voyages of exploration, epitomized by Cabot's 1497 expedition. We are left to ask how late-medieval Europeans, like

Cabot, understood 'discovery,' when the lands they discovered for themselves were already occupied by other peoples.

'DISCOVERY'

Discovery is as much a political act as it is geographical. In fifteenth-century English, 'to discover' was to disclose, to divulge, to make something manifest (or, intransitively, simply to reconnoitre). It was only in the 1550s that 'to discover' took on the modern sense of finding something new, of obtaining for the first time sight or knowledge of the previously unknown.[43] The same was true of cognates like the Portuguese *descobrir*.[44] Attention to what it was 'to discover' in 1500 has often been diverted to discussion of Edmundo O'Gorman's argument that something like a continent cannot be discovered until it has been conceptualized, so that Columbus never discovered America, precisely because he always believed he had reached Asia.[45] This is an interesting point philosophically, which makes it clear that there may be more to discovery than being able to pilot a ship, but it takes for granted a modern sense of what it is to discover something. From the point of view of their contemporaries, Cabot or Columbus discovered lands, because they drew attention to them, whether or not they understood precisely what they were, or whether the worlds they found were new.

The noun 'discovery' was, evidently, a cognate of the modern sense of the verb 'discover,' for it also first appears in the mid-sixteenth century, with an ambiguous sense connoting both the late-medieval making known and the modern finding out of the previously unknown. 'Discovery' in its early sense was like the American legal term, which refers to the public process in which evidence is revealed rather than to the private process by which it was originally obtained.[46] John Cabot's voyage was itself a public exhibition of national claims, in which he 'discovered' new lands to the world, in the original sense of 'discover.' The contemporary observers Raimondo de Soncino, Lorenzo Pasqualigo, and John Day emphasize that 'the discoverer' of the newly reported lands planted a large cross, flew the banner of the Pope, hoisted the royal standard, and so took possession for the king.[47] Day, at least, was aware that other English expeditions had preceded 'the discoverer' to this newly reported territory. All were aware that there were already human inhabitants in the territories found, in fact the whole point of Cabot's expeditions was to find another society to trade with, the known people of Japan (even if they were barely known). Henry VII funded Cabot and required him, by letters patent, 'to set up our ... banners and ensigns in any town, city, castle, island or mainland whatsoever, newly found,' and Henry was surely not expecting his Venetian captain to look for uninhabited towns and cities. Cabot was expected to *discover*, that is make known, these territories; there was no assumption that he would be the first human being to glimpse them.

Planting a cross with national and religious banners is a symbolic act, a deed that is meant to say something. The formulaic language of Henry's patent makes it clear that this was intended as a ritual enactment of possession. It gave John and his sons or their heirs and deputies great powers to 'conquer, occupy and possess whatsoever such towns, castles, cities and islands by them thus *discovered* that they may be able to conquer, occupy and possess, as our vassals and governors lieutenants and deputies therein, acquiring for us the dominion, title and jurisdiction of the same towns, castles, islands and mainlands so *discovered*.'[48] The patent closely resembles the *cartas de doacano* granted by the kings of Portugal to navigators looking to become captains-general of new possessions and it may well be that Cabot's letters patent mimic a Portuguese model.[49] The patent itself was a public statement, in fact that is what 'letters patent' are: open letters as opposed to private 'letters close.'[50] Cabot's raising of the banners of England, Venice, and the Holy See was also a public statement.

It has been argued that these were typically Mediterranean ceremonials, in which the English did not engage.[51] In her analysis of *Ceremonies of Possession*, Patricia Seed maintains that the various European powers favoured distinct rituals of appropriation: the Portuguese celestial observation of geographic position; the Spanish a public reading to Native people of the *Requirimiento*, a text demanding Christian conversion; the French by ceremonial erection of a cross or other marker; the English by the laying-out of fences and the planting of gardens and hedges; the Dutch, in an extension of Portuguese practice, by the drafting of maps and plans.[52] This is a peculiar history, tending to dissolve time and to resemble, a little too much, the story of clan tartans. It over-emphasizes the differences among European colonial powers by ignoring cases, like that of Cabot, that might disconfirm the analysis and by paying scant attention to the inevitable shifts in European ideas about discovery and possession, which came as the realities of interaction with the New World sank in. Leaving the attribution of specific national preferences moot, the analysis is, on the other hand, a useful typology of the ways European powers legitimized appropriation of North and South America at various times in the contact period. It may be true that English colonists of the early seventeenth century based their imperial claims on enclosure; it may even be true that the French often enacted public rituals of possession; there is nevertheless little doubt of either the formality of Cabot's ceremony of 1497 or of the King of England's intention that this ceremony would symbolize some kind of possession.

The character of this putative possession is less clear. It is not necessarily the case that every time an early European visitor to North America raised a flag or cross that he was making a claim of sovereignty. Cartier, for example, may have been interested, at least in part, in creating navigational landmarks when he raised banners and crosses in the Gulf of St Lawrence.[53] Yet these acts were often understood as symbolic acts of possession or, at least, as acts of symbolic possession.[54] John Cabot was, no doubt, happy to report that he had taken possession of the new found land for King Henry and Christendom, but he was certainly even happier that he had not been forced to seal such claims by conquest. 'Since he was with just a few people, he did not dare advance inland beyond the shooting distance of a cross-bow, and after taking in fresh water he returned to his ship,' as the Day Letter reports. Cabot did not know that he was in the territory of small hunter-gatherer bands, few of which would have been able to field the eighteen men of fighting age that Cabot could. From his perspective, the next valley might harbour the army of the Great Khan. In any event, he did not require territory, for his aims were not to found a colony. This was a kind of project that the English worked out conceptually only slowly over the course of the ensuing century.[55] (This in turn implies that English ceremonies of possession were likely to evolve over this period.) What Cabot was interested in was a trading station or *comptoir*, of a type with which he would have been very familiar. Both Venice and Genoa had established by treaty a network of these extraterritorial urban complexes in their Mediterranean trading zones. These represented 'national' interests of an ancient type; they were not colonies in any of the modern senses, either for the settlement of emigrants or for the plantation of staple crops.[56]

Cabot's flag ceremony was, nevertheless, an assertion of national interests. The nineteenth-century British North American nationalists like Samuel Dawson, Moses Harvey, and Daniel Prowse cannot fairly be accused of importing nationalism into their interpretations of a ceremony that celebrated the deliberate and public display of the 'banner of England.' (The Venetian banner of St Mark, noted by Pasqualigo, was probably an assertion of the Cabots' commercial interests, granted by the letters patent.) This event was meant to be recalled and so it was, by every contemporary commentator. It was a staged enactment, meant to say something to an audience. The audience addressed was not the shy people in feathers lurking in the trees; the real audience was Europe. The message was simple: this is our commercial sphere and we dare you to say otherwise. In 1496, the letters patent assumed the lands sought were populated and King Henry gave John Cabot the right to conquer them, though not the men or ships that would actually be needed to do this. In any event, Cabot 'took possession for the king' without a struggle, through a ceremony performed in the discrete absence of Native peoples. Most significantly, for his contemporaries, Cabot publicized his new found land and it was 'discovery,' in this original sense, that gave England a claim precedence in further commercial exploitation of the region. Later, with the passage of time, in the pages of John Dee and Edmund Burke and their successors in 1897, this original sense of discovery-as-disclosure was forgotten and the new modern sense of discovery-as-first-sight became a precedent for British rights of possession. It was only as Britain gradually appropriated eastern North America that actual possession raised overtly the hitherto implicit issue of conquest.

In the end, John Cabot failed to discover either Cipango or Cathay, but he did discover a new industry in the cod fishery. The contemporary great European powers of France, Portugal, and Spain simply ignored Cabot's possessive dare. Portuguese, Breton, and Norman mariners as well the Basques of Guipúzcoa and Gascony rapidly developed a major migratory shore-based transatlantic dry fishery and it was over half a century before English fishermen from Westcountry ports like Dartmouth and Plymouth caught up. Although Bristol merchants did finance a few voyages to this new fishery in the early years of the sixteenth century, the English fell back on the familiar Iceland fishery, which they had dominated since the 1420s and where they turned good profits well into the sixteenth century.[57] Around 1565 the Westcountrymen began to return to Newfoundland in considerable numbers. England managed to displace the Iberians from the Newfoundland shore fishery, but this required a long privateering war between 1580 and 1620.[58] This was the real beginning of English settlement in the New World. Enclosure, conquest, and its natural ally, disease, would be the actual instruments of appropriation, not discovery.

ATLANTIC ASYMMETRY

The arrival of Europeans in North America was a momentous event because it brought a variety of separated and heterogeneous societies into contact. On the European side these were state societies, in some cases with a rapidly evolving bureaucracy and merchant class; in some cases not greatly evolved from the chiefdoms out of which they had emerged; in all cases economically based on peasant agriculture, trade, and the technology of wood and iron. North Americans of the northeastern coasts, on the other hand, lived in smaller, intimate, band societies, based economically on hunting and gathering and, technologically, primarily on wood and stone. These European and American peoples were now drawn into the North Atlantic turbine in a fearful asymmetry. Who were they?

Spain, Portugal, and France were rich and powerful states, centrally ruled by strong monarchs, although economically still dominated by the Mediterranean city-states of Venice and, to a lesser degree, Genoa.[59] (Figure 6.1 presents an image of Venice in this period.) England was a smaller, peripheral power, with a gradually expanding economy based on the export of wool. Henry Tudor, who had seized the throne in 1485, would have liked to govern in the centralizing French fashion but could not, since he was politically dependent on regional magnates.[60] Scotland remained a separate and hostile northern kingdom allied with France; Ireland beyond the Anglo-Norman 'Pale,' a kind of abandoned wild tribal frontier.[61] Norway was now a peripheral dependency of the increasingly powerful Hanse trading ports of the Baltic Sea. Since 1397 and the union of the Scandinavian crowns, Greenland and Iceland were dependencies of Denmark, but Greenland was almost forgotten and Iceland was now allied through Denmark with the Hanse. The Hanse towns displaced Bristol and Hull from the Icelandic supply trade in the 1480s, although the English were able to hang on to their fishery in southwest Iceland and even to expand it in the sixteenth century.[62] Many European societies were already large and complex; by 1500 England had a population of about two million.[63] Europe had the immense advantage of strong internal economic linkages as well as linkages outwards, throughout the Old World, through Portugal and the Islamic empires of the Near East, to Africa and Asia.[64]

The Native societies of the American northeast had relationships one with another, but they were not integrated as Europe was, economically and technologically. The Inuit bands of Greenland and northern Labrador were, in several curious senses, pre-adapted to contact. They had experience in dealings with Europeans and had already begun to make and use iron tools.[65] The Montagnais and Beothuk people of southern Labrador and

6.1 Erhard Reuwich, *City of Venice*, 1486.

Newfoundland were relatively isolated and would have had only infrequent contact with technologically advanced strangers. Their experience would have been limited to the Inuit to their north, the warlike Iroquoian tribes of the St Lawrence River, and, possibly, the Mi'kmaq. The latter were certainly the most complex and the largest of the coastal societies of the Canadian littoral. The Beothuk probably numbered 500 to 1000 at contact, the Mi'kmaq perhaps 6000 to 12,000.[66] Let us look briefly at the Mi'kmaq in order to understand what a Native North American society was. In many respects they can stand for the Beothuk and Montagnais as well, recalling that these were smaller and somewhat less complex societies, even if technologically capable of piecing together a livelihood in a harsh subarctic environment.[67]

Much is remembered of traditional Mi'kmaq political and social organization and much is in dispute, if only because we have only the reports of later observers. Scholars agree that nuclear families allied themselves into extended patrilocal and sometimes polygamous local groups, numbering roughly thirty persons, but, beyond this, disagree about the complexity of Mi'kmaq sociopolitical organization. Some have seen a loose aggregation of egalitarian bands, others a complex 'tribe' on the threshold of becoming a chiefdom.[68] There is little evidence of specialization in Mi'kmaq society; leadership was charismatic rather than the function of an office; they lacked the clans and secret societies that form the horizontal structure of segmentary societies, while residential units remained like one another, largely self-sufficient and autonomous.[69] These are characteristics of band societies rather than chiefdoms. Like other northern Algonkian peoples, they had no traditional concept of personal, family, or band property beyond that which could be carried when the owners in question moved in search of food or a fresh campsite, which they frequently did.[70] On the other hand, in the contact period, the Mi'kmaq used to meet in summer, on the coast, in aggregations of one or two hundred under the sponsorship of a chief or *sagamore*.[71] Traditional band districts appear to reflect such geopolitical practice of long standing, as does the precedence acknowledged the central Cape Breton district and its leader. If this incipient politics gave the Mi'kmaq certain characteristics of more complex societies, they nevertheless retained many characteristics of the band societies to their north.

Cultural tradition served to reinforce Native social structure. The Mi'kmaq, for example, believed that men are equal or should be. Those who spoke with conviction and behaved respectably without arrogance had political authority. Leadership implied a responsibility to redistribute goods to a community of dependents; the prestigious person maintained a large household and shared his wealth through community feasts and personal gifts. Alliances with helpful empowering persons were a major way of acquiring power; marriage a potentially dangerous alliance with relative strangers. Duty to one's kin had great importance. Given a cultural acceptance of ferocity, this implied that revenge was a normal means of restoring the social balance when it was perceived to have been disrupted. In the spiritual realm, the Mi'kmaq believed life or power to be immanent in everything, in various forms understood to be mutable, one into another. They saw the forest as a realm of chaos full of unpredictable changeable beings – which has the interesting implication that Mi'kmaq were traditionally more 'at home' on the coast or at sea. Finally, they remembered their ancestors as great hunters who were (or continued to be in another realm) strong, dignified, healthy, just, brave, and generous role models.[72]

This is, in the last analysis, a complex and resiliant ideology. The societies served by such ideologies were small, but no smaller than the part-societies that Europe sent to North America in the sixteenth century as ships' crews. The asymmetry in the relationship between Europe and America reflected neither ideological weakness nor social incompetence on the part of Native peoples. Europe began to digest the rest of the world, in Fernand Braudel's incisive phrase, because it was technically able and economically inclined to do so.[73] Both the necessary techniques and the economic culture that brought these techniques to bear were new, and these novelties mark the difference between the brief surveys of the medieval Norse and the continuous European exploration of North America after 1497. These techniques included the efficient construction of weatherly ships that could not merely cross the Atlantic to America but could return on a timely and predictable basis as well.[74] Beyond new means of transport and communication, Europe had developed an economic culture that permitted, encouraged, or even required these maritime instruments of appropriation.

It was European technology that most impressed Native peoples. Firearms and other steel weapons and tools made such an impression that in many Native languages the word for the newcomers was 'iron-workers' or 'knife-men' or the like.[75] Native North Americans were also astonished by European ships, which were so much bigger than their own canoes that they saw them at first as floating islands. A nineteenth-century Mi'kmaq elder recalled a legend of these early encounters: 'What should they see but a singular little island, as they supposed, which had drifted near to the land and become stationary there. There were trees on it, and branches to the trees, on which a number of bears ... were crawling about ... What was their surprise to find these supposed bears were men.'[76] It did not take Native peoples very long to figure out what a ship actually was, as Mi'kmaq rock art suggests (figure 6.2). The Montagnais marvelled at these floating islands and called the French *ouemichtigouchiou*: 'men in a wooden boat.'[77]

Native North Americans were right to be impressed with European vessels; the early modern ship was a sophisticated sailing machine. By 1450, the English were using three-masted square-rigged ships with a lateen mizen, that is, a fore-and-aft 'Latin' or southern-style sail on the aft mast. (Reconsider the conjectural plan of Cabot's *Matthew*, figure 2.1.) These were considerably more weatherly than the single-masted medieval cogs or their predecessors, the Norse knarrs: they could tack closer to an inconvenient headwind. Knarrs and early cogs were still guided only by a steering oar, lashed to the 'steer-board' side; the new European ships had the advantage of axial stern-post rudders, which had spread northwards, like the new rig, from the Mediterranean. The three masts of the new ships, which became the standard for centuries, made it possible to drive much larger vessels. English ships roughly doubled in carrying capacity between 1400 and

6.2 Mi'kmaq petroglyph of a European ship, Kejimkujik National Park, Nova Scotia.

1450. Ships of only 30 to 50 tons made early transatlantic voyages, but Bristol was already sending ships of 100 and even 300 tons burthen to Iceland in the fifteenth century.[78]

The early-modern voyage was organized on a three-in-one basis. This formula is meant to emphasize that those involved were committed financially or otherwise only for a single voyage and that there were, in legal terms, three groups of participants in each of these adventures: the owners of the ship, the crew, and the merchants who hired or 'freighted' the ship – in the case of fishing voyages supplying provisions rather than an outward cargo, although of course they expected to see an inward cargo of fish. The legal instrument that brought owners and freighters together for the purposes of a voyage was the charter party, a signed and notarized document specifying the terms and conditions for the lease of the vessel by the owners to the freighters. A vessel of even fifty tons represented a considerable commercial investment at the dawn of the sixteenth century. It is, in fact, difficult to think of larger investments in this period, except perhaps in mining. Property in ships had been organized, since medieval times at least, in shares. In a period before insurance was widespread, this form of ownership constituted a simple hedge against loss, for the part-owner of several ships was much less likely to suffer a total loss than the outright owner of a single vessel. The economic institutions of the voyage, the share, and the legal instrument of the charter party were invisible, of course, to Native Americans, no less than the techniques of navigation used to pilot these ships. European economic innovations have often remained just as invisible in histories of discovery, obscured by the flamboyant bulk of the vessels themselves.[79]

The weatherly three-masted ship, able to sail well into the wind, made economic expansion to the New World possible, but no ship made such a voyage without a pilot skilled in dead reckoning, if not astronomical position finding as well, and no pilot was capable of such navigation without a set of sophisticated instruments and aids. Medieval development of the pivoting compass, portolan charts, and navigation tables had improved techniques of dead reckoning; that is, they made it easier to estimate a course made good. The century between 1450 and 1550 saw the introduction of celestial navigation, a decisive and important transition in European navigational technique, sponsored initially by the Portuguese crown. Most working pilots did not adopt these new techniques until after 1500. In 1492 Columbus, for example, had relied almost entirely on dead reckoning. The Day Letter suggests that Cabot, who had significant Portuguese experience, used astronomical navigation. Pilots trained in the new Iberian techniques, like Sebastian Cabot, played an important role in the spread of astronomical position finding to northern Europe, a process that went on until about 1570.[80]

The astronomical navigational of the late fifteenth century provided a new means of verifying the position or at least the latitude estimated by traditional techniques of dead reckoning. By 1500 or so, navigators had a choice of three astronomical instruments for measuring the altitude of a celestial body and hence determining latitude: the quadrant, the astrolabe, and the cross-staff. The quadrant, a late-medieval astronomers' instrument, went to sea sometime before 1460.[81] It consisted of a thin quarter-circle of metal, with a radius of about 20 centimetres. The observer aligned a pair of sights on the curved edge with a heavenly body, while an assistant took the altitude with a weighted line hung from the centre of the quadrant, read against a scale of degrees marked on its face. This is the only instrument for celestial navigation mentioned in any of the early accounts of the Cabot voyages: Peter Martyr reported that Sebastian sailed 'between the west and the north ... so far that with the quadrant he observed the pole star to be elevated 55 degrees.'[82] Martyr may have been taking the use of this particular instrument for granted; both Sebastian and his father in fact had a choice of instruments. The mariner's astrolabe had already followed the quadrant to sea, in the late fifteenth century. Astrolabes were preferred for observations when the observed body was very high in the sky and were thus favoured by the Portuguese for use in the South Atlantic, where Polaris disappeared over the northern horizon and noon sun sights became essential for estimation of latitude (figure 6.3). One of the chief defects of both quadrant and astrolabe was the need for two observers.

6.3 Observation of solar altitude using an astrolabe.

Furthermore, large astrolabes caught the wind, while small ones could not be read accurately. Even a small astrolabe was a massive bronze object and therefore expensive.

The cross-staff was the simplest and therefore most economical of the early-modern navigational instruments used for determining latitude. Cross-staffs were just beginning to be used by North Atlantic pilots at the end of the fifteenth century.[83] This was a lighter and cheaper wooden device, often purpose-built by or for pilots themselves, most useful in middle latitudes. The cross-staff was constructed of a squared stick, along which the navigator slid a crosspiece, adjusting it so that it just bridged the apparent dis-

6.4 Observation of the altitude of the North Star using a cross-staff.

tance between celestial object and horizon (figure 6.4). Pilots thus 'shot' stars as if they were using a crossbow or *balestela*, which became the Iberian term for the instrument. The altitude was then read off a scale inscribed on the central staff. The cross-staff could be adjusted and read by one observer. Daytime observations were difficult because they required looking almost directly at the sun, but the cross-staff must have been very useful for shooting Polaris in the latitudes of Nova Scotia and Newfoundland.

All of the techniques and many of the instruments of early-modern pilots remained essential to deep-sea navigation well into our own century. The eighteenth-century development of an accurate marine chronometer added significantly to this tradition, by making determination of longitude possible, but it was only in our own times, with the development of depth-sounders, loran C, radar, and electronic geographic positioning systems that navigation changed fundamentally from the techniques worked out during the lifetimes of John and Sebastian Cabot. The origins of this technical tradition reach back to late-medieval times, just as its later developments stretch forwards to our own day. It was one of a number of traditions within which we can locate the events of 1497.

OLD WORLD TRADITIONS

The key technologies of early-modern maritime expansion incorporated inventions from all over the Old World, distilled and transformed in the alembic of Europe. Chinese mariners had invented the axial stern-post rudder and the nautical compass.[84] The lateen rig was not a Mediterranean novelty but an imitation of the rig used by mariners in the Red Sea and farther east. The cross-staff was a modification of the Arabian pilot's *kamal*, which the Portuguese encountered when Bartholomew Diaz reached the Indian Ocean in 1488.[85] The astronomical knowledge so valued by late-fifteenth-century Iberian courts was founded on the scientific groundwork of the medieval astronomers of the Islamic world. The dissemination of geographic and economic information together with the kind of verifiable cheap data storage so necessary for useful navigational tables depended on the printing press, itself the development of another Chinese invention. It is entirely appropriate that the book that seems to have most influenced John Cabot was Marco Polo's account of his travels to

Cathay. It may have been Western Europeans who arrived on the coasts of North America circa 1497, but the technical and intellectual traditions that brought them there were not theirs alone. The Old World was a big place.

Navigators working within oral or even manuscript traditions may have wide geographical concepts, but these concepts are less subject to verification and correction than the geographical ideas of navigators working within a print tradition.[86] The Mi'kmaq in a Basque *chaloupa*, whom Bartholomew Gosnold encountered off the coast of Maine in 1602, may have been able to sketch a map of southern Newfoundland, showing the location of Placentia, but if they drowned on their voyage it is not very certain that their sons would inherit this information.[87] Translucent chert from Ramah Bay in northern Labrador has a wide distribution in pre-contact sites along the eastern littoral of North America as far south as Long Island. From such archaeological finds we know that Native peoples had extensive trading networks, but geographical knowledge was not likely passed on from hand to hand with the treasured artifacts, any more than we learn of China by drinking tea. This is not to deny that geography can be remembered, at least roughly, in an oral tradition. The point is that for others such knowledge remains local and uncertainly close to the realm of myth, as in the Icelandic sagas of Vinland.

This northern tradition of lands to the west of Greenland is another context for Cabot's voyages. Whether or not we will ever be able to determine if Yale's celebrated Vinland Map, with its Vinilanda Insula, is a fake, it represents a genuine medieval tradition of Norse geography. There are other, post-medieval, maps that depict this northern tradition of Helluland, Markland, and a Promentorium Winlandiae resembling Newfoundland's Great Northern Peninsula, where archaeologists uncovered a large camp of Norse turf houses, occupied about the year 1000. Sigurdir Stefansson's *Terrarum Hyperboream*, printed circa 1590, is a good example (figure 6.5).[88] This map has little to do with the cartographic traditions of southern Europe, but seems to be based on accounts of the early Greenland voyages to the west, passed on for centuries in an unwritten bardic tradition and eventually

6.5 Sigurdir Stefansson, *Terrarum Hyperboream*, 1590.

written down in the fourteenth century.[89] The Norse did not forget North America; moreover, archaeological and documentary evidence suggests that medieval Greenlanders continued to use the resources of Labrador and the Canadian Arctic.[90] Most of medieval Europe had nothing to do with North America and no part of Europe had anything to do with most of North America, but this does not mean that Europe had nothing to do with North America. This is true whether we think of Greenland as part of Europe or as part of North America. It lies, of course, between and in this situation it functioned as an intermittent link between Old World and New. Leif's expedition predates Cabot's voyage of 1497 by five centuries, centuries just as long as the five that have now elapsed since Cabot's time, but the Vinland exploration was no more forgotten in the north than we have forgotten Cabot.

This raises the obvious question of whether northern traditions of Vinland were part of John Cabot's geographical conceptions, of his choice of itinerary, and, indeed, of his decision to pursue his projects out of the port of Bristol. This has not been a popular line of thought with American historians, but to deny this we have to treat some very striking coincidences as sheer happenstance.[91] When Cabot and his family moved to Bristol they were coming to one of the English ports that had been most heavily involved in the fifteenth-century Icelandic supply trade.[92] Bristol mariners had ample opportunity to hear of routes to the west, if they had not already heard these stories from the dozens of Icelanders resident in their city in the late fifteenth century.[93] Furthermore, Bristol is the English port most likely to have been involved with illegal (and therefore poorly documented) fifteenth-century trade with the Greenland settlements, which faced Arctic Canada and Labrador across the Davis Strait.[94] These late Greenland voyages were probably the commercial and navigational context for the exploratory expeditions mounted in Bristol in the 1480s and 1490s.[95] It seems very unlikely that John Cabot was in Bristol by accident, any more than it was just coincidence that his voyage should have taken him to the tip of the Great Northern Peninsula, within a few leagues of the Norse camp at L'Anse aux Meadows; or that it would be just coincidence if, on his outward journey, he followed the traditional Norse course for Greenland along a latitude of about 60 degrees north, as suggested by the steady easterly winds attested in the Day Letter.

From the scraps of information that we have about the pre-Cabotian voyages of the 1480s and 1490s, it looks as if Bristol mariners trading or fishing off Greenland knew roughly where their 'Island of Brazil' was, but were not very good at getting back to it. Hence, they employed a series of southern pilots, adept at the new astronomical navigation, who were better at keeping track of their position at sea: Zuan Caboto, João Fernandes, Fransisco Fernandes, João Gonsalves, and, eventually, Zuan's son Sebastian. Cabot's voyage differed from previous intermittent visits to North America, including those of the medieval Norse, in part because it was a reasonable commercial bet that he would get there and back in a single season (although his backers were not so lucky with his third voyage in 1498). Like later deep-sea sailors, the Norse had also used the technique of latitude sailing; but the only instruments they had for the necessary celestial observations were small and cannot have been very accurate. These were hand-held bearing dials, rather like a compass with a gnomon in the centre to cast a shadow.[96] From about 1350 the Norse had compasses, but they would have had the same difficult problems of allowing for magnetic variation that confounded the Cabots, father and son.[97] By the 1480s, Bristol had better ships but perhaps not much better navigational instruments or skills. Admitting that southern European pilots had skills and instruments not yet developed in late-medieval Bristol would explain a lot: not only the hire of Italians and Azoreans but also Bristol's inability to compete in the new transatlantic fishery, which was first exploited by precisely those 'nations' already most skilled in the new navigation, the Bretons and the Portuguese.

Most claims for pre-Columbian contact between Old World and New are suspect because they propose costly and risky voyages of exploration with no plausible socio-economic justification.[98] The great Belgian economic historian Henri Pirenne made a telling joke, when he observed that medieval Europe found North America but immediately lost it again, because there was no use for it.[99] In this sense, a motive for 'discovery' is necessary. We might also add that means and opportunity are needed as well. John Cabot's voyage of 1497 represents the first known intersection of the southern European navigational tradition and the northern geographical tradition. Seen in this way it was a significant step but, nonetheless, only part of a gradual accumulation of technique and geographical knowledge that eventually made the European appropriation of North America possible.

Although it makes good myth, it is arbitrary history to pick out one landfall as a turning point in the complicated history of human interaction. Yet the commemoration of landfalls has a function, of course; it diverts the problematic issue of European appropriation of the New World towards questions of precedent and discovery rather than towards recollection of enclosure and eventual, almost crab-wise, conquest. When Anglo- or Franco-Canadians think about conquest, they think of the victories and defeats of the Seven Years' War, of Louisbourg and Québec and Signal Hill, or even of the treaty of 1763. We recall the triumph of one well-equipped and hard-headed European power over another. If we think about the beginnings of the European appropriation of North America we prefer to quibble about 'discovery.' Like our American cousins, when they celebrated their Columbian 'Man of the Year' in 1992, we turn squeamishly from the most difficult historical issue raised by late-medieval landfalls, which is how Europeans managed to parlay these contacts into possession of a continent.[100]

7

A Memory Perpetual

Oh what a thing it had been then
If that they that be Englishmen
Might have been the first of all
That there should have taken possession
And made first building and habitation
A memory perpetual!

John Rastell, *The Four Elements*, ca. 1525[1]

In the early sixteenth century, Europeans were surprisingly unin-terested in the New World. When they did think about it, they usually thought of the southern continent of Amerigo Vespucci and only rarely of the continent on the other side of the North Atlantic, newly descried.[2] John Rastell was one of the few Englishmen of Cabot's time for whom this was more than a nine days' wonder; indeed he was the first to use the term 'North America.' In his short and merry theatrical interlude, he bemoaned the Spanish precedent set in lower latitudes by Chris-topher Columbus. Although intrigued by news of the new found land to the north, Rastell never saw it himself. He planned a transatlantic adventure, hoping to head onwards from the Breton fishery with a band of armed men, in order to open a trade with

Asia.[3] He would certainly have met resistance by Native people if he had tried to do this, but he could not convince his crew to go farther west than Ireland and so was spared the inconvenience of negotiation and conflict faced by Jacques Cartier a few years later, when he actually attempted what Rastell had planned. To the late-twentieth-century eye, Rastell's verse reads like a prescription for the 'memory perpetual' that Victorian nationalists would make of the landfall of Cabot, although the Tudor poet certainly could not have intended it as such. (More likely, he was expressing regret that Henry VII had not accepted Bartholomew Columbus's offer of his brother's services.) Rastell's verse remains an early example of what we have examined in this book: the sentimental fetish of discovery.

Relationships among various European and Native peoples in northern North America evolved over centuries, as the balance of power and the weight of numbers shifted. As these political realities changed, so changed the ideologies of discovery and conquest. These shifts have affected and continue to affect the use to which the memory of Cabot is put. In this chapter we will consider how the concepts of 'discovery' and 'conquest' have been used as precedents for possession. In order to put these traditions in perspective, we will recall three moments in our national past that reflect the shifting relationship between European and Native peoples in Atlantic Canada. Some closing thoughts on the many landfalls of John Cabot will permit us to conclude that myths of discovery, like other national traditions, have as much to do with forgetting as they do with remembering; indeed, that we often remember in order to forget.[4]

Native peoples tend to remember the European appropriation of the New World more vividly than the heirs, descendants, and assignees of the appropriators do. Within the last few years, elders of the long-isolated Kogi people of the Columbian Andes had a chance to meet Her Royal Highness, the Queen of Spain, when she expressed a desire to see their part of the world. A television production team set up the meeting and the Kogi priests or 'mummers' were particularly pleased to meet her, because the Queen of Spain was one of the few Europeans of whom they had heard. On being presented, one of the Kogi began to ritually lash Her Highness with his ceremonial staff. 'Are you sorry yet?' he cried in his own tongue. 'Have you come to apologize?'[5] This strategy would probably not work in Canada, but the tale of the Kogi elder strikes a nerve, so to speak. Canadians of European extraction have built a society that in many respects excludes Canada's first peoples, making them strangers in their own land.[6] Since this is a situation that many Native people find unendurable, it is probably more than a pious hope to predict that Canadians, of all origins, will sooner or later have to deal with this issue. It is probably also safe to say that in order to face the quintessentially political issue of reconciling competing historical claims to territory, our public memory of the national past will change or, at least, expand. The Kogi have a thought for this too. For them, human existence is a fabric, woven from the weft of memory and the warp of possibility. For them, we see the present through this fabric, through those little holes between memory and possibility.[7] In other words, if we are going to see our present clearly and to understand how this present relates to constructive possibilities for the various peoples who find themselves in what is now Canada, then we will have to remember publicly what happened in the past, beyond a mythic landfall.

This is a difficult challenge at several levels, for there is no simple way of summarizing historically how Europeans appropriated northern or even northeastern North America. Native peoples played a leading role in European discovery, but their part has since been recast, several times. Over a period of three or four centuries Europeans in North America depended on Native peoples for information, communication, and trade. At the same time, Europeans were certainly useful, in some ways, to Native peoples.[8] This is not to minimize the lethal Old World diseases that arrived with European colonists, the corrosion of Native socio-economic structures by merchant capitalism, or the insidious ideological warfare waged by the Christian church.[9] The point is that for many centuries, in most parts of the continent including much of Atlantic Canada, Native and recently arrived North Americans needed each other and interacted in ways that cannot usually be summarized by the cold-hearted finality of conquest. The concepts of coercion, domination, and dependency are more useful for understanding the asymmetrical relationship between European and First Nations.[10] 'Discovery' is not simply a code word for conquest, since many Native peoples (the Innu or the Inuit, for example) were never conquered, at least not in the sense that Cortes conquered the Aztecs. Britain did conquer some Canadian First Nations, particularly those that made the mistake of allying themselves with France during the Seven Years' War (1756–63). Recall, however, that General Amherst, let alone Wolfe and Montcalm, died closer to our own time than to Cabot's. When conquest came, it had little to do with discovery, however hard British North American nationalists would later try to make the landfall a precedent for possession.

There are only so many ways the mutually exclusive claims of competing human groups to a bounded region can be resolved.[11] Briefly, and with no pretensions to morality, the most frequently used justifications for possession might be summarized as follows:

a. First discovery and continuous occupancy (often the claim of 'aboriginals')
b. Conquest (often the claim of 'settlers')
c. A special (divine) relationship with the land (often the claim of 'indigines' – for example, the *québécois*)[12]

The first two rationales, based on discovery or conquest, have the practical advantage that they are universalizable; they do not involve different rules for different peoples. They are, alternatively, idealistic or cruel rules to play by – but they are, at least, logically respectable. The third justification, a divine relationship with the land, is fraught with potential for conflict because it is not universalizable but nationalist, or even racist, insofar as its sets up special rules for one people.

For centuries, the European appropriation of North America was, practically speaking, justified by conquest. There is little to add to the words inscribed on a French gun at Louisbourg: *Ultima*

Ratio Regis – 'the final argument of the King.' Even by the late sixteenth century John Dee was politely disguising this harsh dialectic with the fictive justification of first discovery, in the modern sense. This kind of reasoning involves the beginnings of a racist assumption of special status, since to claim that Columbus or Cabot or Cartier discovered America or North America or Canada, in our distinctively modern sense of 'discovery,' is to discount previous inhabitants as ineligible to be discoverers. Practically speaking, Native peoples could not be discoverers in the original sense of 'discovery,' since they could not bring news to Europe; but it was illogical to deny them the status of discoverers in the new modern sense of finders for the first time. In 1612, the professor of civil law at Oxford, Alberico Gentili, observed sarcastically that the Spanish conquistadors behaved unreasonably, in this sense: 'They regarded it as beyond dispute that it was lawful to take possession of those lands which were not previously known to us; just as if to be known to none of us were the same thing as to be possessed by no one.'[13] There is little doubt that in 1497 the English would have made much the same assumption as the conquistadors, at least if they had been looking for lands to settle. In the words of the 1479 recension of *The Brut*, when the British arrived in the land 'destined and ordained' for them, they 'found neither man nor woman, as the story telleth, but giants & they dwelled in hills and caves.'[14] Technologically backward autochtons simply did not count, either as inhabitants or discoverers. (Curiously enough, the stature of the Beothuk, who were tall but not physically abnormal people, is frequently stressed in early accounts.[15])

In the sixteenth century, apologists for European expansion came up with a definition of Europe's special status in America that at least had the appearance of a universalizable principle. This provided a fourth justification for the appropriation of territory and the one, arguably, with the most life left in it:

d. Efficient use of natural resources, fulfilling nature's destiny to be appropriated for human use (in the end, this is often the claim of the consumer or her henchman the capitalist)

Sir Thomas More devised this argument in his famous *Utopia* of 1514. It represents, perhaps, the hopes that European humanists then had for the 'Others,' recently discovered in the New World:

If the population throughout [Utopia] exceeds the quota, they enroll citizens out of every city and plant a colony under their own laws on the mainland near them, wherever the natives have plenty of unoccupied and uncultivated land. Those natives who want to live with the Utopians are adopted by them. When such a merger occurs, the two peoples gradually and easily blend together, sharing the same way of life, much to the advantage of both. For by their policies the Utopians make the land yield an abundance for all, though previously it had seemed too poor and barren even to support the natives. But those who refuse to live under their laws they drive out of the land they claim for themselves; and against those who resist them, they wage war. They think it perfectly justifiable to make war on people who leave their land idle and waste yet forbid the use and possession of it to others who, by the law of nature, ought to be supported from it.[16]

The Abbé Raynal applied this argument to North America in his widely read *Philosophical and Political History of the British Settlements* (translated into English and published in Edinburgh with Adam Smith's *Wealth of Nations* in that pregnant year 1776):

The first Europeans who went over to settle ... met only with a few savages ... The human race, thinly scattered, fled from each other, or pursued only with intent to destroy. The earth seemed useless ...
    But man appeared, and immediately changed the face of North America. He introduced symmetry, by the assistance of all the instruments of art. The impenetrable woods were instantly cleared, and made room for commodious habitations. The wild beasts were driven away, and flocks of domestic animals supplied their place; whilst thorns and briars made way for rich harvests ... The coasts were covered with towns, and the bays with ships; and thus the new world, like the old, became subject to man.[17]

As the abbé struggles here with the concepts of 'man' and 'the human race,' the fabric of his economic reasoning slips to expose the racism that easily attaches itself to this argument, despite its superficial appeal to an abstract technological imperative.

Racism was relatively new in late-eighteenth-century Europe, having developed in the course of several centuries of exploitation of less technologically sophisticated societies.[18] Note that in 1514 More recommends the blending of human populations. 'Race' in sixteenth- and seventeenth-century English was used to distinguish the human race from other creatures or otherwise to refer to kin descended from a common ancestor. The earliest published example of 'race' meaning a physical division of humanity dates as late as 1774. 'White' had already been used to mean a person of a particular race, but this usage did not appear until the 1670s.[19] Sixteenth-century Europeans assumed that the natives of America were inferior, but this was initially a cultural and religious assessment, rather than a racial one[20] – an elusive distinction, no doubt, to those who bore the brunt of European prejudice, and one which would eventually bear strange and evil fruit. The distinction is, nevertheless, significant if we are to come close to understanding how early-modern Europeans thought about their appropriation of the New World, rather than projecting our own worst fears on them. In any event, the argument from technological efficiency could really only be applied in retrospect, while justifications for appropriation based on race or ethnic destiny were rare before the nineteenth century. The issues of the right of 'nations' to North American territory were thrashed out first in terms of discovery and conquest; and, as we have seen in previous chapters, these issues sustained debate for centuries.[21]

Today we have become cautious about the concept of 'discovery.' Newfoundland's Cabot 500 committee promotes the quincentenary celebration, while its subcontracted public-relations machinery tries to describe what the Venetian pilot did without using the D-word.[22] Any talk of 'discovery' is understood as an endorsement of conquest. A learned society takes exception to the association of a conference in St John's with the quincentenary events, out of concern that 'Cabot 500 will be a celebration of

British colonialism and European settlement.'[23] Few mainland
Canadians share Newfoundlanders' memory of Cabot. The Royal
Canadian Mint decides that the public is not interested in a Cabot
coin. The mint is there to make money, of course, and focus
groups have indicated that a silver-dollar commemoration of a
twenty-five-year-old mythic hockey victory against Russia will be
a better seller. This is a marked thematic departure for the mint,
which issued a commemorative $100 gold coin for the four-
hundredth anniversary of Sir Humphrey Gilbert's farcical visit to
St John's in 1583, when he ran aground on Chain Rock and then
extorted provisions from the Portuguese fishermen who rescued
him. The mint produced not one but two coins to observe the
four-hundred-and-fiftieth anniversary of Cartier's voyages: another $100 gold coin in 1983 and a nickel dollar coin in 1984.[24] Is
Cabot really of less significance than Gilbert? Or is there simply
no plausible opportunity to balance a Cabot coin with yet another
commemoration of Cartier? The decision not to commemorate
Cabot will avoid any possible irritation of the Learned Societies
or First Nations, as well. We are too troubled and probably too
preoccupied to work out whether, how, and why Cabot's 'discovery' might be supposed to have made subsequent 'conquest' possible. Besides, that would require the subtleties of history rather
than the simplifications of myth.

By way of closing this memoir of John Cabot let us reconsider
his 'discovery' as precedent and his landfall as myth. History and
biography apart, what might we make of the late-twentieth-
century remnants of the Cabot tradition? As a politically provoca-
tive context let us recall three moments in our national past that
reflect the shifting implications of discovery, conquest, and our
memories of discovery and conquest. The first is a report of
strangers brought to the court of Henry VII, just after the elder
Cabot disappeared and before his son Sebastian had amounted to
much. The second reflects the outlook of Native peoples conquered by Britain, almost incidentally, during the Seven Years'
War. The third suggests the role that Native people were assigned
during observations of the Cabot quadcentenary in 1897. Of
course there are other events that we might select, from the con-

tinuum of time, to celebrate and make myth of our past, but these will serve as well as many and better than some.

1502/1761/1897: SAVAGE MEN, DOMINION, AND A PICTURESQUE INCIDENT

In 1502 an English transatlantic expedition brought 'three savage men' home and presented them to the king.[25] Richard Hakluyt, who collected a chronicle of this event, erroneously assumed that it was Sebastian Cabot who exhibited his allegiance to Henry Tudor in this generous style. Sebastian was, almost certainly, still in his minority and the collectors of these human souvenirs were likely 'the merchauntes of Bristoll that have bene in the newe founde lande,' who received a reward of £20 from the Royal Household that September.[26] Richard Warde, Thomas Asshehurst, and John Thomas of Bristol, together with the Azorean Portuguese João Fernandes, Fransisco Fernandes, and João Gonsalves, had a current patent for exploration, which gave them authority 'to occupy, possess and subdue' whatever they found in the way of human occupation in the New World.[27] There was at least one other English transatlantic adventure in 1502: the first recorded cargo of cod brought from North America to Europe belonged to the *Gabriel* of Bristol, which came home that year with thirty-six tons of salt fish worth £180, for the persistent transatlantic investor Hugh Elyot.[28] It was, however, more likely the Bristol-Azorean expedition that returned with the first living proof of English contact with Native North Americans. In September, Fraunceys Fernandus and John Guidisalvus, squires, received pensions of £10 from Henry, 'in consideracion of the true service which they have doon unto us to our singler pleasure as Capitaignes into the newe founde lande.'[29] (João Fernandes disappears from the historical record at this point and probably died on the expedition; the Bristol merchants Warde, Asshehurst, and Thomas would have been the financial backers of the Azorean captains who actually led the expedition.)

Although we have a description, we remain uncertain who these Native people returned to England were, because we do not know where Gonsalves and the Fernandes brothers took their ships. Cartographic advances in the period and the appearance of toponyms like 'Cape Spear' suggest that the Azorean pilots may have explored Newfoundland, but the strange cargo they returned to Bristol and London might have come from any part of Atlantic Canada.[30] Whether the three men were Inuit, Innu, Beothuk, or Mi'kmaq, they made a strong impression on a visitor to King Henry's court: 'These were clothed in beastes skinnes, and ate rawe fleshe, and spake such speech that no man coulde understand them, and in their demeanour like to bruite beasts, whom the king kept a time after. Of the which upon two yeeres past after I saw the two apparelled after the manner of Englishmen, in Westminster pallace, which at that time I coulde not discern from Englishmen, till I learned what they were. But as for speech, I heard none of them utter one worde'.[31] There is much to ponder here, but three aspects of the chronicle are particularly striking. First, the English or their Azorean captains had no compunction about taking the people they found in North America from their homes and native land. Yet, once they were dressed like any self-respecting courtier in tights and a robe, the chronicler could not discern them from Englishmen. Dress counted for much in this period and so he reconsidered their status. Finally, the three 'savage men' held their tongues. As in many early chronicles, the Natives are quiet.

For centuries, we hardly hear the voices of the Native people of the Atlantic provinces. They finally become audible amid the din of the eighteenth-century global military struggle between France and Great Britain. This struggle involved many peoples, in several continents. In northeastern North America, the Mi'kmaq acted, with minor exceptions, as allies of France until the British capture of Louisbourg in 1758, which marked the demise of the French colony of Ile Royale (otherwise Cape Breton).[32] While the major belligerents did not sign the Peace of Paris until 1763, the British colonial administration in Nova Scotia had already negotiated a peace treaty with the Mi'kmaq. The representatives of several Mi'kmaq 'tribes' promised, severally, to accept British rule at a ceremony in Halifax, 25 June 1761, 264 years after Cabot's landfall, almost to the day.[33] The commander-in-chief and president of council, Jonathan Belcher, signed for the Crown and Chief Jeannot Picklougawash assented to the terms of the treaty on behalf of a band of about 250 Cape Breton Mi'kmaq.[34] (The role of chief and perhaps even the concept of tribe may have been elicited in Native societies of the northeast only after contact, by the administrative requirements of European state societies.)

This treaty marked a serious defeat for the Mi'kmaq. They had traditionally depended on maritime resources, in an eastern domain of islands, which included, at least in this period, the south coast of Newfoundland.[35] Their relationship with France had undergone a crucial transformation at mid-century, from a trade alliance to a military alliance cemented not only with words of friendship but with annual presents of weapons, clothing, and food. When the war was over and military allies were no longer in demand, the Mi'kmaq no longer had a viable economic base, for the British preferred to avoid annual ceremonials of treaty renewal and the concomitant demand for presents.[36] An abject admission of powerlessness at the Halifax peace ceremony, by Chief Jeannot, suggests that the Cape Breton band was vividly aware of its precarious prospects. This speech was translated for the record by their spiritual adviser Father Maillard, who worked in this period to reconcile the Mi'kmaq to British sovereignty, but it seems nevertheless to reflect a Native perspective. In a long and eloquent speech, Jeannot admitted that it was desperation that brought them '[t]o yield ourselves up ... without requiring any Terms.'[37] The Mi'kmaq and their French allies had lost a war, the British had won: 'You are now Master here such has been the will of God, He has given you Dominion of those vast Countries.' The British could 'dispose of us as you please.'

Yet conquest created responsibilities. On the one hand, Jeannot promised: 'As long as the Sun and the Moon shall endure, as long as the Earth on which I dwell shall exist ... so long will I be your Friend and Ally, Submitting myself to the Laws of your Government, faithful and obedient to the Crown.' At the same time Jeannot emphasized that the Mi'kmaq were bound to the British essentially in two ways. First, because the conquerors permitted 'the free Exercise' of the Roman Catholic faith, which the Mi'kmaq had adopted from their earlier French allies. Second, 'the moderation and lenity wherewith we have been treated has deeply imprinted in our Hearts a becoming Sense of Gratitude – Those good and noble sentiments of yours towards us in our distressed and piteous Circumstances have enboldened us to come out of the Woods.' In essence the Mi'kmaq accepted the British offer of peace because it was endorsed with provisions: 'Our not doubting your Sincerity has chiefly been owing to your Charitable, mercifull & bountifull behaviour to the poor French wandering up and down the Sea Coasts and Woods without any of the necessaries of Life – certain it is that they as well as we must have wretchedly perished unless relieved by your humanity.' This historical perspective on the generosity of the British in victory undercuts Acadian mythology, which recalls the expulsions of 1755 rather than the accommodation after the end of local hostilities. Jeannot's words also emphasize the economic perspective in which the Mi'kmaq placed political relationships. Leaders expressed their good will to those who gave allegiance by sharing with them. The powerful gained status by distributing available goods to those most in need rather than by private accumulation.[38] This is what Jeannot expected after the conquest.

The British had contemplated annual presents when they made their first Mi'kmaq treaties in the early 1750s. In 1752, Governor Peregrine Hopson promised Chief Jean Baptiste Cope: 'When you return here (as a mark of our good Will) we will give you handsome presents of such Things whereof you have most need ... And we hope to brighten the Chain in our Hearts and to confirm our Friendship every year; and for this purpose we shall expect to see here some of your Chiefs to receive annual presents whilst you behave yourselves as good, and faithfull children to our great King – and you shall be furnished with provisions for you and your Families every year.'[39] After the Treaty of Paris in 1763, policy changed and royal instructions to the governors of Nova Scotia for friendly relations with Native peoples were amended to omit earlier references to presents.[40] In July 1764, the Board of

Trade specifically instructed Governor Montagu Wilmot to discourage Mi'kmaq dependence on treaty presents.[41]

The Cape Breton Mi'kmaq might have patched together some kind of subsistence if they had obtained secure access to their traditional maritime resources. The Halifax treaty promised that British laws would be a 'great Hedge' to protect Mi'kmaq rights and, in 1762, Lieutenant-Governor Belcher proclaimed free Mi'kmaq access to the resources of the coast.[42] Neither Belcher nor even Governor Wilmot were the real power in Nova Scotia, however, and settler interests in the person of the powerful merchant Joshua Mauger objected to this 'impudent and unjust' admission of Native rights to coastal access.[43] Mauger had more influence with the Board of Trade in London than Belcher, and that arm of the Privy Council swiftly rescinded the Native economic rights contemplated.[44] It was not that British policy opposed the recognition of 'Indian territories.' In fact, imperial policy, affirmed in an order to North American governors in 1762, required the protection of Native territory.[45] It was just that the Board of Trade misunderstood or ignored the maritime orientation of the Mi'kmaq, accompanying their instructions to Belcher with a stern lecture about how inland territory would be more appropriate for Native peoples: '[I]f it had been necessary or expedient to reserve any lands to the Indians, it should not have been those lying near the coast, but rather the lands among the woods and lakes, where the wild beasts resort and are to be found in plenty.'[46] With hindsight, it is difficult to imagine exactly what game Native people might have expected to find in Nova Scotia after several centuries of trade-driven over-hunting. The Mi'kmaq had been cast adrift. Jeannot and his band set sail for Newfoundland, where they found no treaty presents and few rights but less enforcement and better access to fish and trade with their former allies, the French.[47]

The history of this band is not an epitome of Native experience. In Newfoundland the Mi'kmaq expanded into territories abandoned by the Beothuk, a people who chose to retreat in the face of European appropriation of the coasts and eventually starved in the inhospitable subarctic river valleys of the interior. The Beothuk were never conquered, but could hardly have been worse off, at least after 1763, if they had been. In a sense they were allowed to starve because they had no one to exploit them: no fur traders, no Indian agents, not even a missionary.[48] In Labrador, the Moravian Brotherhood co-opted the Inuit to dependence on European trade, a transition the Naskapi/Montagnais or Innu had begun in the seventeenth century, as suppliers of furs and salmon to the French.[49] If these Native peoples were better off than the Mi'kmaq it was not simply because their rocky hinterland remained unconquered, it was because they were only beginning to be dependent on the North Atlantic economy. Not every Mi'kmaq band could leave for Newfoundland (nor did that turn out to be the promised land for Jeannot and his kin.) Descendants of the other bands who ratified the Halifax Treaty of 1761 pieced together a meagre living, confined to a fraction of the lands and seas on which their ancestors had depended and playing a strictly limited role in the public life of the colony and, later, province of Nova Scotia.[50]

The Mi'kmaq returned to Halifax for a ceremonial re-enactment of the European appropriation of North America, when the Royal Society of Canada invited them to attend the unveiling of the Cabot memorial at Halifax, on 24 June 1897:

A picturesque incident occurred at the close of the ceremony. A group of Micmac Indians, men and women, appeared upon the scene, dressed in the brilliant gala costumes of their tribe, and came forward to present gifts of their own handiwork to the countess [Lady Aberdeen, wife of the governor-general] who received them in a very spirited and gracious manner. The thought that these children of the forest were descended from the people whom Cabot found on these shores made their appearance the occasion of a spontaneous and long-continued outburst of applause.[51]

One can see why representatives of the Mi'kmaq would attend. Here was a ceremony the very meaning of which might have been expected to remind Euro-Canadians of the existence of First

Nations. The Royal Society of Canada made the Mi'kmaq welcome too, but condescended to them as 'children of the forest.' It was easier to think of them this way than as the impoverished losers in a long guerrilla war. By remembering Cabot's landfall, Canadians could put other more problematic issues behind them.

The public memories evoked by the 1897 quadcentenary commemorations were complex. British North American nationalists used elaborate landfall myths as precedents for possession, as Edmund Burke had used the bald fact of Cabot's discovery in the days of Wolfe himself. These memories of the landfall rarely, if ever, served as triumphalist celebrations of conquest, in the worst traditions of the evolutionary racism of the period. More often, as at Halifax, the commemoration of Cabot's landfall ritually minimized the significance of conquest by emphasizing the significance of discovery. The whole point of the landfall myth was that discovery was a precedent: North America was meant to be British; conquest was merely incidental. At least in public, the history of discovery was a substitute for other histories, a useful diversion from the issues of ethnic dominance, coercion, and dependency that we cram clumsily into the concept of conquest. Impatience with that complacent self-deception has led some authorities, the learned society cited above for example, to doubt the value of the Cabot tradition in the late twentieth century. This reaction is natural, but makes little sense, in the last analysis, either logically or symbolically.

CABOT IN 1997

In 1997, as a century ago, Cabot means more to Newfoundland than to Canada, or at least central Canada. In Atlantic Canada, including Cape Breton, the mythic landfalls survive: the reinventions of 1897 gave birth to traditions which have their own life now, independent of the agendas of learned societies or national institutions like the mint. Patterns in the mass production of tradition suggest that modern invention of tradition occurs when vernacular national traditions are weak. This may explain the belligerence Newfoundland and Nova Scotia have displayed in their attachment to their respective landfalls at Bonavista and Cape Breton Island. Although these were among the first North American regions to see a real European presence, the ancestors of most of the present populations of British or Irish origin arrived only in the late eighteenth century and the earlier history of this region is but tenuously documented. The vehemence with which Newfoundland and Nova Scotia have seized their respective Cabot legends may, in part, express popular frustration at the real difficulties of grasping the obscure and complex early-modern history of the Atlantic region. John Cabot, moreover, went to sea; he died at sea; and while he was at sea he began the process of charting the waters of Atlantic Canada. To the extent that Atlantic Canadians continue to define themselves by their relationship with the sea, they are not likely to give up one of their few named early mariners. For these reasons, Cabot traditions in Newfoundland and Nova Scotia are more likely to evolve than to fade away in the face of the indifference of central Canada or the apprehension of Native hostility to his memory.

The late Victorian fetish of discovery also distracted from serious historical attention to the conquest of nature. If Europe tried to digest the rest of the world, it began with a meal of Newfoundland cod. The great natural resource of the Newfoundland fishery once fed millions of people, thousands of miles away, but in 1897 the Canadian public remembered Cabot's landfall better than his baskets of fish. When Newfoundlanders have remembered his fish they have usually remembered them as a precedent. In the words of a commemorative advertisement for Munn's celebrated Medicinal Cod Liver Oil in 1947, 'When John Cabot arrived 450 years ago he reported wonderful fishing – and still going strong.'[52] We now admit to recent and unparalleled over-fishing, but it has taken us a very long time to even consider the idea that Europeans might have over-fished some stocks, to the extent that evolving technologies permitted, pretty well from the beginning.[53] With cod populations so low that they cannot reproduce efficiently and with a moratorium on the fishery within Canadian waters, public memory has begun to trace the trajectory of this industry over half a millennium. This is one of the themes to which Newfoundland's Cabot 500 celebrants have turned, in avoiding the vexed question of discovery. A tradition is reinvented, mythically linking past and present, the better to deal with the uncomfortable realities of change.

When a learned society equates commemoration of Cabot's discovery with the celebration of British colonialism it makes a politically correct symbolic gesture but hardly a logical one. It makes mythic sense, or at least it once made mythic sense, to take the celebration of discovery as a kind of surrogate for the celebration of conquest. But it remains logically possible to commemorate European discovery without celebrating colonialism. Symbolically, in fact, it might be a way of remembering colonialism, which it would be a shame to forget. To forget Cabot would not thereby raise the issue of European appropriation. The Newfoundland government now attempts to disconnect him from the idea of discovery precisely in order to avoid the issue. If we need to reform our public memory of the age of exploration (and we do), it will be more politically useful to remember the asymmetry of contact rather than to attempt to forget that it happened. Asymmetry counts for much: (1) Europeans sailed west and 'discovered' lands and peoples new to them. (2) European weaponry, means of ocean transport, and disease made coercion of Native peoples possible. (3) The long relationship between European- and Native Americans was increasingly characterized by domination on the one hand and dependence on the other. Celebration is neither the only means nor the only reason to remember this asymmetry.

The new tradition which denies that discovery took place or that the results were so terrible that it ought to be forgotten is, like other traditions, itself a means of disguising change. Historically, there was once a time when Europeans were not here in North America, but now they are. The idea that North Americans of Old World ancestry ought not to commemorate their origins elsewhere is, at best, a form of wishful thinking. Of course they will continue to recall this and they will do so, at least in part, with traditions like the ones that have grown up around Columbus and Cabot and Cartier. Zuan Caboto is a good multicultural candidate for commemoration in this sense. His biography and Sebastian's undercut nationalist claims to precedence in European expansion. Their careers (and Columbus's) suggest that it was neither Spain nor England nor France nor Portugal who 'discovered' America; rather the Old World found the New. Such traditions celebrate 'discovery,' in one sense. Tacitly they may even celebrate European settlement. How it would benefit Native peoples for others to forget where they came from, and very approximately how they got here, remains unclear. Better that First Nations continue to reinvent their traditions, the better to remember their own origins and to remind the rest of us of their part in our joint story.

IN SUMMARY

Johnny Burke's perspective on 'The Landfall of Cabot' remains à propos: 'There's an argument unfinished ... for to settle an old grudge.' We will not settle the argument about John Cabot in 1997, because we have not settled the old grudge, but the argument is worth attending. Thanks to the discovery of the Day Letter in the 1950s we now know quite a bit more about the voyage of 1497 than even Henry Harrisse suspected a century ago. We can, if so motivated, construct plausible hypotheses about Cabot's itinerary. More significantly, historically speaking, threads of evidence can be spun together to develop a line of argument that ties Cabot to the medieval Norse voyages that found lands to the west. We can plausibly think of Cabot as the first navigator to apply the new celestial techniques developed by the Portuguese to northern geographic traditions. He brought these together to reach Newfoundland and, perhaps, adjacent parts of the North American mainland. He sought Japan but his greatest discovery was cod. Within a decade of his voyage, the adept pilots of Brittany and Portugal were taking their vessels on annual fishing voyages to the waters he explored.

Despite this achievement, for centuries John Cabot became a footnote to a misleading legend created by his ambitious son Sebastian. Generations honoured the memory of the latter as the father of English navigation, which he was, and as the discoverer of the new found land in 1497, which he was not. With time and many angry words the Sebastiophobes eventually won their historiographic argument with the Sebastiophiles and restored John Cabot to his place in the history of European exploration. This process was complete by the late nineteenth century, just in time for a colourful debate on the exact location of his landfall, launched by various British North American nationalists, partly in imitation of the American celebration of Columbus a few years before and partly as a reaction to the apotheosis of Cartier in French Canada. By this time, what John Rastell had wished for in 1525 had come to pass, at least in the imaginations of anglo-Canadian and Newfoundland intellectuals. They had constructed, of John Cabot and his landfall, 'a memory perpetual.'

Despite the ample evidence for the cynical view that modern nation-states have been particularly adept at the invention of tradition, or perhaps particularly dependent upon it, some browsing in the early historiography of discovery suggests that there is a tradition of invention in these matters. Geoffrey of Monmouth's Brutus was a medieval founder-hero for the British themselves, and a figure who casts a familiar shadow on a landscape previously inhabited only by those who lacked a proper precedent for possession. Cabot later found such an inhabited yet vacant land. One of the most powerful metaphors in the history of his explorations is non-contact. He did not meet Native people. He found their land; he even found their tools and traces of their hearths; but John Cabot and his crew raised King Henry's flag, the Pope's, his own Venetian banner, and a cross in the absence of Native peoples. That was the real precedent.

Notes

A NOTE ON SOURCE REFERENCES

James A. Williamson, *The Cabot Voyages and Bristol Discovery under Henry VII*, Hakluyt Society (2nd series), vol. 120 (Cambridge, 1962), is cited as Williamson, *Cabot Voyages*. When cited here, documents collected in that publication are given the number assigned to them there, to facilitate comparison with Williamson's useful discussion.

George Parker Winship, *Cabot Bibliography with an Introductory Essay on the Careers of the Cabots* [1900], repr. American Classics in History and Political Science no. 14 (New York, 1967), is cited here as Winship, *Cabot Bibliography*.

Citations of some of the more obscure older publications include a reference to 'CIHM' [in brackets]. This refers to the catalogue number of the relevant publication, as it appears in microfiche, in the invaluable series produced by the Canadian Institute for Historical Microreproductions, Ottawa.

CHAPTER 1: AN INTRODUCTION

1 'Cracky' is a small noisy mongrel dog. See G.M. Story, W.J. Kirwin, and J.D.A. Widdowson, eds, *Dictionary of Newfoundland English* (Toronto, 1982).
2 'Turned manus' means to go on strike at sea. A 'jinker' is a person jinxing a vessel. See *Dictionary of Newfoundland English*.
3 The song is given anonymously in Gerald S. Doyle, ed., *The Old Time*

Songs and Poetry of Newfoundland (1927), 71, and in J.R. Smallwood, *The Book of Newfoundland*, vol. 1 (St John's, 1937), 481, with an introduction plagiarized from Doyle. A similar version is ascribed to 'Burke's Popular Songs,' in the *Atlantic Guardian*, August 1945, but is not actually in John Burke, *Burke's Newfoundland Ballads* (St John's, 1912); see Paul Mercer, *Newfoundland Songs and Ballads in Print, 1842–1974: A Title and First-Line Index* (St John's, 1979), 64, 144. John White, *Burke's Ballads* (St John's, 1960), 32, offers a very different version, in a St John's brogue. This is reprinted as Burke's in Paul Mercer, *The Ballads of Johnny Burke: A Short Anthology* (St John's, 1974). Philip Hiscock of the Memorial University of Newfoundland Folklore and Language Archive has evidence that the version reprinted here was in the oral tradition by the early 1920s. One version is probably Burke's. He published a song by this title and a collection called *The Cabot Songster* in 1897; see James E. Candow, *Daniel Woodley Prowse and the Origin of Cabot Tower*, Parks Canada Research Bulletin no. 155 (Ottawa, 1981), 5.

4 *Granta* 32 (1990), 13–56.

5 Jacques Mathieu, 'Un événement fondateur: La découverte du Canada. Le personage de Jacques Cartier et son évolution,' in Claire Dolan, ed., *Evénement, identité et histoire* (Sillery, 1991), 255–67.

6 John Davis, 'History and the People without Europe,' in Kirsten Hastrup, ed., *Other Histories* (London, 1992), 14–28.

7 Eric Hobsbawm, 'Introduction: Inventing Traditions,' in Eric Hobsbawm and Terence Ranger, eds, *The Invention of Tradition* (1983; repr. Cambridge, 1992), 101–64, see p. 13. On *histoire de l'événement*, see Dolan, ed., *Evénement, identité et histoire*.

8 Maurice Halbwachs, *The Collective Memory*, trans. Francis J. Ditter and Vida Yazdi Ditter (New York, 1980), and see the excellent discussion in Patrick H. Hutton, *History as an Art of Memory* (Hanover, VT, 1993), 73–90.

CHAPTER 2: EVERYTHING WE KNOW ABOUT JOHN CABOT

1 Henry Harrisse, *The Discovery of North America by John Cabot* (3rd ed., London, 1897) [CIHM # 12913], 3.

2 But see Ruth Holmes Whitehead, *The Old Man Told Us: Excerpts from Micmac History, 1500–1980* (Halifax, 1991).
3 Virtually all the relevant sources are published, with a judicious introductory commentary, Williamson, *Cabot Voyages*, vol. 120. See introductory note on p. 179, above. For bibliographies of secondary sources see Winship, *Cabot Bibliography* (see introductory note) and W.F. Ganong, *Crucial Maps in the Early Cartography and Place-Nomenclature of the Atlantic Coast of Canada*, ed. Theodore E. Layng (Toronto, 1964).
4 John Day, Letter to the Grand Admiral, ca. 1497, in Williamson, *Cabot Voyages* (25); L.-A. Vigneras, 'The Cape Breton Landfall: 1494 or 1497?: Note on a Letter from John Day,' *Canadian Historical Review* 38(3) (1957), 219–28; cf. 'New Light on the 1497 Cabot Voyage to America,' *Hispanic-American Historical Review* 36(4) (1956), 503–6.
5 Alwyn A. Ruddock, 'John Day of Bristol and the English Voyages across the Atlantic before 1497,' *Geographical Journal* 132 (1966), 224–33. The letter was written in Andalusia; see Williamson, *Cabot Voyages*, 29.
6 For narratives of the voyage not too dependent on must-have-been, see C. Raymond Beazley, *John and Sebastian Cabot; the Discovery of North America* (London, 1898); Henry Harrisse, *The Discovery of North America, a Critical, Documentary, and Historic Investigation* (1892; repr. Amsterdam, 1961); David B. Quinn, *North America from Earliest Discovery to First Settlements: The Norse Voyages to 1612* (New York, 1977), 112–22; Patrick McGrath, 'Bristol and America, 1480–1631,' in K.R. Andrews, N.P. Canny, and P.E.N. Hair, eds, *The Westward Enterprise: English Activities in Ireland, the Atlantic, and America, 1480–1650* (Liverpool, 1978), 81–102; Samuel Eliot Morison, *The European Discovery of America*, vol. 1, *The Northern Voyages* (New York, 1971), 157–209; and Alan F. Williams, *John Cabot and Newfoundland*, Newfoundland Historical Society (St John's, 1997). I am endebted to Dr Williams and the Society for allowing me to see a draft of the latter before publication.
7 E.g., R.A. Skelton, 'Cabot (Caboto), John (Giovanni),' in George W. Brown and Marcel Trudel, eds, *Dictionary of Canadian Biography*, vol. 1, *1000 to 1700* (rev. ed., Toronto, 1979); perhaps following H.P. Biggar, *The Precursors of Jacques Cartier, 1497–1534: A Collection of*

Documents Relating to the Early History of the Dominion of Canada, Publications of the Canadian Archives no. 5 (Ottawa, 1911), vii.

8 Williamson, *Cabot Voyages,* 33. He was sometimes 'Johannes'; no record has survived that calls him 'Giovanni.'

9 Williamson, *Cabot Voyages,* 33; Venetian Archivia de Stato, 13 January 1484, in Williamson, *Cabot Voyages* (11 vii).

10 Pedro de Ayala, Letter to King Ferdinand and Queen Isabella of Spain, 25 July 1498, in Williamson, *Cabot Voyages* (37).

11 King Ferdinand of Spain, Letter to Deigo de Torres, Governor-General of Valencia, 27 September 1492, in Williamson, *Cabot Voyages* (12 i); Robert H. Fuson, 'The John Cabot Mystique,' in Stanley H. Palmer and Dennis Reinhartz, eds, *Essays on the History of North American Discovery and Exploration* (College Station, TX, 1988), 35–51.

12 Williamson, *Cabot Voyages,* 44 and 50, says we have evidence that Cabot was in England by 1495, but this is a 'must have been,' given the grant of letters patent early in 1496; see John Cabotto and sons, Petition to Henry VII, 5 March 1496, Great Britain, Public Record Office (PRO), Chancery Warrants for Privy Seal, series 2, 146, in Williamson, *Cabot Voyages* (17).

13 *The Great Chronicle of London* [1497/1498]; 'Cronicon regnum Anglie,' BL, Cotton ma Vit. A xvi, f. 173; and Robert Fabyan, *Chronicle,* first published in Richard Hakluyt, *Divers Voyages* (London, 1582); all in Williamson, *Cabot Voyages* (31 i–iii). The version quoted is Fabyan's, in Hakluyt.

14 Raimondo de Raimondi de Soncino, Letter to the Duke of Milan, 18 December 1497, in Williamson, *Cabot Voyages* (24).

15 Ferdinand and Isabella, Letter to Gonzales de Puebla, 28 March 1496, in Williamson, *Cabot Voyages* (16).

16 Henry VII, Letters Patent to John Cabot and sons, 5 March 1496, PRO, Treaty Roll 178, 8, trans. H.P. Biggar, in Williamson, *Cabot Voyages* (18).

17 Soncino, Letter to Milan (1497).

18 William Worcestre, *Itinerarium,* Corpus Christi College, Cambridge, ms 210, in Williamson, *Cabot Voyages* (6); David B. Quinn, 'The Argument for the English Discovery of America between 1480 and 1494,' *Geographical Journal* 127 (1961), 227–85.

19 Inquisition at Bristol, 3 September 1481, PRO, Memoranda Roll,

Lord Treasurer's Remembrancer, 22 Edward IV, E 368/255 (10) in Williamson, *Cabot Voyages* (7 ii).

20 Robert Thorne, Memorial addressed to Dr Lee, English ambassador in Spain, 1527, British Library (BL), Cotton ms, Vit. c. vii, ff. 329–45, in Williamson, *Cabot Voyages* (15).

21 John Dee, 'A brief remembrance of sundry foreign Regions ...,' 1578, BL, Cotton ms Aug.I.i, in Williamson, *Cabot Voyages* (14); see the discussion in Williamson, *Cabot Voyages*, 26–9. For a revival of the old view that John Cabot was involved in the venture of 1494, see Harry Kelsey, 'The Planispheres of Sebastian Cabot and Sancho Gutiérrez,' *Terrae Incognitae* 19 (1987), 41–58.

22 See the entries in PRO, Household Books, 1497–1502, E 101/414 and 415, in Williamson, *Cabot Voyages* (26 i–iii).

23 Henry VII, Letters Patent to Richard Warde et al., 19 March 1501, and Letters Patent to Hugh Elyot et al., 9 December 1502, PRO, Patent Roll 16 Henry VII, part 1, 20–1, and Patent Roll 18 Henry VII, part 2, 29–30, both trans. H.P. Biggar, in Williamson, *Cabot Voyages* (43) and (46).

24 Soncino, Letter to Milan (1497).

25 Day, Letter to the Grand Admiral (ca. 1497); Soncino, Letter to Milan (1497); Maurice Toby, 'A brief Chronicle ...,' ca. 1625, Fust ms, in Williamson, *Cabot Voyages* (19); cf. David B. Quinn, 'John Cabot's Matthew,' letter to the editor, *Times Literary Supplement*, 8 June 1967, 517.

26 Soncino, Letter to Milan (1497). Day, Letter to the Grand Admiral (ca. 1497), makes the crew twenty; perhaps there were eighteen from Bristol and Cabot's two continental friends. Williamson, *Cabot Voyages*, 61, maintains that the company included two Bristol merchants, but the evidence for this is not obvious.

27 He dated the voyage to 1496; see Giovanni Battista Ramusio, *Primo Volume delle Navigationi et Viaggi* [Venice, 1550], 398–403; in Williamson, *Cabot Voyages* (56). For discussion, see chapter 3 of this study.

28 E.g., on the 'Paris' world map of 1544, published with his authority, on this occasion dating the voyage to 1494; see Legend 8 on the Paris Map, 1544, in Williamson, *Cabot Voyages* (21). On the map and its history see section 5, 'The Landfall.'

29 Bristol Customs Records, 1503–4, King's Remembrancer, E 122/199, 1, in Williamson, *Cabot Voyages* (20).

30 Colin Mudie, 'Bristol Fashion,' *Classic Boat* 95 (May 1996), 28–36.
31 Day, Letter to the Grand Admiral (ca. 1497); Soncino, Letter to Milan (1497); and see Williamson, *Cabot Voyages*, 61.
32 Soncino, Letter to Milan (1497).
33 Cf. Morison, *Northern Voyages*, 170.
34 D.W. Waters, 'Science and the Techniques of Navigation in the Renaissance,' in Charles S. Singleton, ed., *Art, Science and History in the Renaissance* (Baltimore, 1967), 189–237; see 200–7 and 219.
35 Frederic C. Lane, 'The Economic Meaning of the Invention of the Compass,' *American Historical Review* 68 (1965), 605–17.
36 See Waters, 'Science and Navigation,' 219; Eila M.J. Campbell, 'Discovery and the Technical Setting 1420–1520,' *Terrae Incognitae* 8 (1976), 11–17.
37 Jeffrey Burton Russell, *Inventing the Flat Earth: Columbus and the Modern Historians* (New York, 1991).
38 On Rastell see Kenneth R. Andrews, *Trade, Plunder and Settlement: Maritime Enterprise and the Genesis of the British Empire, 1480–1630* (Cambridge, 1984), 54.
39 John Rastell, *The Four Elements* [ca. 1525], ed. Roger Coleman, (Cambridge, 1971), 58–9.
40 E.G.R. Taylor, *The Haven-Finding Art: A History of Navigation from Odysseus to Captain Cook*, 2nd ed. (London, 1971), 245–63.
41 R.A. Skelton, 'Cabot, Sebastian,' in *DCB* 1.
42 Cited in Morison, *Northern Voyages*, 223.
43 On Day's navigational knowledge see Ruddock, 'John Day.'
44 Soncino, Letter to Milan (1497).
45 For Dursey Head see Morison, *Northern Voyages*, 169; for Achill Head see Melvin Jackson, 'The Labrador Landfall of John Cabot, 1497,' *Canadian Historical Review* 54 (1963), 122–41. Clements R. Markham, 'Fourth Centenary of the Voyage of John Cabot, 1497,' *Geographical Journal* 9(6) (1897), 604–20, assumes Blacksod Bay, just north of Achill Head, see p. 608.
46 Cf. Harrisse, *Discovery of North America* (1892), 7.
47 Soncino, Letter to Milan (1497).
48 R.A. Skelton thought that early Bristol traders used 'the northeasterly winds of early summer ... westward from southern England or Ireland'; see 'The Vinland Map,' 234, in R.A. Skelton, Thomas E.

Marston, and George D. Painter, *The Vinland Map and the Tartar Relation*, 2nd ed. (New Haven, 1995), 107–240.

49 Hans-Jörg Isemer and Lutz Hasse, *The Bunker Climate Atlas of the North Atlantic Ocean*, vol. 1, *Observations* (Berlin, n.d., ca. 1986), 189, chart 152.

50 *Hauksbók*, ed. F. Jónsson (Copenhagen, 1892), 4, cited in G.J. Marcus, *The Conquest of the North Atlantic* (New York, 1981), 95.

51 Marcus, *Conquest of the North Atlantic*, 93–6.

52 Isemer and Hasse, *Climate Atlas*, 1: 190, chart 153.

53 Morison, *Northern Voyages*, 168–9.

54 Day, Letter to the Grand Admiral (ca. 1497).

55 Taylor, *Haven-Finding Art*, 172–91; Waters, 'Science and Navigation,' 196, 223.

56 E.g., Samuel Edward Dawson, 'The Voyages of the Cabots in 1497 and 1498; with an Attempt to Determine Their Landfall and to Identify Their Island of St John,' *Transactions of the Royal Society of Canada* (1st ser.) 12 (1894), sect. II, 51–112.

57 Paris Map (1544), Legend 8.

58 Legend 8 on the Paris Map, 1544, identifies the landfall as Cape Breton. The history of this map and some of the reasons for distrusting this information are discussed later in this section.

59 Williamson, *Cabot Voyages*, 9–10; Donald S. Johnson, *Phantom Islands of the Atlantic* (Fredericton, NB, 1994), 131–50.

60 Day, Letter to the Grand Admiral (ca. 1497) says, literally, 'is west of' rather than 'is in the same latitude as.'

61 Henry Harrisse, *Découverte et évolution cartographique de Terre-Neuve et des pays circonvoisins, 1497–1501–1769* (1900; repr. Ridgewood, NJ, 1968), 203–13. The Avalon is shown as an island on the Paris Map of 1544.

62 Morison, *Northern Voyages*, 172–3.

63 This assumes Cabot used the generally accepted Ptolemaic mile of 5000 feet. The nautical mile of 6080 feet was a seventeenth-century invention; see David W. Waters, *The Art of Navigation in England in Elizabethan and Early Stuart Times* (London, 1958), 423–5 and 487–8.

64 The distance is given as 400 leagues in 'News received from England,' 24 August 1497, Milan Archives, trans. in A.B. Hinds, *Calendar of State Papers, Milan*, vol. 1 (London, 1912), no. 535, in

Williamson, *Cabot Voyages* (23). Is this another copyist's error of 'iiii' for 'vii,' as in the famous 1494/1497 controversy?

65 On sea leagues see E.G.R. Taylor, 'Where Did the Cabots Go? A Study in Historical Deduction,' *Geographical Journal* 129 (1963), 339–41.

66 Soncino, Letter to Milan (1497).

67 Under very favourable conditions black spruce can grow to over 30 metres, although 18 metres would be a large specimen in Newfoundland or Labrador. See R.C. Hosie, *Native Trees of Canada* 7th ed., Canadian Forestry Service (Ottawa, 1969), 72; A. Glen Ryan, *Native Trees and Shrubs of Newfoundland and Labrador*, Parks Division, Department of Tourism, Newfoundland (St John's, 1978), 15.

68 Soncino, Letter to Milan (1497).

69 Charles Deane, 'The Voyages of the Cabots,' in Justin Winsor, ed., *Narrative and Critical History of America* (Boston, 1884), 3: 1–58; see 20. Cf. Kelsey, 'Planispheres of Cabot and Gutiérrez,' 41–2.

70 Winship, *Cabot Bibliography*, 13–16 (no. 39).

71 On Sebastian Cabot's voyage of 1508, see Williamson, *Cabot Voyages*, 145–72.

72 Joannes Ruysch, *Universalior Cogniti Orbis Tabula ex Recentibus Confecta Observationibus* [1508], in A.E. Nordenskiöld, *Facsimile-Atlas to the Early History of Cartography* (1889; repr. New York, 1973), plate xxxii. Henry Harrisse, *L'atterage de Jean Cabot au continent américain en 1497*, Mémoire lu à la Société royale des sciences de Goettingen dans sa session du 30 octobre 1897 et extrait de ses *Nachrichten* (Göttingen, 1897), 5, give Ribeiro (1529) and Viegas (1534) as other early examples. On the early cartography see Harrisse, *Découverte et évolution cartographique*.

73 Day, Letter to the Grand Admiral (ca. 1497).

74 Lorenzo Pasqualigo, Letter to his brothers in Venice, 23 August 1497, in Marin Sanuto, ms *Diarii*, Venice, Biblioteca Marciana, mss Ital. Cl. VII, Cod. 417 (vol. 1), f. 374v, trans. H.P. Biggar, in Williamson, *Cabot Voyages* (22). According to Sebastian's later description of the landfall area, 'the people of it are dressed in the skins of animals; they use in their wars bows and arrows, lances and darts, and certain clubs of wood, and slings'; see Eighth Legend, Paris Map, 1544, in

Williamson, *Cabot Voyages* (21). Since John Cabot did not actually encounter Native people in 1497, this description must be based on later voyages.

75 James A. Tuck, *Maritime Provinces Prehistory* (Ottawa, 1984), 79, 90, and *Newfoundland and Labrador Prehistory* (Toronto, 1976), 62, 70.

76 Tuck, *Newfoundland and Labrador Prehistory*, 87–8, 109–18. My argument makes an assumption about the vexed question of the distribution of the Inuit in the contact period; on which see Ralph Pastore, 'The Sixteenth Century: Aboriginal Peoples and European Contact,' in Phillip A. Buckner and John G. Reid, eds, *The Atlantic Region to Confederation: A History* (Toronto and Fredericton, 1994), 22–39, n. 7 (p. 390).

77 Day, Letter to the Grand Admiral (ca. 1497) and cf. Pasqualigo, Letter to Venice (1497).

78 A century ago, Bishop Michael Howley argued for roughly this itinerary, although he put the landfall variously as Cape St John, Bonavista, or St John's. See M.F. Howley, 'Cabot's Landfall,' *Magazine of American History* 26 (1891), 267–88 [CIHM # 17806], and 'Latest Lights on the Cabot Controversy,' *Transactions of the Royal Society of Canada* (2nd ser.) 9 (1903), sect. II, 205–15.

79 On the case for a Grates Cove landfall, see chapter 4.

80 Charles Deane, trans., 'The Legends of the Cabot Map of 1544,' *Proceedings of the Massachusetts Historical Society* (2nd ser.) 6 (1890–1), repr. in *Transactions of the Royal Society of Canada* (2nd ser.) 3 (1897), 430–50; see no. 17, p. 449.

81 Dawson, 'Voyages of the Cabots,' 87, 88; cf. Williamson, *Cabot Voyages*, 58.

82 Harrisse, *L'atterage de Jean Cabot*, 16–17.

83 Robert Thorne, *Orbis Universalis Descriptio*, 1527, in Nordenskiöld, *Facsimile-Atlas*, plate xli: 'Terra hec ab Anglis primus fuit inventa.' Cf. Harrisse, *Discovery by John Cabot* (1897).

84 Harrisse, *L'atterage de Jean Cabot*, 4.

85 Jacopo Gastaldi, Mappemonde, 1546, in Harrisse, *Découverte et évolution cartographique*, 250–2; cf. Williams, *John Cabot and Newfoundland*, 43.

86 Henry VII, Letters Patent, 5 March 1496.

87 The Day Letter does not give these latitudes as limits of exploration,

although they are read as such by some scholars, e.g., Andrews, *Trade, Plunder and Settlement*, 47.

88 Deane, 'Voyages of the Cabots,' 8; Winship, *Cabot Bibliography*, 38–9.

89 H.P. Biggar, 'The Voyages of the Cabots and of the Corte-Reals to North America and Greenland 1497–1503,' *Revue Hispanique* 10 (1903), 485–92, and *Precursors of Cartier*, vii–x; Ganong, *Crucial Maps*; John T. Juricek, 'John Cabot's First Voyage,' *Smithsonian Journal of History* 2(4) (1968), 1–22.

90 Shane O'Dea, 'Judge Prowse and Bishop Howley: Cabot Tower and the Construction of Nationalism,' lecture to Newfoundland Historical Society, St John's, 25 April 1996.

91 Harrisse, *Discovery by John Cabot* (1897); George E. Nunn, *The Mappemonde of Juan de la Cosa: A Critical Investigation of Its Date* (Jenkintown, PA, 1934), 2, 28–41, 51–2. For an argument against Nunn's dating of ca. 1508, see Williamson, *Cabot Voyages*, 75–6.

92 Samuel Edward Dawson, 'The Voyages of the Cabots in 1497 and 1498 – a Sequel to a Paper in the "Transactions" of 1894,' *Transactions of the Royal Society of Canada* (2nd ser.) 2 (1896), sect. II, 3–29; Ganong, *Crucial Maps*; G.R.F. Prowse, 'Cabot's Surveys,' typescript (Winnipeg, 1931); Bernard G. Hoffman, *Cabot to Cartier: Sources for an Historical Ethnography of Northeastern North America, 1497–1550* (Toronto, 1961), 87–97; Quinn, *North America to 1612*, 116; Juricek, 'John Cabot's First Voyage'; Frederic Kidder, 'The Discovery of North America by John Cabot,' *New England Historical and Genealogical Register*, October 1878 (repr. Boston, 1878) [CIHM # 19008]; David O. True, 'Cabot Explorations in North America,' *Imago Mundi* 13 (1955), 11–25; A. Davies, 'The "English Coasts" on the Map of Juan de la Cosa,' *Imago Mundi* 13 (1956), 26–29; Lucien Campeau, 'Les Cabot et l'Amérique,' *Revue d'histoire de l'Amérique française* 14(3) (1960), 317–52.

93 E.R. Seary, *Place Names of the Avalon Peninsula of the Island of Newfoundland* (Toronto, 1971), 27–33.

94 Soncino, Letter to Milan (1497); Day, Letter to the Grand Admiral (ca. 1497); Pasqualigo, Letter to Venice (1497); Williamson, *Cabot Voyages*, 5–7, 87–8. For another view see Taylor, 'Where Did the Cabots Go?'

95 Peter Martyr, *Summario della Generale Istoria dell' Indie Occidentali* (Venice, 1534), f. 65, in Williamson, *Cabot Voyages* (53).

96 Day, Letter to the Grand Admiral (ca. 1497).
97 For a brief discussion see Taylor, 'Where Did the Cabots Go?'
98 'Item to hym that founde the new Isle,' Daybook Entry, Household Books, 10–11 August 1497, PRO E 101/414, 16, in Williamson, *Cabot Voyages* (26 i); Pasqualigo, Letter to Venice (1497); Day, Letter to the Grand Admiral (ca. 1497).
99 Soncino, Letter to Milan (1497).
100 Entry, Household Books, 10–11 August 1497; Henry VII, Grant of Pension to John Cabot, 13 December 1497, PRO, Privy Seals, 13 Henry VII, in Williamson, *Cabot Voyages* (27). Soncino calls Henry 'wise and not prodigal.'
101 'A Bristol Rental 1498–9. The property of Mrs Chester-Master,' in Williamson, *Cabot Voyages* (30).
102 Soncino, Letter to Milan (1497).
103 Again, it was Soncino who explicitly noted that Cabot went west in order to reach the east, *pace* Campeau, 'Les Cabot et l'Amérique.'
104 Soncino, Letter to Milan (1497).
105 Soncino, Letter to Milan (1497); Day, Letter to the Grand Admiral (ca. 1497).
106 Henry VII, Letters Patent to John Kabotto, 3 February 1498, PRO, Warrants for Privy Seal, C. 82/173, 13 Henry VII, February, in Williamson, *Cabot Voyages* (35).
107 Fabyan, *Chronicle* (1498).
108 McGrath, 'Bristol and America, 1480–1631,' 90.
109 Polydore Vergil, *Anglica Historia*, trans. Denys Hay, in Williamson, *Cabot Voyages* (33).
110 David B. Quinn, 'Sebastian Cabot and Bristol Exploration,' Bristol Branch of the Historical Association (1968, rev. ed. Bristol, 1993), 34, reports: 'It appears that John Cabot did survive the 1498 voyage, though the evidence for it has not yet been published.'
111 Fabyan, *Chronicle*, re 1502 as reprinted in Hakluyt's *Divers Voyages* [1582], in Williamson, *Cabot Voyages* (31 iii).
112 Williams, *John Cabot and Newfoundland*, 48, appears to have slipped on this matter.
113 Pietro Pasqualigo [Venetian ambassador in Portugal], Letter to his brothers in Venice, 19 October 1501, *Paesi nouamente retrouati* (Vicenza, 1507), lib. vi, cap. cxxvi, in Williamson, *Cabot Voyages* (38).

114 For this and some other evidence, see Williamson, *Cabot Voyages*, 106–13.
115 Bristol Customers, Accounts, 1496–9, Westminster Chapter Archives, Chapter Muniments, 12243, in Williamson, *Cabot Voyages* (29 ii).

CHAPTER 3: LEGENDS OF SEBASTIAN

1 Richard Biddle, *A Memoir of Sebastian Cabot* (Philadelphia and London, 1831), iv.
2 On Sebastian's voyage, see Williamson, *Cabot Voyages*, 145–72.
3 Edmund Burke, *An Account of the European Settlements in America* (London, 1757) [CIHM # 32610], 133.
4 Henry Gardener, *New-Englands vindidation* [*sic*] (London, 1660), 1.
5 Peter French, *John Dee, the World of an Elizabethan Magus* (1972; repr. London, 1987), 180–7; Kenneth R. Andrews, *Trade, Plunder and Settlement: Maritime Enterprise and the Genesis of the British Empire 1480–1630* (Cambridge, Eng., 1984), 35.
6 John Dee, 'A brief remembrance of sundry foreign Regions ...,' 1578, British Library (BL), Cotton ms, Aug.I.i.1, in Williamson, *Cabot Voyages* (14).
7 French, *John Dee*, 43–61.
8 Robert Fabian, 'A note of Sebastian Cabots first discoverie of part of the Indies ...,' in Richard Hakluyt, *The Principal Navigations Voyages Traffiques & Discoveries of the English Nation* [1599–1600] (Edinburgh, 1885–1890; repr. New York, 1965), 7: 154. Cf. Robert Fabyan, 'Note of Sebastian Gabotes Voyage of Discoverie,' *Divers Voyages* [London, 1582], in Williamson, *Cabot Voyages* (31 iii) and p. 222n.
9 Peter Martyr, *De Orbe Novo Decades* (Alcalá, 1516), Dec. III, lib. vi, f. 52 and *Historia dell' Indie Occidentali*, vol. 1 (Venice, 1534), f. 65, in Williamson, *Cabot Voyages* (52 and 53).
10 Francisco Lopez de Gomara, *La historia general de las Indias* [Saragossa, 1552], f. xx, and André Thevet, *Les Singularitez de la France Antarctique, autrement nommé Amérique* [Paris, 1558], f. 148b; both in Williamson, *Cabot Voyages* (58 and 59).
11 Winship, *Cabot Bibliography*, 52–3, 71.
12 Winship, *Cabot Bibliography*, 84–9.

13 Alonso de Santa Cruz, 'Islario General de todas las Islas de Mundo' [1541], Vienna, Nationalbiblioteck, ms 7195; Giovanni Battista Ramusio, *Primo Volume delle Navigationi et Viaggi* [Venice, 1550], ff. 398–403; Antonio Galvao, *Tratado* [Lisbon, 1563], trans. C.R.D. Bethune; and Jean Ribault, *The Whole and true discovery of Terra Florida* [London, 1563], sig. A ii–iii; all in Williamson, *Cabot Voyages* (39, 56, 60, and 62).

14 Winship, *Cabot Bibliography*, 51, 89.

15 John Smith, *The Generall Historie of Virginia, New England and the Summer Isles* [1624], in Philip L. Barbour, ed., *The Complete Works of Captain John Smith (1580–1631)*, Institute of Early American History and Culture, vol. 2 (Chapel Hill, 1983), 62.

16 Samuel Purchas, *Hakluytus Posthumus or Purchas his Pilgrimes: Contayning a History of the World in Sea Voyages and Lande Travells by Englishmen and Others* [1625], Hakluyt Society (extra series), vol. 16 (Glasgow, 1906), 106.

17 Purchas, *Pilgrimes*, vol. 14 (Glasgow, 1906), 300–1.

18 Luke Fox, *North-west fox, or, Fox from the North, west passage* [London, 1635] in Miller Christy, ed., *The Voyages of Captain Luke Foxe of Hull and Captain Thomas James of Bristol, in Search of a North-west Passage, in 1631–32*, Hakluyt Society (1st ser.), nos. 88–9 (London, 1894), 1: 31–3; Rev. William Hubbard, *General History of New England*, in *Collections of the Massachusetts Historical Society* (2nd ser.) 5–6 (1815) (repr. New York, 1972), 8.

19 John Oldmixon, *The British Empire in America* (1708; repr. London, 1741), 11; Thomas Lediard, *The Naval History of England* (London, 1735), vol. 1, chap. 20, 84–9; Thomas Prince, *The Chronological History of New England* [Boston, 1736], 80, the latter cited in Winship, *Cabot Bibliography*, 51, 162.

20 Lediard, *Naval History*, 1: 86.

21 As was the author of *The History of the British dominions in North America* [London, 1773], cited in Winship, *Cabot Bibliography*, 142–3. William Douglass, *Summary, Historical and Political, of the First Planting, Progressive Improvements, and Present State of the British Settlements in North America*, vol. 1 (1749; repr. New York, 1972), 5, 273, makes a similar argument.

22 John Campbell, 'The History of Sir John Cabot' and 'Sebastian

Cabot,' in *Lives of the Admirals and other Eminent British Seamen*, 2nd ed. (London, 1750) vol. 1 [CIHM # 33212], 326–31, 385–91. John's role was also recognized in Henry Ellis, *A Voyage to Hudson's-Bay* (London, 1748), 3–4.

23 William Mavor, *Historical Account of the Most Celebrated Voyages, Travels, and Discoveries, from the Time of Columbus to the Present Period* (London, 1796), vol. 1 [CIHM # 37595], 97–101.

24 John Reinhold Forster, *History of the Voyages and Discoveries Made in the North*, trans. from the German [Frankfurt, 1784] (Dublin, 1786) [CIHM # 35172], 266–9. On Forster's influence, see Winship, *Cabot Bibliography*, 130.

25 [Etienne Maurice Chompré], *Histoire générale des voyages* (Paris, 1746–1761) [CIHM # 50060–79]; see vol. 12 (1754), 99, and vol. 15 (1759), 92–3.

26 Abbé Guillaume-Thomas-François Raynal, *A Philosophical and Political History of the British Settlements and Trade in North America* (Edinburgh, 1776), vol. 1 [CIHM # 27344], 68; Alexander von Humboldt, *Examen critique de l'histoire de la géographie du nouveau continent* (Paris, 1836–9), cited in Winship, *Cabot Bibliography*, 145. There were French authors who recognized John, e.g., Georges-Marie Butel-Dumont, *Histoire et commerce de colonies angloises dans l'Amérique septentrionale* (London, 1755), 28.

27 Biddle, *Memoir of Sebastian*. Roberto Perin, 'La découverte canadienne de Jean Cabot ou les emplois de l'histoire,' in R. Momoli Zorzi and U. Tucci, eds, *Venezia e I Caboto: Le relazioni Italo-Canadesi* (Venice, 1992), 103–18, a thought-provoking discussion of the later historiography of the Cabots, blunders on this issue, seeing Biddle as the paladin of John.

28 Biddle, *Memoir of Sebastian*, 41–52.

29 Ibid., 44.

30 Winship, *Cabot Bibliography*, 111–12.

31 J.F. Nicholls, *The Remarkable Life, Adventures and Discoveries of Sebastian Cabot of Bristol* (London, 1869); Henry Stevens, 'Sebastian Cabot – John Cabot = 0,' *Boston Daily Advertiser*, 19 March 1870 (repr. London, 1870). Stevens was a biased reviewer; he had just published *Historical and Geographical Notes on the Earliest Discoveries in America, 1453–1530* ... (1869; repr. New York, 1970).

32 R.A. Skelton, 'Cabot, Sebastian,' in George W. Brown and Marcel Trudel, eds, *Dictionary of Canadian Biography,* vol. 1, *1000 to 1700* (rev. ed., Toronto, 1979), 153–8.

33 Henry Harrisse, *John Cabot, the Discoverer of North America and Sebastian his Son, a Chapter of the Maritime History of England under the Tudors, 1496–1557* (London, 1896; repr. 1968).

34 Winship, 'Careers of the Cabots,' xvi, in *Cabot Bibliography,* observes that 'there is no evidence of any value to suggest that he did or did not take part ... in the voyages to America in 1497 and 1498.'

35 Wardens of the Drapers Company, 'Answer made to by 1 sent by the Wardens of Mercers,' March 1521, Records of the Drapers' Company of London, transcribed by H.P. Biggar, in Williamson, *Cabot Voyages* (71), conventional contractions, 'joperd,' 'v,' and 'hard' expanded here.

36 Martyr, *Decades* (1516) and 3rd ed. (Alcalá, 1530), Dec. VII, f. xcii b, in Williamson, *Cabot Voyages* (52 and 54); George Best, *A True Discourse of the Late Voyages of Discoverie* (London, 1578), in Williamson, *Cabot Voyages* (66).

37 Winship, 'Careers of the Cabots,' xvii–xviii, in *Cabot Bibliography;* Williamson, *Cabot Voyages,* 159–72; David B. Quinn, *Sebastian Cabot and Bristol Exploration* (1968; rev. ed., 1993), 13; Alwyn A. Ruddock, 'The Reputation of Sebastian Cabot,' *Bulletin of the Institute of Historical Research* 47 (1974), 93–9. Despite the evidence, Samuel Eliot Morison, *The European Discovery of America,* vol. 1, *The Northern Voyages* (New York, 1971), 220, doubts the reality of Sebastian's Labrador voyage of 1508.

38 For the others see Skelton, 'Cabot, Sebastian,' 154.

39 David B. Quinn, *North America from Earliest Discovery to First Settlements: The Norse Voyages to 1612* (New York, 1977), 133–6. Williamson, *Cabot Voyages,* 136, argues that the Bristol expeditions of 1503 to 1505 were already attempts to find a northwest passage. He has no doubt that the voyage of 1508 was such an attempt; see ibid., 152. Andrews, *Trade, Plunder and Settlement,* 49–50, 55, argues that there was no conception of a northwest passage before ca. 1505 and that John Rut's expedition of 1527 was 'the first well-attested English attempt.'

40 Quinn, 'Sebastian Cabot and Bristol Exploration'; Patrick McGrath, 'Bristol and America, 1480–1631,' in K.R. Andrews, N.P. Canny, and

P.E.H. Hair, eds, *The Westward Enterprise: English Activities in Ireland, the Atlantic, and America, 1480–1650* (Liverpool, 1978), 81–102; see p. 89.

41 Henry VII, Writ of Privy Seal to Bristol Customer, 3 April 1505, Public Record Office (PRO) Exchequer, E 368/279, in Ruddock, 'Reputation of Sebastian Cabot,' 98–9. A truncated version recorded in King's Remembrancer, Memoranda Roll, 20 Henry VII, in Williamson, *Cabot Voyages* (51), unfortunately implies that Sebastian had the pension for services simply 'in and aboute' Bristol.

42 Henry VII, 'Of Licence to discover unknown Land,' 9 December 1502, PRO, Patent Roll 18 Henry VII, p. 2, membr. 29–30, trans. H.P. Biggar, in Williamson, *Cabot Voyages* (47).

43 Ruddock, 'Reputation of Sebastian Cabot.'

44 Andrews, *Trade, Plunder and Settlement*, 54–7.

45 Skelton, 'Cabot, Sebastian.'

46 On the *padrón real* see Harry Kelsey, 'The Planispheres of Sebastian Cabot and Sancho Gutiérrez,' *Terrae Incognitae* 19 (1987), 41–58.

47 Winship, 'Careers of the Cabots,' xviii–xvix. On the *Casa de Conratación* and the duties of the *piloto mayor* see D.W. Waters, 'Science and the Techniques of Navigation in the Renaissance,' 213, in Charles S. Singleton, ed., *Art, Science and History in the Renaissance* (Baltimore, 1967), 189–237, and Ursula Lamb, 'The Sevillian Lodestone: Science and Circumstance,' *Terrae Incognitae* 19 (1987), 29–39.

48 Waters, 'Science and Navigation.'

49 Winship, 'Careers of the Cabots,' xxi–xxii and xxxiii; Williamson, *Cabot Voyages*, 150–1.

50 Winship, 'Careers of the Cabots,' xix–xx; Skelton, 'Cabot, Sebastian,' 155.

51 The discovery was not reported until 1522, with the return of the the survivors of the expedition.

52 Roger Barlow, who accompanied Sebastian on the expedition, wrote up new observations on the region in his *Brief Summe of Geographie* (1541); see Andrews, *Trade, Plunder and Settlement*, 54. On de Solis, see Waters, 'Navigation in the Renaissance,' 213.

53 Winship, 'Careers of the Cabots,' xxii–xxxii.

54 Ursula Lamb, 'Science by Litigation: A Cosmographic Feud,' *Terrae Incognitae* 1 (1969), 40–58.

55 Skelton, 'Cabot, Sebastian,' 157.

56 For discussions of these issues see C. Koeman, 'The Chart Trade in Europe from Its Origins to Modern Times,' *Terrae Incognitae* 12 (1980), 49–64, and Elizabeth L. Eisenstein, *The Printing Revolution in Early Modern Europe* (1983; repr. Cambridge, 1993), 197–205.

57 'Censorship over Spanish maps' is propounded by Samuel Edward Dawson, 'The Voyages of the Cabots – Latest Phases of the Controversy,' *Transactions of the Royal Society of Canada* (2nd ser.) 3 (1897), sect. II, 139–267, and has crept into some subsequent Canadian discussions. For a contemporary rebuttal, see Harrisse, *John Cabot* (1896), 71–5.

58 Lamb, 'Science by Litigation.'

59 Kelsey, 'Planispheres of Cabot and Gutiérrez.'

60 Harrisse, *John Cabot* (1896), 86–108, and *Découverte et évolution cartographique dè Terre-Neuve et des pays circonvoisins, 1497–1501–1769* (1900; repr. Ridgewood, NJ, 1968), 177–80; R.A. Skelton in Williamson, *Cabot Voyages*, 59n.

61 Charles Deane, 'The Voyages of the Cabots,' in Justin Winsor, ed., *Narrative and Critical History of America* (Boston, 1884), 3: 1–58; see p. 20.

62 Harrisse, *Evolution cartographique de Terre-Neuve*, 179.

63 Kelsey, 'Planispheres of Cabot and Gutiérrez.' Sancho was the son of Diego Gutiérrez.

64 Cited in Skelton, 'Cabot, Sebastian,' 157.

65 E.G.R. Taylor, *The Haven-Finding Art: A History of Navigation from Odysseus to Captain Cook*, 2nd ed. (London, 1971), 194; D.W. Waters, 'The English Pilot: English Sailing Directions and Charts and the Rise of English Shipping, 16th to 18th Centuries,' *Journal of Navigation* 42(1) (1989), 317–54.

66 David W. Waters, *The Art of Navigation in England in Elizabethan and Early Stuart Times* (London, 1958), plate 1, facing p. 3, and 83–6.

67 Henry Harrisse, 'The Date of Cabot's Discovery of the American Continent' and 'An alleged forgery by Chatterton. A rejoinder,' reprinted from *Notes and Queries*, 14 August 1897 (London, 1897) [CIHM # 06775], 12; but see Winship, 'Careers of the Cabots,' xxii.

68 Andrews, *Trade, Plunder and Settlement*, 223–55; C.R. Boxer, *The Dutch Seaborne Empire, 1600–1800* (1965; repr. London, 1988), 1–33.

69 Ferdinand of Spain, Letter to Sebastian Cabot, 13 September 1512, Seville, Archivo General de Indias, est. 139, caj. I, leg. 5, liv. IV, f. 19v, transcribed by H.P. Biggar, in Williamson, *Cabot Voyages* (69); Winship, 'Careers of the Cabots,' xxiv; Williamson, *Cabot Voyages*, 150.
70 Winship, 'Careers of the Cabots,' xxxii–xxxiii.
71 Martyr, *Decades* (1516); cf. Gerald Panting, 'The Italians as Free-lancers in the Opening of the North Atlantic, 1400–1600,' in Zorzi and Tucci, *Venezia e I Caboto*, 47–51.
72 *The Voyages of Jacques Cartier*, with an introduction by Ramsay Cook (Toronto, 1993); Fernand Braudel and Michel Mollat du Jourdin, eds, *Le monde de Jacques Cartier: L'aventure au XVIe siècle* (Montreal, 1984).
73 Andrews, *Trade, Plunder and Settlement*, 64–75. There was an English trade to the Levant, ca. 1511–34, and to Brazil, ca. 1530–42; see ibid., 59, 87–8.
74 Stephen Borough, 'The Navigation and discoverie toward the river of Ob,' in Hakluyt, *Principal Navigations*, 2: 322–44.
75 The original Latin reads: 'Effigie. Sebastiani Caboti Angli. Filii. Johanis Caboti. Veneti. Militis Avrati. Primi. inventoris. Terrae nova sub Henrico VII. Angllae Rege' (conventional contractions expanded and word divisions regularized); see Winship, *Cabot Bibliography*, 28. The translation is from Morison, *Northern Voyages*, 223.
76 Andrews, *Trade, Plunder and Settlement*, 7.
77 The title is borrowed from G.W.F. Prowse, 'Sebastian Cabot Lied,' typescript (Winnipeg, 1942), on file at Centre for Newfoundland Studies, Memorial University of Newfoundland.
78 Williamson, *Cabot Voyages*, passim.
79 Harrisse, 'Date of Cabots Discovery,' 12.
80 Paris World Map, 1544, Legend 8, trans. C. Raymond Beazley, in Williamson, *Cabot Voyages* (21). For a slightly different translation and the original texts, given in Latin and Spanish, see Charles Deane, 'The Legends of the Cabot Map of 1544,' *Transactions of the Royal Society of Canada* (2nd ser.) 3 (1897), 430–50.
81 The landfall is identified by the words 'Prima Tierra Vista' inscribed on the map in the Gulf of St Lawrence, near Cape Breton.
82 Williamson, *Cabot Voyages*, 25–9.
83 Kelsey, 'Planispheres of Cabot and Gutiérrez.'

84 Winship, *Cabot Bibliography,* 13–16; R.A. Skelton, 'The Cartography of the Voyages,' in Williamson, *Cabot Voyages,* 295–325; see pp. 322–4.
85 Clement Adams, 'An extract taken out of a map of Sebastian Cabot ...,' in Hakluyt, *Principal Navigations,* 7: 146.
86 Williamson, *Cabot Voyages,* 25.
87 M. d'Avezac, 'Les navigations terre-neuviennes de Jean and Sébastien Cabot. Lettre au révérend Léonard Woods' (Paris, 1869), repr. in *Documentary History of the State of Maine,* vol. 1, J.G. Kohl, *History of the Discovery of Maine,* Collections of the Maine Historical Society (2nd ser.) (Portland, 1869) [CIHM # 07362], 121–63; Harrisse, 'Date of Cabot's Discovery.'
88 He may also have used experiences from his possible voyage of 1504.
89 Martyr, *Decades* (1516) and (1530) and *Historia* (1534).
90 Martyr, *Decades* (1516).
91 Miren Egaña Goya and Brad Loewen, 'Dans le sillage des morutiers basques du Moyen Age: Une perspective sur l'origine et la diffusion du mot bacallao,' in Jean Bourgoin and Jacqueline Carpine-Lancre, eds, *L'aventure maritime, du golfe de Gascogne à Terre-Neuve* (Paris, 1995), 235–50.
92 Martyr, *Historia* (1534).
93 Harrisse made this point, and others reconsidered in this chapter, in spades, in *John Cabot* (1896), 115–25.
94 On Ribault and Sebastian see Taylor, *Haven-Finding Art,* 194.
95 Richard Eden, *The Decades of the newe worlde or west India* [London, 1555], sig. cl, in Williamson, *Cabot Voyages* (62).
96 Giovanni Battista Ramusio, *Primo Volume delle Navigationi et Viaggi* [Venice, 1550], ff. 398–403, in Williamson, *Cabot Voyages* (56). The land at 56 degrees north does not actually turn east, although it might be said to in terms of local magnetic north. 'Florida' at this time often meant the whole Atlantic seaboard, north to Maine.
97 'A discourse of Sebastian Cabot ...,' in Hakluyt, *Principal Navigations,* 7: 147–9.
98 Winship, *Cabot Bibliography,* 28–9. Waters, *Art of Navigation,* xiii, sticks by the attribution.
99 The copy made in 1838 for the Massachusetts Historical Society is reproduced in Morison, *Northern Voyages,* 223; the copy made for the

New York Historical Society in 1841 is reproduced as the frontis-
piece to Waters, *Art of Navigation*, plate 1, facing p. 3. I suspect the
Massachusetts version is somewhat idealized.

100 John M. Walsh and John G. Butt, *Newfoundland Specialized Stamp
Catalogue* (St John's, 1992), 8; Thomas F. Nemec, 'Postage Stamps,'
in Cyril F. Poole, ed., *Encyclopedia of Newfoundland and Labrador*, vol.
4 (St John's, 1993), 412–25.

101 On Ord see Williamson, *Cabot Voyages*, 29.

102 Daybook Entry, Household Books, 10–11 August 1497, PRO E 101/
414, in Williamson, *Cabot Voyages* (26). Ord's transcript is in the
British Library, Add ms 7099, 12 Henry VII, f. 41; see Winship,
Cabot Bibliography.

103 Lorenzo Pasqualigo, Letter to his brothers in Venice, 23 August
1497, in Marin Sanuto, ms *Diarii*, Venice, Biblioteca Marciana, mss
Ital. Cl. VII, Cod. 417 (vol. 1), f. 374v, trans. H.P. Biggar; Raimondo
de Raimondi de Soncino, Letter to the Duke of Milan, 18 December
1497; both in Williamson, *Cabot Voyages* (22 and 24).

104 Winship, *Cabot Bibliography*, 7–8.

105 *Mémoires des commissaires du roi et de ceux de sa majesté Britannique*,
vol. 4, *Contenant les derniers Mémoires sur l'Acadie* ... (Paris, 1757)
[CIHM # 36851].

106 *Mémoires des commissaires*, 4, 488–9.

107 Winship, *Cabot Bibliography*, 154–5. 'Diplomatist' in the first line is
probably an error for 'diplomats' or 'diplomatists.'

108 D'Avezac, 'Les navigations terre-neuviennes' (1869); Kohl, *Discov-
ery of Maine* (1869); Richard Henry Major, 'The True Date of the
English Discovery of the American Continent under John and
Sebastian Cabot,' repr. from *Archaeologia* 43 (1871), 17–42 (London,
1870) [CIHM # 26558]; Henry Harrisse, 'When Did John Cabot Dis-
cover North America?' *Forum* (April, 1897), 463–75, and Henry
Harrisse, *The Discovery of North America by John Cabot*, 3rd ed.
(London, 1897) [CIHM # 12913].

CHAPTER 4: THE MANY LANDFALLS

1 H.A. Innis, 'Recent Books on the American Arctic,' *Canadian Historical Review* 22 (1941), 187.

2 Edmund Burke, *An Account of the European Settlements in America*, (London, 1757) [CIHM # 32610], 133.

3 Charles Leigh, 'A Voyage to Cape Breton' [1597], in Richard Hakluyt, *The Principal Navigations* ... [1600], vol. 8 (London, 1904), 166–80, and Franscisco de Cazanova, Examination, Public Record Office (PRO), High Court of Admiralty, HCA 13/91; both in D.B. Quinn, ed., *New American World: A Documentary History of North America to 1612*, vol. 4, *Newfoundland from Fishery to Colony. Northwest Passage Searches* (New York, 1979), 68–75 and 78–9.

4 For 'Terres Neufves' see Y. Raymond (1533) in H.P. Biggar, *The Precursors of Jacques Cartier, 1497–1534: A Collection of Documents Relating to the Early History of the Dominion of Canada*, Publications of the Canadian Archives no. 5 (Ottawa, 1911), 181–2.

5 Marc Lescarbot, *Histoire de la Nouvvelle-France*, in W.L. Grant, ed., *The History of New France by Marc Lescarbot*, Champlain Society (1907–14; repr. New York, 1968), 580.

6 PRO, Household Books, 1502, E 101/415, and Daybook, 1503, British Library (BL), Add ms 7099; both in Williamson, *Cabot Voyages* (26 iii and iv). Cf. G.M. Story, W.J. Kirwin, and J.D.A. Widdowson, eds, *Dictionary of Newfoundland English* (Toronto, 1982), 'newfoundland.'

7 PRO, Household Books, 1497–8, E 101/414 6 and 16, in Williamson, *Cabot Voyages* (26 i).

8 For an example of this argument see Daniel W. Prowse, 'The Discovery of Newfoundland by John Cabot in 1497,' repr. from the *Royal Gazette* (St John's, 1897), 9; for an early critique see C. Raymond Beazley, *John and Sebastian Cabot; the Discovery of North America* (London, 1898), 71; cf. D.B. Quinn, 'Newfoundland in the Consciousness of Europe in the Sixteenth and Seventeenth Centuries,' in G.M. Story, ed., *Early European Settlement and Exploitation in Atlantic Canada* (St John's, 1982), 9–30.

9 [Richard Biddle], *A Memoir of Sebastian Cabot* (London, 1831), 52.

10 John Dee, 'A brief remembrance of sundry foreign Regions ...,' 1578, BL, Cotton ms Aug.I.i.1, in Williamson, *Cabot Voyages* (14).

11 Robert Fabyan, 'Chronicle,' in Richard Hakluyt, 'A note of Sebastian Cabots first discoverie of part of the Indies ...' [1599–1600], in Williamson, *Cabot Voyages* (31 iii).

12 David B. Quinn, 'John Cabot's Matthew,' letter to the editor, *Times*

Literary Supplement, 8 June 1967, 517; Samuel Purchas, *Hakluytus Posthumus or Purchas his Pilgrimes: Contayning a History of the World in Sea Voyages and Lande Travells by Englishmen and Others* [1625], Hakluyt Society (extra ser.), vol. 14 (Glasgow, 1906), 300.

13 Thomas Lediard, *The Naval History of England* (London, 1735), 1: 86; John Campbell, 'The History of Sir John Cabot,' in *Lives of the Admirals*, vol. 1 (London, 1750) [CIHM # 33212], 326–31; cf. William Mavor, *Historical Account of the Most Celebrated Voyages, Travels, and Discoveries, from the Time of Columbus to the Present Period*, vol. 1 (London, 1796) [CIHM # 37595], 98.

14 [Etienne Maurice Chompré], *Histoire générale des voyages* (Paris, 1746–61) [CIHM # 50060–79]; see vol. 12 (1754), 99, and vol. 15 (1759), 92–3; Abbé Guillaume-Thomas-François Raynal, *A Philosophical and Political History of the British Settlements and Trade in North America* (Edinburgh, 1776), vol. 1 [CIHM # 27344], 68; William Canniff, *History of the Province of Ontario* (Toronto, 1872), 3, and William Kingsford, *The History of Canada* (Toronto, 1887), 2, both cited in Roberto Perin, 'La découverte canadienne de Jean Cabot ou les emplois de l'histoire,' in R. Momoli Zorzi and U. Tucci, eds, *Venezia e I Caboto: Le relazioni Italo-Canadesi* (Venice, 1992), 103–18; Edward John Payne, *History of the New World Called America* (Oxford, 1892), 213. It took Payne 210 pages to get to the Cabots.

15 John Reinhold Forster, *History of the Voyages and Discoveries Made in the North* (1784; trans. from the German, Dublin, 1786), 267.

16 Lewis Amadeus Anspach, *A History of the Island of Newfoundland* (London, 1819), 27–8.

17 On Anspach see 'Anspach, Rev. Lewis Amadeus,' in Joseph R. Smallwood and Robert D.W. Pitt, eds, *Encyclopedia of Newfoundland and Labrador*, vol. 1 (St John's, 1981). Winship, *Cabot Bibliography*, 130, describes Forster's *Voyages and Discoveries* as an 'important work, which exerted a considerable influence at the time of its appearance.'

18 Anspach, *History of Newfoundland*, 8 and 20, cites Forster, *History of Discoveries in the North* on the Norse voyages.

19 Philip Tocque, *Newfoundland: As It Was and as It Is in 1877*, (Toronto, 1878), 1–2; Rev. Charles Pedley, *The History of Newfoundland, from the Earliest Times to the Year 1860* (London, 1863), 5–6.

20 M.F. Howley, 'Cabot's Landfall,' *Magazine of American History* 26
    (1891) [CIHM # 17806], 267–88; *Cabot's Voyages: A Lecture Delivered in
    St Patrick's Hall for the Athenaeum, St John's, Newfoundland* (St John's,
    1897); 'Latest Lights on the Cabot Controversy,' *Transactions of the
    Royal Society of Canada* (2nd ser.) 9 (1903), sect. II, 205–15.
21 'Prowse, Daniel Woodley,' in Cyril F. Poole and Robert H. Cuff, eds,
    Encyclopedia of Newfoundland and Labrador, vol. 4 (St John's, 1993).
22 D.W. Prowse, *A History of Newfoundland from the English, Colonial and
    Foreign Records* (1895; repr. Belleville, ON, 1972), 30n, 106; 'Discovery
    of Newfoundland' (1897); 'Cabot's Landfall, the Claims of New-
    foundland Stoutly Defended and Those of Cape Breton Strongly
    Contested,' Halifax *Morning Chronicle*, 7 August 1897.
23 Prowse, 'Discovery of Newfoundland,' 10.
24 Samuel Edward Dawson, 'The Voyages of the Cabots – Latest Phases
    of the Controversy,' *Transactions of the Royal Society of Canada* (2nd
    ser.) 3 (1897), sect. II, 139–267; see p. 142. Cf. Beazley, *John and
    Sebastian Cabot*, 71.
25 Cf. Daniel Prowse, Letter to Archbishop Michael Howley, 27 April
    1909, Roman Catholic Archdiocesan Archives, St John's, Howley
    Papers 106/5/11.
26 James E. Candow, *Daniel Woodley Prowse and the Origin of Cabot
    Tower*, Parks Canada Research Bulletin no. 155 (Ottawa, 1981); Jiri
    Smrz, 'Cabot and Newfoundland Identity: The 1897 Celebrations,'
    unpub. honours B.A. dissertation, Memorial University of New-
    foundland, 1994.
27 *Times* (London), 27 June 1897, and Marquis of Dufferin and Ava,
    Scribner's Magazine, July 1897, 72–5; both cited in Henry Harrisse,
    The Outcome of the Cabot Quater-Centenary, repr. *American Histori-
    cal Review* 4 (1898), 38–61 (New York, 1898) [CHIM # 06777], 17.
28 G.R.F. Prowse, 'The Voyage of John Cabot in 1497 to North America,
    the Time Occupied in Coasting also the Island of St John,' repr. from
    Notes and Queries (8th ser.) 12 (1897), 208–10 (Bradford, 1897); 'The
    Cabot Landfall,' in *Report of the Eighth International Geographic Con-
    gress, held in the United States 1904* (1905; repr. Nendeln, Liechten-
    stein, 1972), 905–12.
29 G.R.F. Prowse, 'Cabot's Surveys,' self-pubished typescript (Win-
    nipeg, 1931); 'Sebastian Cabot Lied' (Winnipeg, 1942), etc. These are

on file at the Centre for Newfoundland Studies, Memorial University of Newfoundland.

30　W.A. Munn, 'John Cabot's Landfall,' paper presented to the Newfoundland Historical Society, 1936, *Newfoundland Quarterly* 36(1) (1936), 5–11; *John Cabot Supplement, 1497–1947, Evening Telegram,* St John's, 23 June 1947.

31　Cf. Marshall McLuhan, *The Mechanical Bride: Folklore of Industrial Man* (Boston, 1968).

32　W.A. Munn, 'John Cabot's Landfall,' *Newfoundland Quarterly* 36(1) (1936), 5–11; Shannon Ryan, 'Newfoundland, Fishery to Canadian Province,' 9, in E. Boyde Beck, Greg Marquis, Joan M. Paysant, and Shannon Ryan, *Atlantic Canada at the Dawn of a New Nation* (Halifax, 1990), 7–43; Fabian O'Dea, 'Cabot's Landfall – Yet Again,' in Barbara Farrell and Aileen Desbarats, eds, *Explorations in the History of Canadian Mapping: A Collection of Essays,* Association of Canadian Map Libraries and Archives (Ottawa, 1988), 55–68.

33　E.g., Newfoundland and Labrador [Department of Tourism], 'Cabot and His World Symposium' (St John's, n.d., ca. 1996).

34　Innis, 'Recent Books'; M.F. Howley, 'Latest Lights on Cabot.'

35　Curtis Rumbolt, 'No "debate" over Cabot's landfall,' *Express* (St John's), 10 July 1996.

36　W.E. Cormack, *Narrative of a Journey Across the Island of Newfoundland* (St John's, 1856), 6. Rev. Moses Harvey edited a later reprint (St John's, 1873).

37　L.E.F. English, *Historic Newfoundland,* Newfoundland Tourist Development Division (St John's, 1955), 14.

38　Anon., 'The Grates Cove Stone,' *Newfoundland Quarterly* 54(4) (1955), 48; Allan R. Guy, 'The "Cabot Rock" at Grate's Cove,' *Atlantic Guardian* 13(4) (1956), 27–8. I am endebted to Joan Ritcey of the Centre for Newfoundland Studies for drawing my attention to these useful articles and to Ken Reynolds for discussion of the evidence.

39　Peter E. Pope, 'The South Avalon Planters, 1630 to 1700: Residence, Labour, Demand and Exchange in Seventeenth-Century Newfoundland,' unpub. Ph.D. dissertation, Memorial University of Newfoundland, 1992, 282–3.

40　Samuel Eliot Morison, *The European Discovery of America,* vol. 1, *The Northern Voyages* (New York, 1971), 202–3. For a very weak argument

that Cabot was marooned near Grates Cove in 1498, see Arthur
Davies, 'The Last Voyage of John Cabot and the Rock at Grates
Cove,' *Nature* 176(4491) (1955), 996–9. For an explanation of why
scholars are wary of such historically convenient inscriptions, see
Birgitta Linderoth Wallace, 'The Vikings in North America: Myth
and Reality,' in Ross Samson, ed., *Social Approaches to Viking Studies*
(Glasgow, 1991), 207–19.

41 Guy, 'Cabot Rock,' 28.
42 Beazley, *John and Sebastian Cabot*, 73; E.G.R. Taylor, 'Where Did the
    Cabots Go? A Study in Historical Deduction,' *Geographical Journal*
    129 (1963), 339–41.
43 Jack Dodd, *Cabot's Voyage to Newfoundland* (n.p., 1974), 41–5.
44 Jeremy Belknap, 'John Cabot and Sebastian Cabot,' *American
    Biography: or, An Historical Account of Those Persons Who Have
    Been Distinguished in America* (Boston, 1794), vol. 1 [CIHM # 48979],
    149–58.
45 Biddle, *Memoir of Sebastian*, 52–6.
46 I have not seen George Bancroft, *A History of the United States of
    America, from the Discovery of the American Continent to the Present
    Time* (Boston, 1834), vol. 1; but have used *History of the United States
    of America, from the Discovery of the Continent* (New York, 1883), vol. 1
    [CIHM # 61407], 9–11.
47 Bancroft is described as 'le grand historien des Etats Unis' by M.A.P.
    d'Avezac, *Les navigations terre-neuviennes de Jean and Sébastien Cabot.
    Lettre au révérend Léonard Woods*, L'Institut de France (Paris, 1869), 6.
    On the encylopedia articles see Winship, *Cabot Bibliography*, 107–8.
48 J.G. Kohl, *Documentary History of the State of Maine*, vol. 1, *History of
    the Discovery of Maine*, Collections of the Maine Historical Society
    (2nd ser.) (Portland, 1869) [CIHM # 07362], 121–63; see pp. 126, 132.
49 Henry Harrisse, *The Discovery of North America by John Cabot*, 3rd ed.
    (London, 1897) [CIHM # 12913], 3.
50 Brian Cuthbertson, 'John Cabot and His Historians, Five Hundred
    Years of Controversy,' paper presented to the Royal Nova Scotia
    Historical Society, 15 May 1996.
51 Henry Harrisse, *Jean et Sébastien Cabot, leur origine et leurs voyages*
    (Paris, 1882; repr. Amsterdam, 1968); *The Discovery of North America,
    a Critical, Documentary, and Historic Investigation* (London and Paris,

1892; repr. Amsterdam, 1961); *Découverte et évolution cartographique de Terre-Neuve et des pays circonvoisins, 1497–1501–1769* (Paris, 1900; repr. Ridgewood, NJ, 1968)

52 Harrisse treats Dawson courteously, although he does not really take him seriously; he does not mention Prowse, at whom Dawson pokes such fun; see Harrisse, 'Outcome of the Cabot Quater-Centenary.'

53 Harrisse, *Jean et Sébastien Cabot*, 61–96. He is wrongly accused of accepting a Cape Breton landfall in this work by Samuel Edward Dawson, 'The Voyages of the Cabots in 1497 and 1498; with an Attempt to Determine Their Landfall and to Identify Their Island of St John,' *Transactions of the Royal Society of Canada* (1st ser.) 12 (1894), sect. II, 51–112, see p. 54, and 'Voyages of the Cabots' (1897), 141; cf. Henry Harrisse, 'The Cabots,' *Transactions of the Royal Society of Canada* (2nd ser.) 4 (1898), sect. II, 103–6.

54 Harrisse, *Jean et Sébastien*, 96; *Discovery of North America* (1892), 6–9; *John Cabot, the Discoverer of North America and Sebastian His Son, a Chapter of the Maritime History of England under the Tudors, 1496–1557* (1896; repr. London, 1968), plate 1, facing p. 108, and passim; *Discovery by John Cabot* (1897), 26; and 'When Did John Cabot Discover North America?' *Forum*, April 1897, 463–75.

55 Samuel Edward Dawson, 'The Voyages of the Cabots in 1497 and 1498 – a Sequel to a Paper in the "Transactions" of 1894,' *Transactions of the Royal Society of Canada* (2nd ser.) 2 (1896), sect. II, 3–29; Harrisse, 'The Cabots,' 104, and *Discovery of North America* (1892), plate 1, facing p. 8; John Boyd Thacher, 'The Cabotian Discovery,' *Transactions of the Royal Society of Canada* (2nd ser.) 3 (1897), 279–307.

56 John Day, Letter to the Grand Admiral, ca. 1497 in Williamson, *Cabot Voyages* (25).

57 For another view see Taylor, 'Where Did the Cabots Go?'

58 J.-B.-A. Ferland, *Cours d'histoire du Canada* (Québec, 1861) [CIHM # 44499]; C.-H. Laverdière, *Histoire du Canada* (Québec, 1869) [CIHM # 08878]; cf. Dawson, 'Voyages of the Cabots' (1897), 144.

59 James Patrick Howley, 'The Landfall of Cabot,' *Bulletin-Transactions of the Geographical Society of Quebec* 1 (1889), 67–78, proposes a landfall near Domino.

60 Payne, *History of the New World*, 210–13; M.F. Howley, 'Cabot's Landfall' (1891) and 'Latest Lights' (1903); Theodore Layng,

'Charting the Course to Canada,' *Congresso Internacional de História dos Descobrimentos, Lisbon, 1960. Actas* 1(2) (1961), 255–76; Robert McGhee, *Canada Rediscovered* (n.p. [Montreal], 1991), 88–90; G.J. Marcus, *The Conquest of the North Atlantic* (New York, 1981); Kirsten A. Seaver, *The Frozen Echo, Greenland and the Exploration of North America, ca. A.D. 1000–1500* (Stanford, CA, 1996). This approach is discussed in chapter 6.

61 Melvin Jackson, 'The Labrador Landfall of John Cabot, 1497,' *Canadian Historical Review* 54 (1963), 122–41. The itinerary proposed for the rest of the voyage, down the west coast of Newfoundland, leaving the Gulf by the Cabot Strait, is not very convincing.

62 Belknap, 'John and Sebastian Cabot,' 153.

63 Thomas C. Haliburton, *An Historical and Statistical Account of Nova-Scotia* (Halifax, 1829), 2–4. Winship, *Cabot Bibliography,* 134, is in error in ascribing a landfall of 'Trinity Bay, Nova Scotia' (*sic*) to Haliburton, as is Cuthbertson, 'Cabot and His Historians.'

64 William Canniff, *History of the Province of Ontario* (Toronto, 1872), 3, and William Kingsford, *The History of Canada* (Toronto, 1887), 2; both cited in Perin, 'La découverte de Jean Cabot,' 105.

65 Dawson, 'Voyages of the Cabots' (1897), 142.

66 Richard Brown, *A History of the Island of Cape Breton with Some Account of the Discovery and Settlement of Canada, Nova Scotia, and Newfoundland* (London, 1869) [CIHM # 314], 8–11.

67 James Hannay, *The History of Acadia: From Its First Discovery to Its Surrender to England by the Treaty of Paris* (Saint John, NB, 1879), 4–5.

68 Charles Deane, 'The Voyages of the Cabots,' in Justin Winsor, ed., *Narrative and Critical History of America* (Boston, 1884), 3: 1–58, see p. 20; Winship, *Cabot Bibliography,* 105–6.

69 d'Avezac, *Les navigations terre-neuviens.*

70 Charles Deane, 'Remarks on Sebastian Cabot's Mappe-monde,' repr. from *Proceedings of the American Antiquarian Society,* April 1867 (Cambridge, 1867) [CIHM # 27819].

71 Winship, *Cabot Bibliography,* 13–16, cites 'Jomard, *Monuments de la Géographie* [1862], plate xx.' Deane, 'Sebastian Cabot's Mappe-monde,' 1n, notes that Jomard omitted the marginal legends.

72 Frederic Kidder, 'The Discovery of North Ameica by John Cabot,' lecture to Maine Historical Society, Bath, 17 February 1874 (repr. in

New England Historical and Genealogical Register, October 1878 [CIHM # 19008], 10), cites J. Carson Brevoort, 'Early Voyages from Europe to America. 2. John Cabot's Voyage of 1497,' *Historical Magazine* (Morrisania, NY) (2nd ser.) 3 (1868), 129–35, cf. Winship, *Cabot Bibliography,* 114; J.F. Nicholls, *The Remarkable Life, Adventures and Discoveries of Sebastian Cabot of Bristol* (London, 1869), 59.

73 Henry Stevens, *Historical and Geographical Notes on the Earliest Discoveries in America 1453–1530, with comments on the earliest charts and maps; the mistakes of the early navigators & the blunders of the geographers ...* (1869; repr. New York, 1970), plate iv, no. 1.

74 On the facsimiles see Dawson, 'Voyages of the Cabots' (1897), 143; Douglas Brymner, *Report on Canadian Archives 1897,* Appendix to Report of the Minister of Agriculture (Ottawa, 1898).

75 Nicholls, *Remarkable Life of Sebastian Cabot,* 63; Henry Stevens, 'Sebastian Cabot – John Cabot = 0,' repr. from *Boston Daily Advertiser,* 19 March 1870 (London, 1870), 17, and cf. *Earliest Discoveries in America* (1869), 17–18.

76 Kidder, 'Discovery of North America,' 10–11.

77 Deane, 'Voyages of the Cabots,' 24.

78 J.G. Bourinot, 'Cape Breton and Its Memorials of the French Regime,' *Transactions of the Royal Society of Canada* 9 (1891), 173–343; see 176–80.

79 Clements R. Markham, *The Journal of Christopher Columbus (during the First Voyage, 1492–93), and Documents Relating to the Voyages of John Cabot and Gaspar Corte Real,* Hakluyt Society (London, 1893), xv; 'Fourth Centenary of the Voyage of John Cabot, 1497,' presidential address, *Geographical Journal* 9(6) (1897), 604–20, see p. 608.

80 Dawson, 'Voyages of the Cabots' (1894), (1896), and (1897).

81 In this he followed Stevens, *Earliest Discoveries* (1869).

82 Dawson, 'Voyages of the Cabots' (1897), 163.

83 George E. Nunn, *The Mappemonde of Juan de la Cosa: A Critical Investigation of Its Date* (Jenkintown, PA, 1934), 2; Winship, *Cabot Bibliography,* 38–9; Stevens, *Earliest Discoveries,* plate 1.

84 H.P. Biggar, 'The Voyages of the Cabots and the Corte-Reals to North America and Greenland 1497–1503,' *Revue Hispanique* 10 (1903), 485–92; *Precursors of Cartier,* vii–x; W.F. Ganong, 'Crucial Maps in the Early Cartography and Place-Nomenclature of the Atlantic Coast of

Canada,' I and II, *Transactions of the Royal Society of Canada* (3rd ser.) 23 (1929), 135–75, and 24 (1930), sect. II, 135–88, repr. in W.F. Ganong, *Crucial Maps in the Early Cartography and Place-Nomenclature of the Atlantic Coast of Canada* (Toronto, 1964); John T. Juricek, 'John Cabot's First Voyage,' *Smithsonian Journal of History* 2(4) (1968), 1–22. Because the Day Letter suggests that Cabot believed himself to have been in the latitude of the Strait of Belle Isle, Quinn's revised version of this theory has him coasting eastern Newfoundland northwards on his return trip: see David B. Quinn, *North America from Earliest Discovery to First Settlements: The Norse Voyages to 1612* (New York, 1977), 116.

85 Ganong, *Crucial Maps*; Juricek, 'Cabot's First Voyage.'
86 Winship, *Cabot Bibliography*, 13–16, and cf. xiv; Brymner, *Report on Canadian Archives 1897*.
87 Joseph Hatton and Rev. M. Harvey, *Newfoundland, The Oldest British Colony, Its History, Its Present Condition and Its Prospects for the Future* (London, 1883), 5–6; Rev. M. Harvey, *A Short History of Newfoundland: England's Oldest Colony* (London, 1890), 16, and 'Voyages and Discoveries of the Cabots,' *Collections of the Nova Scotia Historical Society* 9 (1895), 17–37.
88 Charles Deane, 'The Legends of the Cabot Map of 1544,' *Proceedings of the Massachusetts Historical Society* (2nd ser.) 6 (1890–1), repr. in *Transactions of the Royal Society of Canada* (2nd ser.) 3 (1897), 430–50.
89 Archbishop [Cornelius] O'Brien, 'Presidential Address on Cabot's Landfall,' *Proceedings of the Royal Society of Canada* (2nd ser.) 3 (1897), cv–cxxxix; 'Cabot's Landfall and Chart: Some Criticisms Answered,' *Transactions of the Royal Society of Canada* (2nd ser.) 5 (1899), 427–55; quotation from the latter, p. 427.
90 Among twentieth-century scholars this interpretation survives only in aberrant or reverse forms, in Arthur Davies, 'The "English Coasts" on the Map of Juan de la Cosa,' *Imago Mundi* 13 (1956), 26–9, and in Jackson, 'Labrador Landfall.'
91 Francesco Tarducci, *John and Sebastian Cabot. Biographical Notice with Documents* (Detroit, 1893), 56. The original Italian edition was published in 1892; see Winship, *Cabot Bibliography*, 172.
92 L'Abbé J.-D. Beaudouin, 'Jean Cabot,' *Le Canada français* 1 (1888), 608–61, cited in Perin, 'La découverte de Jean Cabot,' 107, and *Jean Cabot* (Lévis, 1898), 50–60.

93 Biggar, 'Voyages of Cabots and Corte-Reals'; *Precursors of Cartier,*
    vii–x; W.F. Ganong, *Crucial Maps.*
94 Innis, 'Recent Books,' 187.
95 In, e.g., Harrisse, *Discovery by John Cabot* (1897).
96 Ian McKay, 'History and the Tourist Gaze: The Politics of Com-
    memoration in Nova Scotia, 1935–1964,' *Acadiensis* 22(2) (1993),
    102–38.
97 L.-A. Vigneras, 'The Cape Breton Landfall: 1494 or 1497: Note on a
    Letter from John Day,' *Canadian Historical Review* 38(3) (1957),
    219–28.
98 Williamson, *Cabot Voyages,* 54–83; R.A. Skelton, 'The Cartography
    of the Voyages,' in Williamson, *Cabot Voyages,* 295–325.
99 Pietro Pasqualigo, Letter to Venice, 19 October 1501, in Williamson,
    Cabot Voyages (38); cf. Williamson, *Cabot Voyages,* 59, 69, and R.A.
    Skelton, 'Cabot (Caboto), John (Giovanni),' in George W. Brown
    and Marcel Trudel, eds, *Dictionary of Canadian Biography,* vol. 1, *1000
    to 1700* (Toronto, 1979), 146–52; see p. 150.
100 Williamson, *Cabot Voyages,* 69. This is to account for a 'wide margin
    of error,' although the northern latitude remains somehow simply
    'northern Newfoundland.'
101 Williamson came to the theory later in his career; he had opted for
    Cape Breton or Newfoundland in a pre-war discussion of the
    subject; see J.A. Williamson, 'The Voyages of John and Sebastian
    Cabot,' Historical Association Pamphlet no. 106 (London, 1937).
102 The only notable exception to this generalization is the Miami his-
    torian David O. True. He accepts the conventional Cape Breton
    landfall, but then takes John Cabot on a coastal voyage south to
    Florida, making this the *reductio ad absurdum* of southern interpre-
    tations of the voyage. See David O. True, 'Some Early Maps
    Relating to Florida,' *Imago Mundi* 11 (1954), 73–84, and 'Cabot
    Explorations in North America,' *Imago Mundi* (1956), 11–25.
103 David B. Quinn, *Sebastian Cabot and Bristol Exploration,* Bristol
    Branch of the Historical Association (1968; rev. ed. 1993), 8; cf.
    Quinn, *North America,* 116; Ian Wilson, *The Columbus Myth: Did Men
    of Bristol Reach America before Columbus?* (London, 1991) and *John
    Cabot and the Matthew* (Tiverton, 1996), 37. I have heard, by word of
    mouth, that Professor Quinn has repented of these views.

104 Skelton, 'Cabot, John.'

105 R.I. Ruggles, 'Exploring the Atlantic Coast,' plate 19 in R.C. Harris and G.J. Matthews, eds, *Historical Atlas of Canada*, vol. 1, *From the Beginning to 1800* (Toronto, 1988); McGhee, *Canada Rediscovered*, 81–92.

106 The Strait of Belle Isle is just south of Harrisse's proposed landfall near Sandwich Bay in southern Labrador. Although the Day Letter almost certainly rules out Harrisse's proposed northern itinerary, it is quite consistent with a landfall in the Strait of Belle Isle.

107 Samuel Eliot Morison, *Admiral of the Ocean Sea, a Life of Christopher Columbus* (Boston, 1942). Brown, *History of Cape Breton* (1869), 11, had put the landfall 'near the northern end of the Straits of Belle Isle,' on the basis of the Pasqualigo letter and the descriptions of Native peoples in the Eighth Legend of the 1544 map, quoted by Hakluyt.

108 Morison, *Northern Voyages*, 157–208

109 Bernard G. Hoffman, *Cabot to Cartier: Sources for an Historical Ethnography of Northeastern North America, 1497–1550* (Toronto, 1961), 16; cf. Harrisse, *Discovery of North America*, 3; Beazley, *John and Sebastian Cabot*, 69.

110 Objections based on the dangers of 'fierce tides' and heavy fogs, raised by an academic who spends his summers on an island in the St Lawrence River, do not seem decisive; but see Jake T.W. Hubbard, 'John Cabot's Landfall: Cape Dégrat or Cape Bonavista? Some Observations,' *American Neptune* 33(3) (1973), 174–7.

111 E.g., Kenneth R. Andrews, *Trade, Plunder and Settlement: Maritime Enterprise and the Genesis of the British Empire, 1480–1630* (Cambridge, 1984), 45

112 Quinn, *North America*, 116–19.

CHAPTER 5: TRADITIONS OF INVENTION, 1897

1 Rev. M. Harvey, 'Voyages and Discoveries of the Cabots,' paper to Nova Scotia Historical Society (1893), in *Collections of the Nova Scotia Historical Society* 9 (1895), 17–37.

2 Simon Schama, 'The Many Deaths of General Wolfe,' *Granta* 32 (1990), 13–56; Roberto Perin, 'La découverte canadienne de Jean

Cabot ou les emplois de l'histoire,' in R. Momoli Zorzi and U. Tucci, eds, *Venezia e I Caboto: Le relazioni Italo-Canadesi* (Venice, 1992), 103–18; cf. Robert H. Fuson, 'The John Cabot Mystique,' in Stanley H. Palmer and Dennis Reinhartz, eds, *Essays on the History of North American Discovery and Exploration* (College Station, TX, 1988), 35–51.

3 Eric Hobsbawm, 'Introduction: Inventing Traditions,' in Eric Hobsbawm and Terence Ranger, eds, *The Invention of Tradition* (1983; repr. Cambridge, Eng., 1992), 1–14, see p. 13.

4 Edward G. Porter, 'The Cabot Quadri-Centenary Celebrations of 1897 at Bristol, Halifax and St John's,' *New England Magazine* 17 (1898), 653–71 (repr. Boston, 1898) [CIHM # 12128]; quotation p. 670.

5 Hobsbawm, 'Introduction: Inventing Traditions' and 'Mass-Producing Traditions: Europe, 1870–1914,' in Hobsbawm and Ranger, eds, *Invention of Tradition*, 263–307.

6 D.W. Prowse, *A History of Newfoundland from the English, Colonial and Foreign Records* (1895; repr. Belleville, ON, 1972).

7 James E. Candow, *Daniel Woodley Prowse and the Origin of Cabot Tower*, Parks Canada Research Bulletin no. 155 (Ottawa, 1981); Jiri Smrz, 'Cabot and Newfoundland Identity: The 1897 Celebrations,' unpub. honours B.A. dissertation, Memorial University of Newfoundland, 1994, 22–34; Shane O'Dea, 'Judge Prowse and Bishop Howley: Cabot Tower and the Construction of Nationalism,' lecture to Newfoundland Historical Society, St John's, 25 April 1996.

8 Cf. Hobsbawm, 'Introduction: Inventing Traditions,' 9.

9 Hobsbawm, 'Mass-Producing Traditions,' 281.

10 E.J. Hobsbawm, *Nations and Nationalism since 1780* (Cambridge, 1990), 101–30; on the word see p. 102.

11 Henry Harrisse, *The Discovery of North America by John Cabot*, 3rd ed. (London, 1897) [CIHM # 12913], 26; Melvin Jackson, 'The Labrador Landfall of John Cabot, 1497,' *Canadian Historical Review* 54 (1963), 122–41. Jackson was Associate Curator of Naval History at the Smithsonian Institution in Washington when he published this article. A notable exception to this generalization is the most coherent version of the la Cosa argument for a Cape Breton landfall: John T. Juricek, 'John Cabot's First Voyage,' *Smithsonian Journal of History* 2(4) (1968), 1–22.

12 Samuel Edward Dawson, 'The Voyages of the Cabots – Latest Phases

of the Controversy,' *Transactions of the Royal Society of Canada* (2nd ser.) 3 (1897), sect. II, 139–267; see pp. 143–5.

13 Samuel Edward Dawson, 'The Voyages of the Cabots in 1497 and 1498 – a Sequel to a Paper in the "Transactions" of 1894,' *Transactions of the Royal Society of Canada* (2nd ser.) 2 (1896), sect. II, 3–29; see p. 5.

14 Samuel Edward Dawson, 'The Voyages of the Cabots in 1497 and 1498; with an Attempt to Determine Their Landfall and to Identify Their Island of St John,' *Transactions of the Royal Society of Canada* (1st ser.) 12 (1894), sect. II, 51–112; see pp. 51–2 and cf. 'Voyages of the Cabots' (1896), 7, 10.

15 M.F. Howley, *Cabot's Voyages: A Lecture Delivered in St Patrick's Hall for the Athenaeum, St John's, Newfoundland* (St John's, 1897), 31.

16 Dawson, 'Voyages of the Cabots' (1897), 219.

17 Dawson, 'Voyages of the Cabots' (1897), 141; *Handbook for the Dominion of Canada* (Montreal, 1884) [CIHM # 03776].

18 Samuel Edward Dawson, *The Northern Kingdom, by A Colonist* (Montreal, 1866); *Episcopal Elections, Ancient and Modern* (Montreal, 1877); *Copyright in Books, an Inquiry into Its Origin, and an Account of the Present State of the Law in Canada* (Montreal, 1882); *A Study, with Critical and Explanatory Notes, of Alfred Tennyson's Poem The Princess* (Montreal, 1882); all in University of Toronto Library catalogue, which lists other similar early publications. In later life Dawson seems to have concentrated on serious travel books, notably the 700-page *Canada and Newfoundland* (London, 1897).

19 'The Cabot Celebration,' *Proceedings of the Royal Society of Canada* (2nd ser.) 2 (1896), xxix–xxxii. Dawson Brothers printed the 1894 *Transactions* for the Royal Society of Canada.

20 Dawson, 'Voyages of the Cabots' (1894), 92.

21 Perin, 'La découverte de Cabot.'

22 Henry Harrisse, *The Outcome of the Cabot Quater-Centenary,* repr. in *American Historical Review* 4 (1898), 38–61 (New York, 1898) [CIHM # 06777], 1. The recent London fabrication would be George Edward Weare, *Cabot's Discovery of North America* (London, 1897); the Bristol contribution to 'barefaced plagiarism' might be J.F. Nicholls, *The Remarkable Life, Adventures and Discoveries of Sebastian Cabot of Bristol* (London, 1869).

23 Isabella published 'John Cabot's Discovery,' in *A Cabot Souvenir Number* (St John's, 1897); Robert Thorburn, 'In Memoriam John Cabot,' *Evening Herald* (St John's), 25 June 1897; both cited in Winship, *Cabot Bibliography* 118, 167–8, 173–4, and see Winship for the reviews and articles that escaped Harrisse's count. Obviously neither had heard Johnny Burke's 'Landfall of Cabot.'

24 Claudia Bushman, *America Discovers Columbus: How an Italian Explorer Became an American Hero* (Hanover, NH, 1992), 158–90. The quotes are from pp. 158 and 182.

25 Perin, 'La découverte de Cabot.'

26 Porter, 'Cabot Celebrations,' 661, cites an article in the *Maritime Monthly Magazine* (1874); Rev. M. Harvey, Letter to S.E. Dawson, *Proceedings of the Royal Society of Canada* 12 (1894), xvii, and cf. M. Harvey, Letter to Dr Bourinot, *Proceedings of the Royal Society of Canada* (2nd ser.) 2 (1896), xxvi–xxviii, and Perin, 'La découverte de Cabot,' 108–9.

27 'Harvey, Moses,' in Joseph R. Smallwood et al., eds, *Encyclopedia of Newfoundland and Labrador*, vol. 2 (St John's, 1984).

28 Winship, *Cabot Bibliography,* 129.

29 Candow, *Origin of Cabot Tower,* 3.

30 Bushman, *America Discovers Columbus,* 22–4, 81–97.

31 O.A. Howland, 'The Fourth Century of Canadian History' and 'The Canadian Historical Exhibition 1897,' *Canadian Magazine* 4, January 1895, and 5, June 1896; the latter repr. Toronto, 1896.

32 'The Canadian Historical Exhibition, 1897,' *The Week*, 8 November 1895 (repr. Toronto, 1895).

33 O.A. Howland and David Boyle, 'The Canadian Historical Exhibition, 1897,' form letter, December 1895, copy in Howley Papers, Roman Catholic Archdiocesan Archives, St John's, 106/5/11; 'Canada's History, A Great Exhibition to Take Place Next Year,' *Globe* (Toronto), 11 February 1896; 'Cabot Anniversary,' *Catholic Register* (Toronto), 13 February 1896.

34 Howland, 'The Canadian Historical Exhibition, 1897,' 4.

35 Quoted in Joseph Pope, 'The Cabot Celebration,' *Canadian Magazine* 8(2) (1896), 158–64.

36 *Catalogue, Canadian Historical Exhibition* (Toronto, 1899) [CIHM # 06968].

37 *First Canadian Historical Exhibition: Held at Victoria College, Queen's Park, Toronto June, 1899, Report of the Secretary and Treasurer* (Toronto, 1900) [CIHM # 06969].

38 Perin, 'La découverte de Jean Cabot,' 111.

39 *Globe* (Toronto), 24 and 25 June 1897. The *Globe* also ran a picture of the proposed Cabot Memorial in Bristol England.

40 Marie Elwood, 'The State Dinner Service of Canada, 1898,' *Material History Bulletin* 3 (1977), 41–9; Elizabeth Collard, *Nineteenth-Century Pottery and Porcelain in Canada*, 2nd ed. (Kingston and Montreal, 1984), 320–1.

41 Archbishop O'Brien, Letter to S.E. Dawson, 31 January 1896, National Archives of Canada, MG 27 I I 36, cited in Perin, 'La découverte de Cabot,' 111.

42 Royal Society of Canada, 'Cabot Celebration' (1896).

43 Harry Piers, 'The Discovery of the Continent,' *Halifax Herald*, part 2, 25 June 1897, 10–11.

44 Royal Society of Canada, 'Cabot Celebration' (1896); 'The Cabot Celebration. Unveiling of the Tablet in Honour of the Italian Navigator,' repr. from Halifax *Herald*, 25 June 1897, in *Proceedings of the Royal Society of Canada* (2nd ser.) 3 (1897), xci–ciii.

45 Porter, 'Cabot Celebrations,' 661–2; Winship, *Cabot Bibliography*, 127; Harrisse, *Outcome of the Cabot Quater-Centenary*, 1.

46 Candow, *Origin of Cabot Tower*, 5, 17, 22.

47 M. Howley, *Cabot's Voyages*; Daniel Woodley Prowse, *The Discovery of Newfoundland by John Cabot in 1497*, repr. from *Royal Gazette* (St John's, 1897).

48 Candow, *Origin of Cabot Tower*, 19.

49 Smrz, 'Cabot and Newfoundland Identity,' 39–42; the quote is cited from *Evening Herald* (St John's), 26 June 1897.

50 Winship, *Cabot Bibliography*, 167–8.

51 Arthur English, *Evening Telegram* (St John's), 4 March 1897, 4, cited in Candow, *Origin of Cabot Tower*, 13.

52 Candow, *Origin of Cabot Tower*, 12ff.

53 *Evening Herald* (St John's), 24 June 1897, cited in Smrz, 'Cabot and Newfoundland Identity,' 39.

54 Cited in Candow, *Origin of Cabot Tower*, 18.

55 'Howley, Most Rev. Michael Francis,' in Smallwood et al., *Encyclopedia of Newfoundland*, vol. 2.
56 M. Howley, *Cabot's Voyages*, 39.
57 M. Howley, *Cabot's Voyages*, 5.
58 S.J.R. Noel, *Politics in Newfoundland* (Toronto, 1971), 21–5.
59 'Cabot Anniversary,' 13 February 1896.
60 'Badge' and 'Flags,' in Smallwood et al., *Encyclopedia of Newfoundland*, vols 1 and 2. I am endebted to James Hiller for drawing these interesting parallels to my attention.
61 *History of Newfoundland*, 6.
62 Prowse, *Discovery by John Cabot*, 1; cf. Joseph Hatton and Rev. M. Harvey, *Newfoundland, the Oldest British Colony, Its History, Its Present Condition, and Its Prospects for the Future* (London, 1883), 2.
63 Moses Harvey, *Text-Book of Newfoundland History, for the Use of Schools and Academies* (London, 1890), v.
64 John Boyd Thacher, 'The Cabotian Discovery,' *Transactions of the Royal Society of Canada* (2nd ser.) 3 (1897), 279–307; see pp. 281, 295.
65 Harvey, 'Voyages of the Cabots,' 20–1. For similar remarks by the United States consul in Bristol and by Lord Dufferin, on laying the cornerstone for the Cabot Memorial Tower there, see Porter, 'Cabot Celebrations,' 661–3.
66 Moses Harvey, *Newfoundland in 1897* (London, 1897), 4–7.
67 Dawson, 'Voyages of the Cabots' (1894), 51, 52.
68 Dawson, 'Voyages of the Cabots' (1896), 12, argues unconvincingly against this reading. Cf. Perin, 'La découverte de Cabot,' 111–12.
69 Jacques Robert, 'L'invention d'un héros,' in Fernand Braudel and Michel Mollat du Jourdin, eds, *Le monde de Jacques Cartier: L'aventure au XVIe siècle* (Montreal, 1984), 295–306; Jacques Mathieu, 'Un événement fondateur: La découverte du Canada. Le personage de Jacques Cartier et son évolution,' in Claire Dolan, ed., *Evénement, identité et histoire* (Sillery, 1991), 255–67.
70 Joseph Olivier Chanveau, cited in Robert, 'L'invention d'un héros,' 301; translation mine.
71 Mathieu, 'Un événement fondateur,' 260.
72 'Cabot Monument in Montreal,' *Newfoundland Quarterly* 55(4) (1956), 5.

73 'The Proposed Cabot Celebration,' *Proceedings of the Royal Society of Canada* (2nd ser.) 2 (1896), xxiii–xxviii; see p. xxviii.

74 N.-E. Dionne, 'Cartier vs Cabot,' *Journal des Campagnes* (Quebec City), ca. 1896, copy on file: RC Archdiocesan Archives, St John's, Howley Papers 106/5/3; cf. *John and Sebastian Cabot* (Quebec, 1898) [CIHM # 18870].

75 *La presse québécoise des origines à nos jours,* vol. 3, *1880–1895* (Quebec, 1977), 55.

76 Translation mine, emphasis in Dionne.

77 Pope, 'Cabot Celebration.'

78 Lucien Campeau, 'Les Cabot et l'Amérique,' *Revue d'histoire de l'Amérique française* 14(3) (1960), 317–52. On Groulx, see Serge Gagnon, *Quebec and Its Historians, 1840 to 1920* (Montreal, 1982), 111–21.

79 Yves Lamontagne, 'History Gives Gaspar Cortereal Credit for Cabot's Discovery of Newfoundland,' *Montreal Star,* 27 July 1959. This mythic effrontery drew the inevitable return fire, in the form of a rebuttal by D.L. Jackman, a Newfoundland-born Montrealer and tireless proponent of a national monument to Cabot; see 'Holds Criticism of Cabot Puts Cart Before Horse,' Letter to the editor, *Montreal Star,* July 1959; both repr. in *Newfoundland Quarterly* 58(3) (1959), 25–6, and cf. Jackman, Letters to editor, *Newfoundland Quarterly* 60(2) (1961), 19, and 60(3) (1961), 19.

80 Porter, 'Cabot Celebrations,' 667.

81 Hobsbawm, 'Mass-Producing Traditions.'

82 Hugh Trevor-Roper, 'The Invention of Tradition: The Highland Tradition of Scotland'; Prys Morgan, 'From a Death to a View: The Hunt for the Welsh Past in the Romantic Period'; David Cannadine, 'The Context, Performance and Meaning of Ritual: The British Monarchy and the "Invention of Tradition," c. 1820–1977,' in Hobsbawm and Ranger, eds, *Invention of Tradition,* 12–42, 43–100, and 101–64.

83 Linda Colley, *Britons: Forging the Nation, 1707–1837* (New Haven, 1992).

84 Carl Berger, *The Sense of Power: Studies in the Ideas of Canadian Imperialism, 1867–1914* (Toronto, 1970), 89–99.

85 Berger, *Sense of Power,* 99.

86 Smrz, 'Cabot and Newfoundland Identity,' 9–18.

87 Hugh Kearney, *The British Isles, a History of Four Nations* (1989; repr. Cambridge, 1995).

88 Samuel Edward Dawson, *The Saint Lawrence, Its Basin & Borderlands: The Story of Their Discovery, Exploration and Occupation* (Toronto, 1905), 13–34; J.G. Bourinot, 'The Makers of the Dominion of Canada,' part 1, *The Canadian Magazine* 10(1) (1897), 2–15.

89 Ian McKay, 'History and the Tourist Gaze: The Politics of Commemoration in Nova Scotia, 1935–1964,' *Acadiensis* 22(2) (1993), 102–38. McKay's assertion that government officials promoted the Cabot Trail 'in the absence of authoritative evidence' is puzzling. How many articles in the *Transactions of the Royal Society of Canada* does it take to establish an historical 'fact'? Surely it was historians who tailored myth, not the civil servants.

90 Cf. Candow, *Origin of Cabot Tower*, and Smrz, 'Cabot and Newfoundland Identity.'

91 Halifax *Herald*, 'Cabot Celebration,' 25 June 1897.

92 There is an interesting parallel, in his *History of Newfoundland*, in which Prowse uses historical evidence in a similar way to make his case that Newfoundland was long oppressed by West Country merchants – but that is another story; see Keith Matthews, 'Historical Fence Building: A Critique of the Historiography of Newfoundland,' *Newfoundland Quarterly* 74 (1978), 21–30.

93 Judge [D.W.] Prowse, 'Cabot's Landfall, the Claims of Newfoundland Stoutly Defended and Those of Cape Breton Strongly Contested,' *Morning Chronicle* (Halifax), 7 August 1897.

94 Cf. Prowse's remarks quoted in the *Daily News* (St John's), 14 April 1897, 4, cited in Candow, *Origin of Cabot Tower*, 14.

95 Or, at least, so Prowse claims; see Prowse, 'Cabot's Landfall.' Cf. [Clements R. Markham], 'Fourth Centenary of the Voyage of John Cabot, 1497,' presidential address, *Geographical Journal* 9(6) (1897), 604–20, and, for Lord Dufferin's acceptance of Bonavista, Porter, 'Cabot Celebrations,' 663.

96 Hobsbawm, 'Introduction: Inventing Traditions,' 11.

97 See Cyril Williams-Wood, *English Transfer-Printed Pottery and Porcelain* (London, 1981); Schama, 'Many Deaths of General Wolfe'; and Colley, *Britons*, for other examples.

98 Hobsbawm, 'Mass-Producing Traditions'; see table 1.

99 *Stanley Gibbons Stamps of the World 1981* (London, 1981).
100 Thomas F. Nemec, 'Postage Stamps,' in Cyril F. Poole, ed., *Encyclopedia of Newfoundland and Labrador*, vol. 4 (St John's, 1993), 412–25.
101 Lyse Rousseau and Emanuel Darnell, *Stamps of Canada* (Ottawa, 1996), 3, 7.
102 Clifford F. Brown, *The Newfoundland Stamp Album* (St John's, 1989).
103 Donald J. Lehnus, *Angels to Zepplins: A Guide to the Persons, Objects, Topics and Themes on United States Postage Stamps, 1847–1980* (Westport, CN, 1982), 57, and 13, table 2.

CHAPTER 6: THE HISTORY OF DISCOVERY

1 Geoffrey of Monmouth, *The History of the Kings of Britain*, trans. Lewis Thorpe (Harmondsworth, 1966), 72.
2 Benedict R. O'G. Anderson, *Imagined Communities: Reflections on the Origin and Spread of Nationalism*, 2nd ed. (London, 1991).
3 Linda Colley, *Britons: Forging the Nation, 1707–1837* (New Haven, 1992).
4 Colette Beaune, *The Birth of an Ideology, Myths and Symbols of Nation in Late-Medieval France* (Berkeley, 1991), 226–41.
5 E.J. Hobsbawm, *Nations and Nationalism since 1780* (Cambridge, Eng., 1990), 1–14.
6 'Ernest Renan, *Qu'est que c'est une nation?* (Paris, 1882), 7–8, cited in Hobsbawm, *Nations and Nationalism*, 12; translation mine.
7 The work was not published until 1508 and available only in Latin until an English translation appeared in 1718; Geoffrey, *History of the Kings of Britain*, 9, 31–3. On the pervasive influence of the *History*, see Laura Keeler, *Geoffrey of Monmouth and the Late Latin Chroniclers, 1300–1500* (1946; repr. Folcroft, PA, 1974) and Hugh A. MacDougall, *Racial Myth in English History: Trojans, Teutons, and Anglo-Saxons* (Hanover, NH, 1982).
8 Geoffrey, *History*, 65–72.
9 Keeler, *Geoffrey and the Late Latin Chroniclers*, 1.
10 Geoffrey, *History*, 51 and 284; MacDougall, *Racial Myth*, 7.
11 Michael J. Curley, *Geoffrey of Monmouth* (New York, 1994).
12 Friedrich W.D. Brie, ed., *The Brut or the Chronicles of England* (London, 1906 and 1908).

13 MacDougall, *Racial Myth*, 7–8.
14 Keeler, *Geoffrey and the Late Latin Chroniclers*, 80–5.
15 MacDougall, *Racial Myth*, 7–27, 53–70.
16 Brie, ed., *The Brut*, 1: x and 8–11.
17 William Caxton, *The Description of Britain* [1480], trans. M. Collins (New York, 1988), 30, 48, 61. Caxton's text was actually an extract from John Trevisa's translation of the first book of Ranulp Higden, *Polychronicon*; see Caxton, p. 9.
18 Beaune, *Birth of an Ideology*, 226–41. At the turn of the sixteenth century, French humanists were just beginning to have doubts about their Trojan origins; see ibid., 338–40.
19 Colin Renfrew, *Archaeology and Language: The Puzzle of Indo-European Origins* (New York, 1988), 288.
20 Beaune, *Birth of an Ideology*, 241–4; MacDougall, *Racial Myth*, 7–27; Curley, *Geoffrey of Monmouth*, 14–18.
21 Beaune, *Birth of an Ideology*, 310.
22 Beaune, *Birth of an Ideology*, 320–1.
23 Eviatar Zerubavel, *Terra Cognita: The Mental Discovery of America* (New Brunswick, NJ, 1992).
24 Jennifer Kaylin, 'Tales of the "Un-fake,"' *Yale Alumni Magazine* 59(7) (1996), 30–5. I am endebted to Stuart Pierson for drawing this article to my attention. Cf. R.A. Skelton, Thomas E. Marston, and George D. Painter, *The Vinland Map and the Tartar Relation*, 2nd ed. (New Haven, 1995).
25 I made this up, but students will recognize the trope.
26 Robert H. Fuson, 'The John Cabot Mystique,' in Stanley H. Palmer and Dennis Reinhartz, eds, *Essays on the History of North American Discovery and Exploration* (College Station, TX, 1988), 35–51.
27 Eric R. Wolf, *Europe and the People without History* (Berkeley, CA, 1982).
28 Robert Paine, 'Columbus and Anthropology and the Unknown,' *Journal of the Royal Anthropological Institute*, new ser. 1 (1995), 47–65, and 'Dilemmas of "Discovery": Europeans and "America,"' in Vered Amit-Talai and Caroline Knowles, eds, *Re-Situating Identities: The Politics of Race, Ethnicity and Culture* (Peterborough, ON, 1996), 240–62.
29 Stephen A. Davis, 'Early Societies: Sequences of Change,' in Phillip A. Buckner and John G. Reid, eds, *The Atlantic Region to Confederation: A History* (Toronto and Fredericton, NB, 1994), 3–21.

30 James A. Tuck, *Maritime Provinces Prehistory* (Ottawa, 1984).
31 Bruce Bourque, 'Ethnicity on the Maritime Peninsula, 1600–1759,' *Ethnohistory* 3(3) (1989), 257–84.
32 Philip K. Bock, 'Micmac,' in Bruce G. Trigger, ed., *Handbook of North American Indians*, vol. 15, *Northeast* (Washington, 1978), 109–22; Peter Bakker, '"The language of the coast tribes is half Basque": A Basque-American Indian Pidgin in Use between Europeans and Native Americans in North America, ca. 1540–ca. 1640,' *Anthropological Linguistics* 31(3–4) (1989), 117–47.
33 Alfred Goldsworthy Bailey, *The Conflict of European and Eastern Algonkian Cultures, 1504–1700* (Toronto, 1969); J.R. Miller, *Skyscrapers Hide the Heavens: A History of Indian-White Relations in Canada* (Toronto, 1991).
34 Bruce G. Trigger, 'American Archaeology as Native History, a Review Essay,' *William and Mary Quarterly* (3rd ser.) 40(3) (1983), 413–52; see p. 443.
35 Tuck, *Maritime Provinces Prehistory* and *Newfoundland and Labrador Prehistory* (Toronto, 1976).
36 Robert McGhee, *Canadian Arctic Prehistory* (Toronto, 1978), 24.
37 Ralph Pastore, 'The Sixteenth Century: Aboriginal Peoples and European Contact,' in Buckner and Reid, *Atlantic Region*, 22–39; Bryan C. Hood, 'The Maritime Archaic Indians of Labrador: Investigating Prehistoric Social Organization,' *Newfoundland Studies* 9(2) (1993), 155–62.
38 Ralph T. Pastore, 'The Collapse of the Beothuk World,' *Acadiensis* 19(1) (1989), 52–71.
39 Ralph T. Pastore, 'Archaeology, History, and the Beothuks,' *Newfoundland Studies* 9(2) (1993), 260–78. Samuel Eliot Morison, *The European Discovery of America*, vol. 1, *The Northern Voyages, A.D. 500–1600* (New York, 1971), 184–5, is mistaken on this issue and is followed in error, unfortunately, in Kirsten A. Seaver, *The Frozen Echo: Greenland and the Exploration of North America, ca. A.D. 1000–1500* (Stanford, CA, 1996), 272.
40 Birgitta Linderoth Wallace, 'The Vikings in North America: Myth and Reality,' in Ross Samson, ed., *Social Approaches to Viking Studies* (Glasgow, 1991), 207–19.
41 Pastore, 'Aboriginal Peoples,' 28.

42 Thomas H. McGovern, 'The Vinland Adventure: A North Atlantic Perspective,' *North American Archaeologist* 2(4) (1981), 285–308.

43 J.A. Simpson and E.S.C. Weiner, eds, *Oxford English Dictionary,* 2nd ed. (Oxford, 1989), vol. 4.

44 Samuel Eliot Morison, *Portuguese Voyages to America in the Fifteenth Century* (Cambridge, MA, 1940), 4–10; M.W.G.L. Randles, 'Sur l'idée de la découverte,' in Michel Mollat and Paul Adam, eds, *Les aspects internationaux de la découverte océanique aux XV et XVI siècles* (Paris, 1966), 15–21.

45 Edmundo O'Gorman, *The Invention of America* (Bloomington, IN, 1961); Wilcomb E. Washburn, 'The Meaning of "Discovery" in the Fifteenth and Sixteenth Centuries,' *American Historical Review* 68(1) (1962), 1–21.

46 Henry Campbell Black, *Black's Law Dictionary,* 5th ed. (St Paul, 1979), 419.

47 Raimondo de Raimondi de Soncino, Letter to the Duke of Milan, 18 December 1497; Lorenzo Pasqualigo, Letter to Venice, 23 August 1497; John Day, Letter to the Grand Admiral, ca. 1497; all in Williamson, *Cabot Voyages,* (22), (24), and (25).

48 Henry VII, Letters Patent 'For John Cabot and his sons,' 5 March 1496, in Williamson, *Cabot Voyages* (18); emphasis mine.

49 Morison, *Northern Voyages,* 159–60.

50 Patricia Seed, 'Taking Possession and Reading Texts: Establishing the Authority of Overseas Empires,' *William and Mary Quarterly* (3rd ser.) 49(2), 183–209.

51 Seed, 'Taking Possession' compares Columbus's practice in the 1490s with Humphrey Gilbert's 1583 visit to St John's, mis-characterized as an attempt at settlement.

52 Patricia Seed, *Ceremonies of Possession in Europe's Conquest of the New World, 1492–1640* (New York, 1995).

53 Brian Slattery, 'Did France Claim Canada upon "Discovery?"' in J.M. Bumsted, ed., *Interpreting Canada's Past,* vol. 1, *Before Confederation,* 1st ed. (Toronto, 1986), 2–26.

54 L.C. Green, 'Claims to Territory in Colonial America,' in L.C. Green and Olive P. Dickason, *The Law of Nations and the New World* (Edmonton, 1989), 1–139; see pp. 7–17.

55 D.B. Quinn, 'Renaissance Influences in English Colonization,'

Transactions of the Royal Historical Society (5th ser.) 26 (1976), 73–93.

56 M.I. Finley, 'Colonies – an Attempt at a Typology,' *Transactions of the Royal Historical Society* (5th ser.) 26 (1976), 167–88; see pp. 176–7.

57 G.J. Marcus, *The Conquest of the North Atlantic* (New York, 1981), 144–9.

58 Kenneth R. Andrews, *Trade, Plunder and Settlement: Maritime Enterprise and the Genesis of the British Empire, 1480–1630* (Cambridge, Eng., 1984), 223–55, 304–7.

59 Fernand Braudel, *Civilization and Capitalism, 15th–18th Century,* vol. 3, *The Perspective of the World* (New York, 1984), 116–50.

60 Christine Carpenter, 'Henry VII and the English Polity,' in Benjamin Thompson, ed., *The Reign of Henry VII,* (Stamford, 1995), 11–30.

61 Hugh Kearney, *The British Isles: A History of Four Nations* (Cambridge, Eng., 1995), 116–38.

62 Marcus, *Conquest of the North Atlantic,* 150–4.

63 Best estimates back-project a population of 2,773,851 for 1541; see E.A. Wrigley and R.S. Schofield, *The Population History of England 1541–1871* (Cambridge, MA, 1981), 208, table 7.8.

64 Wolf, *Europe and People without History,* 24–58.

65 Robert McGhee, 'Contact between Native North Americans and the Medieval Norse: A Review of the Evidence,' *American Antiquity* 49(1) (1984), 4–26.

66 Pastore, 'Aboriginal Peoples,' 35.

67 See Ingeborg Marshall, *A History and Ethnography of the Beothuk* (Montreal and Kingston, 1996). This is a very useful compendium of almost everything that is known about the Beothuk, although unfortunately it sometimes misrepresents and often underestimates the contributions of other scholars.

68 For discussion and sources see Pastore, 'Aboriginal Peoples,' 36–7.

69 Bock, 'Micmac.'

70 This is a vexed question, but my bald summary reflects the current consensus. See Elisabeth Tooker, 'History of Research,' in Trigger, *Northeast,* 4–13; Alfred Goldsworthy Bailey, 'Social Revolution in Early Eastern Canada,' *Canadian Historical Review* 19 (1938), 264–76 and *Conflict of Cultures,* xix ff.; T.J. Brasser, 'Early Indian-European Contact,' in Trigger, *Northeast,* 78–88; Bruce G. Trigger, 'Alfred G.

Bailey – Ethnohistorian,' *Acadiensis* 18(2) (1989), 3–21; cf. Pastore, 'Aboriginal Peoples,' 37.

71 Bernard G. Hoffman, 'Historical Ethnography of the Micmac of the Sixteenth and Seventeenth Centuries,' Ph.D. dissertation, University of California at Berkeley, 505–16; Bock, 'Micmac,' 114ff.

72 Bock, 'Micmac,' 117; Hoffman, 'Historical Ethnography'; Harold F. McGee, 'The Micmac Indian: The Earliest Migrants,' in Douglas F. Campbell, ed., *Banked Fires – the Ethnics of Nova Scotia* (Port Credit, ON, 1978), 15–33; Ruth Holmes Whitehead, *Stories from the Six Worlds, Micmac Legends* (Halifax, 1988), 2–15.

73 Fernand Braudel, *Civilization and Capitalism*, vol. 1, *The Structures of Everday Life: The Limits of the Possible* (New York, 1982), 457.

74 Richard W. Unger, *The Ship in the Medieval Economy, 600–1600* (Toronto, 1980), 201–50; Williamson, *Cabot Voyages*, 4.

75 James Axtell, 'Imagining the Other: First Encounters in North America,' in *Beyond 1492, Encounters in Colonial North America* (New York, 1992), 57.

76 Josiah Jeremy, 26 September 1869, cited in Ruth Holmes Whitehead, *The Old Man Told Us: Excerpts from Micmac History, 1500–1980* (Halifax, 1991), 2.

77 Axtell, 'Imagining the Other,' 35.

78 Marcus, *Conquest of the North Atlantic*, 134–6.

79 Peter E. Pope, 'The 16th-Century Fishing Voyage,' in Carol Corbin, ed., *How Deep Is the Ocean? History of the Northwest Atlantic Fishery* (Sydney, NS, in press).

80 D.W. Waters, 'Science and the Techniques of Navigation in the Renaissance,' in Charles S. Singleton, ed., *Art, Science and History in the Renaissance* (Baltimore, 1967), 189–237; E.G.R. Taylor, *The Haven-Finding Art: A History of Navigation from Odysseus to Captain Cook*, 2nd ed. (London, 1971), 122–71; Frederic C. Lane, 'The Economic Meaning of the Invention of the Compass,' *American Historical Review* 68 (1965), 605–17, and 'Progrès technologique et productivité dans les transports maritimes de la fin du Moyen Age au début des Temps modernes,' *Revue historique* 251(1) (1974), 277–302.

81 W.F.J. Mörzer Bruyns, *The Cross-Staff: History and Development of a Navigational Instrument* (Netherlands, 1994), 14.

82 Peter Martyr, *historia dell'Indie Occidentali* [1534], vol. 1, f. 65, in

Williamson, *Cabot Voyages* (53). Seaver, *The Frozen Echo*, 270, asserts that Cabot navigated with quadrant and astrolabe, but she goes somewhat beyond the evidence here, as elsewhere.

83 Waters, 'Science and Navigation,' 208–10, dates the cross-staff to the 1490s; Bruyns, *Cross-Staff*, 14, gives a date of 1515 for the first known use.

84 Joseph Needham, *Science and Civilization in China*, vol. 4, *Physics and Physical Technology*, part 1, *Physics* (Cambridge, 1962), 279–93.

85 Waters, 'Science and Navigation,' 210n.

86 Elizabeth L. Eisenstein, *The Printing Revolution in Early Modern Europe* (1983; repr. Cambridge, Eng., 1993), 187–206.

87 Gabriel Archer, 'The Relation of Captain Gosnols Voyage,' in David B. Quinn and Alison M. Quinn, eds, *The English New England Voyages 1602–1608*, Hakluyt Society, 2nd ser., no. 161 (London, 1983), 112–38.

88 Cf. Robert McGhee, *Canada Rediscovered* (Montreal, 1991), 62–70.

89 Gwyn Jones, *The Norse Atlantic Saga*, 2nd ed. (London, 1986).

90 Seaver, *The Frozen Echo*, 28–43.

91 Morison, *Northern Voyages*, is especially hostile; e.g., p. 192.

92 Williamson, *Cabot Voyages*, 13–14; Marcus, *Conquest of the North Atlantic*, 132–43.

93 McGhee, *Canada Rediscovered*, 90.

94 Marcus, *Conquest of the North Atlantic*, 155–63; Seaver, *The Frozen Echo*, 225–53; cf. Williamson, *Cabot Voyages*, 116–19.

95 David B. Quinn, *North America from Earliest Discovery to First Settlements: The Norse Voyages to 1612* (New York, 1977), 114–15; Marcus, *Conquest of the North Atlantic*, 164–73; Seaver, *The Frozen Echo*, 265–70.

96 Seaver, *The Frozen Echo*, 16–19.

97 Marcus, *Conquest of the North Atlantic*, 117–18.

98 Stuart C. Brown, 'Far Other Worlds and Other Seas: The Context of Claims for Pre-Columbian European Contact with North America,' *Newfoundland Studies* 9(2) (1993), 235–59. For an epitome of pre-Columbian fantasy see the forthcoming pastiche by Gunnar Thompson, *The Friar's Map of Ancient America, 1360 AD*, to be published by Stonehenge Viewpoint Press. (I am not making this up.)

99 Henri Pirenne, *Economic and Social History of Medieval Europe* (New York, 1937).

100 Garry Wills, 'Man of the Year,' *New York Review of Books* 38(19) (1991), 12–18.

CHAPTER 7: A MEMORY PERPETUAL

1 John Rastell, *The Four Elements* [ca. 1525], ed. Roger Coleman, (Cambridge, Eng., 1971), 49.
2 Peter Burke, 'America and the Rewriting of World History,' in Karen Ordahl Kupperman, ed., *America in European Consciousness, 1493–1750* (Chapel Hill, NC, 1995), 33–51.
3 David B. Quinn, 'Renaissance Influences in English Colonization,' *Transactions of the Royal Historical Society* (5th ser.) 26 (1976), 73–93; *North America from Earliest Discovery to First Settlements: The Norse Voyages to 1612* (New York, 1977), 350; 'Newfoundland in the Consciousness of Europe in the Sixteenth and Seventeenth Centuries,' in G.M. Story, ed., *Early European Settlement and Exploitation in Atlantic Canada* (St John's, 1982), 9–30.
4 Benedict R. O'G. Anderson, *Imagined Communities: Reflections on the Origin and Spread of Nationalism,* 2nd ed. (London, 1991), 200–1, and recall Renan's *bon mot,* quoted above.
5 I owe this instructive story to Alan Ereira of Sunstone Films, who saw this incident after he had completed his own film on the Kogi, *From the Heart of the World.*
6 Cf. Jennifer Reid, *Myth, Symbol, and Colonial Encounter: British and Mi'kmaq in Acadia, 1700–1867* (Ottawa, 1995), 9–21.
7 Alan Ereira, personal communication.
8 J. R. Miller, *Skyscrapers Hide the Heavens: A History of Indian-White Relations in Canada* (Toronto, 1991).
9 On which see Bruce G. Trigger, *Natives and Newcomers: Canada's 'Heroic Age' Reconsidered* (Montreal and Kingston, 1985) and Denis Delâge, *Le pays renversé: Amérindiens et Européens en Amérique du nord-est – 1600–1664* (Quebec, 1991).
10 Bruce G. Trigger, 'The Historian's Indian: Native Americans in Canadian Historical Writing from Charlevoix to the Present,' *Canadian Historical Review* 67(3) (1986), 315–42.
11 For a historical review see L.C. Green and Olive P. Dickason, *The Law of Nations and the New World* (Edmonton, 1989).

12 I have applied Robert Paine's aboriginal/settler/indigene terminology to my abstract of claims for possession.

13 Alberico Gentili, *De Jure Belli* [1612], vol. 1, 122–6, in Green and Dickason, *Law of Nations*, 49, 135; cf. David P. McGinnis, 'International Law as It Is Related to Discovery and Exploration in Cabot's Time,' in R. Momoli Zorzi and U. Tucci, eds, *Venezia e I Caboto: Le Ralazioni Italo-Canadesi* (Venice, 1992), 61–9.

14 Friedrich W.D. Brie, ed., *The Brut or the Chronicles of England*, vol. 1, Early English Text Society no. 131 (London, 1906), 8–10; translation mine.

15 Sonja Jerkic, 'Burials and Bones: A Summary of Burial Patterns and Human Skeletal Research in Newfoundland and Labrador,' *Newfoundland Studies* 9(2) (1993), 213–34.

16 Thomas More, *Utopia*, ed. George M. Logan, Robert M. Adams, and Clarence H. Miller (Cambridge, Eng., 1995), 135–7; cf. M.I. Finley, 'Colonies – an Attempt at a Typology,' *Transactions of the Royal Historical Society* (5th ser.) 26 (1976), 167–88.

17 [Abbé Guillaume-Thomas-François Raynal], *A Philosophical and Political History of the British Settlements and Trade in North America*, vol. 1 (Edinburgh, 1776) [CIHM # 27344], 45–6.

18 Eric R. Wolf, 'Unforeseen Americas: The Making of New World Societies in Anthropological Perspective,' *Proceedings of the National Academy of Science* (Anthropology) 93 (1996), 2603–7.

19 J.A. Simpson and E.S.C. Weiner, eds, *Oxford English Dictionary*, 2nd ed. (Oxford, 1989), vols 13 and 20.

20 James Axtell, 'Imagining the Other: First Encounters in North America,' in *Beyond 1492: Encounters in Colonial North America* (New York, 1992), 25–74; see p. 58.

21 Trigger, 'The Historians' Indian'; Green and Dickason, *Law of Nations*.

22 I was asked by a servant of the P.R. industry in June 1996 to summarize Cabot's achievement without using the term. She told me it had been banned.

23 Canadian Association of Schools of Social Work (CASSW), Resolution, Annual General Meeting, St Catharines, Ontario, 1996.

24 W.K. Cross, *Charlton Standard Catalogue of Canadian Coins*, 51st ed. (Toronto, 1997), 530, 560.

25 Robert Fabyan, *Chronicle*, 1502, as repr. in Richard Hakluyt, *Divers Voyages* [1589], in Williamson, *Cabot Voyages*, (31 iii).

26 Public Record Office (PRO), Household Books, E 101/415, 3, 25–30 September 1502, in Williamson, *Cabot Voyages* (26 iii).

27 Henry VII, Letters Patent to Richard Warde et al., 19 March 1501, PRO, Patent Roll 16 Henry VII, part 1, 20–1. The 1502 patent to Hugh Elyot, Asshehurst, Gonsalves, and F. Fernandes was not issued until December; see Letters Patent to Hugh Elyot et al., 9 December 1502, Patent Roll 18 Henry VII, part 2, 29–30. Both patents trans. H.P. Biggar, in Williamson, *Cabot Voyages* (43) and (46).

28 Alwyn A. Ruddock, 'The Reputation of Sebastian Cabot,' *Bulletin of the Institute of Historical Research* 47 (1974), 93–9; cf. Quinn, *North America from Earliest Discovery*, 125.

29 Henry VII, Warrant for Issue of Pension, 26 September 1502, PRO, E 404/84, I, in Williamson, *Cabot Voyages* (46).

30 Samuel Eliot Morison, *The European Discovery of America: The Northern Voyages* (New York, 1971), 218–19, puts the voyage in Newfoundland. Quinn, *North America from Earliest Discovery*, 127, suggests that the Native people were Mi'kmaq.

31 Fabyan, *Chronicle*, re 1502.

32 Olive P. Dickason, 'Amerindians between French and English in Nova Scotia, 1713–1763,' *American Indian Culture and Research Journal* 10(4) (1986), 31–56.

33 Lieutenant Governor Jonathan Belcher and Chiefs of the Micmac Indians, 'Ceremonials at Concluding a Peace,' 25 June 1761, PRO CO 217/18, 276–83v; cf. Stephen E. Patterson, 'Indian-White Relations in Nova Scotia, 1749–61: A Study in Political Interaction,' *Acadiensis* 23(1) (1993), 23–59.

34 Order Book, Memorandum of a Treaty, 12 October 1761, Public Archives of Nova Scotia (PANS), RG 1/165, 187.

35 Charles A. Martijn, 'An Eastern Micmac Domain of Islands,' in William Cowan, ed., *Actes du vingtième congrès des algonquinistes* (Ottawa, 1989), 208–31; Ralph T. Pastore, *Newfoundland Micmacs: A History of Their Traditional Life*, Newfoundland Historical Society Pamphlet no. 5 (St John's, 1978), 10.

36 Dickason, 'Between French and English,' 40–6; Patterson, 'Indian-White Relations,' 54.

37 Chief Jeannot, Remarks at the Ceremonials of Peace, 25 June 1761, CO 217/18, 281–3v; Patterson, 'Indian-White Relations,' 56–7.

38 Bill Wicken, '26 August 1726: A Case Study in Mi'kmaq–New England Relations in the Early 18th Century,' *Acadiensis* 23(1) (1993), 5–22.

39 Chief Jean Baptiste Cope and Governor Peregrine Hopson, Treaty, 16 September 1752, in Thomas B. Akins, ed., *Selections from the Public Documents of the Province of Nova Scotia* (Halifax, 1869), 672–4; cf. L.F.S. Upton, *Micmacs and Colonists: Indian-White Relations in the Maritimes, 1713–1867* (Vancouver, 1979), 54, and Patterson, 'Indian-White Relations,' 37–41.

40 Leonard Woods Labaree, ed., *Royal Instructions to British Colonial Governors, 1670–1776*, American Historical Association (1935; repr. New York, 1967), 2: 469–70; Dickason, 'Between French and English'; Patterson, 'Indian-White Relations.'

41 Lord Hillsborough, for Committee for Trade and Plantations (CTP), Letter to Governor Montagu Wilmot, 13 July 1764, PANS RG 1/31 (34).

42 Lieutenant Governor Jonathan Belcher, Proclamation, 2 July 1762, CO 217/19, 27v.

43 Joshua Mauger, Letter from the General Assembly to CTP, 28 September 1763, CO 217/20, 202–3v.

44 CTP, Minutes, vol. 69, 275–8, 3 December 1762, in HMSO, *Journal of the Commissioners for Trade and Plantations from January 1759 to December 1763* (London, 1935), 308.

45 George III in Council, '... Instruction for the Governors of Nova Scotia [etc.] ...,' 19 June 1762, PRO WO 34/72, 169–70v.

46 CTP, Minutes, 3 December 1762.

47 Dennis A. Bartels and Olaf Uwe Janzen, 'Micmac Migration to Western Newfoundland,' *Canadian Journal of Native Studies* 10 (1990), 69–94; Stephen E. Patterson, '1744–1763: Colonial Wars and Aboriginal Peoples,' in Phillip A. Buckner and John G. Reid, eds, *The Atlantic Region to Confederation: A History* (Toronto, 1994), 125–55.

48 Ralph T. Pastore, 'The Collapse of the Beothuk World,' *Acadiensis* 19(1) (1989), 52–71.

49 James K. Hiller, 'Early Patrons of the Labrador Eskimos: The Moravian Mission in Labrador, 1764–1805,' in Robert Paine, ed., *Patrons and Brokers in the East Arctic* (St John's, 1971), 74–111.

50 Upton, *Micmacs and Colonists.*
51 Edward G. Porter, 'The Cabot Celebrations of 1897 at Bristol Halifax and St John's,' *New England Magazine* 17 (1898), 653–71 [CIHM # 12128]; see p. 666.
52 'John Cabot Supplement, 1497–1947,' *Evening Telegram*, St John's, 23 June 1947.
53 Jeffrey A. Hutchings and Ransom A. Myers, 'The Biological Collapse of Atlantic Cod off Newfoundland,' in Ragnar Arnason and Lawrence Felt, eds, *The North Atlantic Fisheries: Successes, Failures, and Challenges* (Charlottetown, PEI, 1995), 39–83; Peter Pope, 'Early Estimates: Assessment of Catches in the Newfoundland Cod Fishery, 1660–1690,' *Marine Resources and Human Societies in the North Atlantic since 1500*, Institute for Social and Economic Research Conference Paper no. 5 (St John's 1997), 7–40.

Credits and Permissions

The author wishes to thank the following:

The Hakluyt Society and David Higham Associates, for permission to quote from James A. Williamson, *The Cabot Voyages and Bristol Discovery under Henry VII*, Hakluyt Society (2nd series), vol. 120 (Cambridge, 1962).

Penguin Books, for permission to quote from Geoffrey of Monmouth, *The History of the Kings of Britain*, trans. Lewis Thorpe (Harmondsworth, 1966).

Cambridge University Press, for permission to quote from Thomas More, *Utopia*, ed. George M. Logan, Robert M. Adams, and Clarence H. Miller (Cambridge, 1995).

University of Toronto Press Incorporated, for permission to quote from the *Canadian Historical Review.*

The Manuscript Department of the Royal Library, Copenhagen, Denmark, for permission to reproduce Sigurdir Stefansson, *Terrarum Hyperboeam*, 1590 (Gl. kgl. Saml. 2881, 4°, f. 10v).

Colin Mudie for permission to reproduce his design of a reconstruction of the *Matthew.*

National Archives of Canada, for permission to reproduce W.H. Greene's plan for Cabot Tower, 1898 (C97397).

Nova Scotia Museum, Historical Collection, for permission to reproduce the Mi'kmaq petroglyph from Kejimkujik National Park, Nova Scotia.

Smallwood Centre for Newfoundland Studies, for permission to reproduce Jacopo Gastaldi's map *La nuova Francia* of 1558 (map 75) and John Mason's map *Newfound Land* of 1625 (map 25).

Stanford University Libraries, Special Collections, for permission to reproduce Erhard Reuwich, *City of Venice*, 1486 (KA 1486.B73f).

The Roman Catholic Archdiocesan Archives, St John's, for permission to reproduce part of a letter dated 21 February 1896 from W.R. Harris to Bishop Michael Howley (Howley Papers, 106/5/11).

Index